D0792864

Don Quijote in America

Don Quijote in America

Plays in English and Spanish,
Grades 1·6

Resurrección Espinosa

Drawings by Dorothy Louise Hall

Music by Charles Frink

2002
Teacher Ideas Press
Libraries Unlimited
A Division of Greenwood Publishing Group, Inc.
Greenwood Village, Colorado

MONTROSE LIBRARY DISTRICT
320 So. 2nd St.
Montrose, CO 81401

Copyright © 2002 Libraries Unlimited
All Rights Reserved
Printed in the United States of America

No part of this publication may be reproduced, stored in a retrieval system, or transmitted, in any form or by any means, electronic, mechanical, photo-copying, recording, or otherwise, without the prior written permission of the publisher. An exception is made for individual librarians and educators, who may make copies of scripts for classroom use in a single school. Other portions of the book (up to 15 pages) may be copied for in-service programs or other educational programs in a single school or library. Standard cita-tion information should appear on each page.

TEACHER IDEAS PRESS
Libraries Unlimited
A Division of Greenwood Publishing Group, Inc.
7730 East Belleview Avenue, Suite A200
Greenwood Village, CO 80111
1-800-225-5800
www.lu.com/tips

Library of Congress Cataloging-in-Publication Data

Espinosa, Resurrección.
    Don Quijote in America : plays in English and Spanish, grades 1-6 / Resurrección Espinosa.
      v. cm.
    Includes bibliographical references and index.
    Contents: The farmer finds his true friends = El granjero descubre a sus verdaderos amigos — The princess is sad = La princesa esta triste — Clothes do not make the man = El habito no hace al monje — Cinderella in modern times = Cenicienta en tiempos modernos — El Bully = El valenton — The coming of Winter = La llegada del invierno — Where did they go? Where did I put them? = Donde se fueron? Donde los puse yo? — What happened in the garden this summer? = Que paso en el jardin este verano? — Ay, Carmelo! = Ay, Carmelo! — Don Quijote in America = Don Quijote en America.
    ISBN 1-56308-927-0 (paper)
    1. Children's plays, American—Translations into Spanish. 2. Children's plays, American. [1. Plays. 2. Spanish language materials—Bilingual.] I. Title.

PS3555.S5452 D66.2002
812'.54—dc21

                                 2002017361

To the many young actors, singers, and designers of all ages who, with enthusiasm and hard work, made great productions of these plays with Providence City Arts, the Charles Fortes After School Troupe, and the Educational Center for Arts and Sciences 2001 Workshop for International Theater Week in Providence, Rhode Island; and with Teatro Latino de New London, the Edgerton After School Bilingual Troupe, and the Winthrop Drama Club in New London, Connecticut.

And to my cat, Gato, who continuously reminds me that all children love to be patted on the head and told that they are good.

Contents

viii   Contents

List of Figures

Illustrations of several costumes and instructions for making them are provided as examples only, and thus no attempt was made to depict all the costumes required in any of the plays. As in all aspects of theater, the imagination of every participant should be exercised as fully as possible. So, please—experiment, invent, and enjoy!

Acknowledgments

I want to extend my thanks to Charles Frink, composer and editor, and to Dorothy Louise Hall for their contributions to this book. I thank the Holleran Center for Public Policy and Community Challenges and the Office of Volunteer Services at Connecticut College, the United Way of Southeastern Connecticut, the New London Public Schools, and the Palmer and Bodenwein Funds for their generous support. I thank Patricia Harper, William Wuyke, Diane Klotz, Tracee Reiser, Wilma Hodge, Jean Jordan, Cindy Samul, Meghan Flynn, and many others who have helped with productions of these plays. I thank John Adamson for his ongoing and unfailing technical assistance. And I thank Suzanne Barchers for her help in preparing the manuscript and for her faith in the prospects for these plays.

The Spanish version of the play *The Princess Is Sad* is reprinted here by permission of University Press of America.

Preface

The youngest member of the theater group, a small, dark Dominican boy who was playing the role of the governor's son, suddenly looked up from his script, a very serious look on his face, and asked me, "What do you want to be when you grow up?" I said, "Just what I am." He nodded, satisfied by my answer, and went back to studying his part. When I thought about this on my way home, I was surprised to realize that I had the answer ready to such a deep question. I was 43 at the time.

Introduction I:
For Directors and Teachers

We recommend that anyone who is about to direct or supervise a multicultural theater project for children read the following suggestions, although your experience and preferences may lead you to supplement or modify them. At the end of this introduction is a section dedicated to the children, to be read by them or to them if the conditions are right. We have found that young people who decide to join a theater group like to feel that they are authorities on the subject. And they are right. Once, two "starlets" who had been rather disruptive showed up at a rehearsal delivering the following line with great pride: "There are no small parts, just small people." Everyone nodded wisely. After that, they began to take their participation in the troop more seriously. Things were much easier within the group.

VALUES

Keep in mind the contributions that participating in multicultural theater can make to children's quality of life, especially children who live in the inner city. We are involved with much more than entertainment; we are carrying on education according to the original meaning of the Latin word: to bring out the best in all concerned. Some of the educational values that theater promotes in this context are the following:

1. Improved Reading and Greater Clarity of Speech

Although theater rehearsal provides little opportunity for systematic instruction in reading, taking part in a play does provide exciting motivation to practice reading that many inner-city children might not otherwise encounter. Exercising whatever reading skills he or she has already acquired gives a child the immediate and continuous gratification of developing a character in a story shared with others. Under these conditions, noticeable improvement in reading often occurs rapidly. The same can be said for clarity of speech: the actors will know whether they are communicating well, and they will hear from their peers promptly if their speech is not readily understandable.

2. Cooperative Behavior as a Member of a Group

Cooperative behavior fosters many good habits, such as listening silently and attentively while others speak, making constructive suggestions, refraining from criticizing others, and participating punctually and regularly in a long-term project. It also teaches systematic practice, self-discipline, and greater trust in others. Cultivation of these aspects of cooperative behavior will almost certainly call for patience on the part of the director and his or her assistants, for the environment of inner-city children often systematically evokes the opposite of these virtues.

3. Greater Insight into, and Understanding of, the Thoughts and Feelings of Others

Theater cultivates these attributes in at least three ways: learning about the character one is working to portray, learning about other characters in the play, and learning about the other participants in the project (a result of practicing the modes of cooperative behavior described in value 2).

4. Self-Confidence in a Challenging Situation

Children develop self-confidence when they undertake new activities in a supportive environment and contribute to that support by practicing the kinds of behavior described in values 2 and 3 above.

5. Discovery, Acknowledgment, and Cultivation of a Wide Range of Individual Abilities

Theater is much more than acting. It involves designing and constructing the set; designing and making costumes and props; writing program notes, press releases, and flyers; and managing the house. It involves organizing receptions, making and serving refreshments, composing or performing music, and planning stage movements. There are also opportunities to edit or create episodes and scenes for those who can rise to the occasion.

We know of no other single activity for children that calls for a greater variety of skills than theater. We believe that with sufficiently observant and supportive direction, every child can discover that he or she has a gift for some aspect of theater. This discovery on the part of the participant reinforces everything discussed in the other values described here.

6. Higher Self-Esteem

Higher self-esteem results from all of the aforementioned values and is of special importance to those children who do not find adequate self-esteem in the course of their customary activities at home or school and so turn to the street and its dangers.

7. Improved Concentration, Longer Attention Span, and Greater Resistance to Distraction

These values, too, are developed in conjunction with all of the foregoing ones and are of fundamental importance to many children whose environment consists largely of swiftly overlapping sounds and events that show little or no logical connection. Many of these children also have few or no opportunities for considered, patient, sequential communication.

8. Constructive Interaction with Parents or Other Proximate Adults in Activities of Shared Interest

Shared activities with adults at home often develop in connection with practice of memorization and characterization or the making of costumes, props, publicity pieces, refreshments, and so forth. The importance of such interaction for all children should be self-evident. The lack of such interaction for many children is, in today's hurried society, all too apparent.

WHEN, WHERE, AND FOR HOW LONG?

Numerous locations for theater programs with children are usually available—community centers, recreation departments, churches, social service centers, performing arts facilities, and so forth. Schools are probably the most convenient locations. The children are already there, and transportation and assistance are usually available; funding can often be obtained if the goals of the activity are presented well to administrators.

Nonetheless, there are conditions to be negotiated and problems to be avoided. First, it is probably not a good idea to conduct a theater program during the school day, when too many other activities are going on and there is insufficient time for practice. Theater should be an after-school activity.

Fortunately, there is a growing perception nationwide that after-school activities are much needed. Common situations such as single-parent households or households in which both parents work mean that many children have no one at home for several hours after the close of the regular school day. This can result in children's watching too much television or their taking part in unsafe street activities. A theater program cannot, in itself, solve this problem—but it can help. There is one other factor in favor of placing theater programs in schools with big minority and multilingual populations, especially if the children come from low-income families: the parents often do not have the economic resources or the understanding and education necessary to take their children to an arts center.

We have found that the ideal length for a theater rehearsal with children is about an hour and a half; the most effective frequency is once a week, and the best number of rehearsals for one complete program is from ten to twelve. This schedule fits easily into a school semester. The classroom, because of its small size and its crowded furniture, may not be the best place. A cafeteria or gym may be best, although these should be avoided if there are several children in the group with behavioral problems or if there are other things going on at the same time. Of course, a cafeteria may be the only place available, and then the thing to do is to discuss the situation with any disruptive children, and, if necessary, ask an assistant to bring them to a classroom or other available space and rehearse privately with them until they calm down. It may also be necessary to inform them that they will have to leave the group if they don't cooperate. But for the rest of the children, a cafeteria with minimal distractions works well. This is also a good place for the final performance, because a traditional stage is too frightening and impractical for young actors. If a clear space on the floor is designated as the stage, decorated appropriately, and surrounded by low chairs or risers where their classmates, teachers, and families can sit, it is almost certain that a new generation of talented actors and an enthusiastic following will be born.

The idea of continuity should be carefully considered and talked about with the administration or whoever is funding or supporting the program. A large part of the population participating in programs such as those we are discussing here does not have a sense of continuity in life. Yet many children ask me, whenever we stage a play, when we will start rehearsing the next one. Working with school administrators and community and arts organizations to ensure you will have the resources for the next play is one of the best ways to promote continuity in children's lives and to address their feelings of powerlessness. It also restores culture to their lives, which does not happen in an atmosphere of helplessness.

WHO IS THE DIRECTOR?

The first characteristic of a good director, of course, is that he or she has a love of the theater and enough experience to guide young actors. A second—and very important—characteristic is an understanding of the life and culture of the group with whom one is working. It is a very different thing to conduct a theater workshop for upper-middle-class children than one for inner-city youths. People with a lot of professional training can fail if they do not keep this factor in mind and prepare themselves accordingly. One of the realities of directing theater at an inner-city school is that one may have to start at the beginning several times, even as "opening night" looms. The continuity of a theater program in a particular school or community will lessen this problem, given sufficient time and a lot of persistence.

An assistant is almost always necessary. Among parents and teachers, one can usually find someone willing to help children memorize lines, keep order, and make props. If a play includes a special feature such as music or dancing, it is wise to contact local art schools or colleges, where one may find a talented student who wants the experience. If there is enough money in the budget to pay a movement or music instructor, that's great. But the person hired must not do the job mechanically; children notice this right away, and it is detrimental to the objectives outlined above.

FUNDING

Most school systems do not have readily available funding for a program such as this. Almost everywhere, provisions have been made for sports programs to take place on a structured basis, but the possibilities a theater program with the objectives outlined above offers to children and their communities have seldom been brought to the attention of those who can help. School principals and community-center directors need to be made aware that we are dealing with much more than the entertainment provided by, say, a Christmas play. Only then will the conditions change and adequate funding become available. The program can be included in the school's budget, and money can also be found from state arts commissions, community foundations, and special funds at nearby colleges and universities.

A director may have to start with almost nothing. If he or she can afford to do this and is fortunate enough to have a group of youngsters interested in the project from the outset, then the sense of pride and accomplishment once adequate support is received can be satisfying and instructive.

One more thing: if you are a teacher, librarian, or parent who understands the value of this kind of theater but cannot implement it for some reason, bring the matter to the attention of an administrator or community director. The right individual to start the program can be found.

REHEARSAL STRUCTURE

The substance and sequence of events during rehearsals will vary with the participants' skills and weaknesses, with the play to be performed, with the personality and technique of the director, and so forth. But we believe that all rehearsals should have three parts: a brief introduction, the main body of work on the play, and a brief conclusion.

The introduction has two purposes: to focus attention on the play and to develop qualities of movement, vocalization, thought, and feeling that are basic to all theater performance. Certain simple exercises can advance both purposes. Many are available, and each director should choose the exercises most appropriate for the situation, feeling free to modify them if necessary. (An exercise sequence in the short essay directed to the children follows.) Keep in mind that what is needed are exercises that improve the volume of the voice without straining it, that relax the body and help a young actor find the movements and positions required by his or her character, and that help with concentration and improve cooperative behavior. Other important activities include exercises or games designed to help young people tell or create a story and improvisational exercises that can be assigned as homework or as group work. Consider asking the actors to develop a scene that takes place in a dentist's office, a television commercial, a conversation between a mother and son, or a monologue on how they feel about a new friend or neighbor.

The rehearsals should be designed to allow time for studying and memorizing the text and for working on movement. Then, text and movement should be put together. One important consideration is that the young actors should be encouraged to do their best at all times and to understand that they are participating in a team effort. They will do well in performance if their shortcomings (such as difficulty memorizing lines) are not emphasized at any time.

Designing and building the stage set and making costumes and props with the actors is rewarding because, among other things, the children take ownership of the performance, which helps them achieve success. Of course, they also learn other theater skills from these activities.

Especially in the final weeks of rehearsals, it is a good idea to finish each session by reviewing which tasks have been finished and which still need to be completed, which aspects of the performance still need work, and who can help those who have not yet memorized their parts. Also, discuss exactly when and where the play will be performed and who will be invited to it. In short, the best way to conduct a theater workshop is to help the actors become aware of the many details involved in producing a play and to delegate responsibility whenever possible.

Nine of the plays in this collection have been written for, and most of them have been performed by, elementary school children. If they are to be used by groups made up of different age levels, some of the plays may require adaptation, either by adding a narrator or by shortening a scene that may lengthen the play beyond young actors' capabilities. Some advice in this regard is given at the beginning of some of the plays. The tenth play, *Don Quijote in America,* was written for a community group that aimed to integrate all ages in a theater project. This play was performed for an enthusiastic, multicultural, all-ages audience on May 12, 2001. The group gave their performance at Connecticut College Downtown in New London for Main Street Spring Fever Day, and the cast of twenty-eight ranged in age from 6 to 73 years old. The play can also serve as a collaborative effort among students from different grade levels. We have included it here to contribute material that may foster this very desirable type of project.

Resurrección Espinosa
Charles Frink

Introduction II:
For the <u>Children Who Will Perform These Plays</u>

Dear Children:

Maybe you have participated in a play before, have seen one performed, or both—or neither. But in any case, have you ever wondered what a play is?

A play is a story told with words and movement by people, the actors, each of whom plays the part of another person to tell the story. There may also be scenery and props, the latter being objects the actors use.

Through the movements, words, and facial expressions of the actors, we know how the characters feel about themselves and about others in the story, whether they are people we like or dislike, whether they are telling the truth or not. We know what actions they take in a particular situation and what the consequences of their actions are. We also can see right away when a character is presented well, that is, we can see not only whether the actor is good at acting, but if he or she has chosen the right costume, voice, expressions, and movements. We know that something is wrong if, let's say, someone is playing the part of a cat and starts to bark.

If you are to participate in a play, there are a few things that you should think about, because they will help you become a good actor. The first is that not all actors talk at once or come out in front of the audience at the same time, unless this is part of the story. Usually, each actor or group of actors comes out on the stage at a different time and waits for his or her turn to speak. That's one reason why everyone has to be aware of what the other actors are doing.

To get ourselves ready to do the best job we can, we should start rehearsals with a few exercises that will put us in a good mood and prepare our bodies and voices for our character.*

So, please stand up and form a semicircle in front of your instructor, or a big circle around your instructor, depending on the number of participants. Bend your arms in front of your body, and shake your hands, letting them hang from your wrists as if they were asleep. Do this for as long as it feels good, and don't think about anything else. If you start to giggle while doing this exercise, that's a good sign. Giggle!

Now, stand with your feet about one foot apart and bend your knees. Move your body gently up and down. You may place your hands on your legs if you are more comfortable that way. If you do this well, you may find yourself smiling and looking at others who are smiling, too. Go ahead, smile!

Straighten up and shake your shoulders a few times. Then let your head hang down slowly, followed by your arms. Your head and your arms feel heavy, and you bring them down, down, down, very slowly. Can you touch the floor with your fingertips? If you can, touch it, but don't force your body to do it. Now, very slowly, bring up your arms and head.

Breathe deeply through your nose, and bring your shoulders up so that your head is caught between them. Bring the shoulders down and let the air out through your mouth at the same time. Do this three times. How about picking a few apples now? Imagine that you are under a tree, and the branches are at arm's reach if you stretch your body all you can and bring your arm as high as

---

Note: I thank Charles Frink for introducing me to warming up before a rehearsal and the children of all ages who have enjoyed these and other exercises and who, in many cases, have provided wonderful ideas to get ready to act.

it can go, sometimes even having to stand on your toes to reach the apple you want. Do this once with your right hand, and place the "apple" on an imaginary basket at your feet. Now you are a left-handed apple picker, then a right-handed one, and so on, until you have stretched your body enough. Yawn at the end of the job.

Keeping your position in the circle, turn to your right and look at your fellow actor, who has turned his or her back to you to look at his or her fellow actor. Look at how the person is dressed, how tall he or she is, and how far this actor is standing from you. Try not to change this distance when you move: don't bump into anyone. Start walking when your instructor tells you to. Move at a normal pace, keeping in mind that there are people behind and in front of you. Next, your instructor tells you to walk as if you were very tired, or as if you were feeling very happy or sad, or in a great hurry. Whatever the instructor tells you to feel, try to act out the best way you can, and within your own space.

Face the inside of the circle now, and hold hands with the two people next to you. Bring your right leg forward, then backward. Do the same with the left one. Try not to lose your balance. Do this three times with each leg. Then, bend your right leg and bring your knee up, at a ninety-degree angle with your body. You are still holding hands, and probably smiling at one another. Roll your ankle around, to the right and to the left. Your back and your head should feel very good while you do this. Repeat this with the left leg and ankle.

Sit on the floor, placing your hands just behind your body. You are all still in a circle, so you can see everyone. If you have not already taken off your shoes, do so now. Look at your toes, which are just in front of you. Wiggle them. Is there a volunteer to count them? From one to ten, and from ten to one. So, if you have all your toes on, bring them all toward your body, and say HI! as loud as you can without yelling. Then, bring them away from your body, and say GOOD-BYE!, also as loud as you can without straining your voice. Move your toes back and forth several times, as many times as you want and as fast as you can! Before moving on to something else, who is nimble enough to say good-bye to your toes by touching them without bending your legs?

Now we are coming to the end of the exercises that you should do to warm up before a rehearsal. It is not necessary to do them all at every rehearsal, but some of them, done in the right combination, will help you become a good performer. So, sitting down as you are now, lie on your back, with your hands by your side. Close your eyes and think only of what you are doing. Place your right hand on your belly button. Breathe deeply through your nose, bringing the air inside your body until your belly feels like a big balloon. Hold the air in for as long as it takes you to count slowly to three in your mind, then release the air through your mouth. Do this again: The third time you are ready to let the air go; do so while softly saying "wow-wow-wow- wow-wow" without straining your throat. Breathe in two more times, and every time you exhale, say the "wow-wows" a little bit louder. Open your eyes, and slowly sit up. Do this by placing both hands on the floor to your right and propping up your body.

Now that you are warmed up, you are ready to start rehearsing. Please keep a few important things in mind: the other people who are doing the play with you also need to learn the lines and movements of their characters. So, concentrate on the work at hand. Don't speak loudly or become disruptive. Save some of that wonderful extra energy that you have for exercising outdoors. If someone starts bothering you, don't respond. It takes two to fight.

And what happens if you want to play the part that someone else is playing? Or you think that your best friend should be the princess, instead of that other person? Or what if you have been fighting for two days with someone who is in the play, and you think that the other person should leave the group? I've been through all that—and worse. Should I tell you what I did? No; you must decide what should be done in your situation. Ask the director for advice, talk it over with your parents. Perhaps you should suggest to the director that you start the next rehearsal by talking about whatever it is with the whole group while sitting on the floor in a circle. That should be an interesting warm-up exercise.

Good luck, and don't hesitate to invite me to your next performance.

R. Espinosa
New London, Connecticut
March 13, 2001

The Farmer Finds His True Friends

El granjero descubre a sus verdaderos amigos

Cow

(Directions for the horns
are shown below.)

A white long-sleeved top
and white pants (or long
johns) are painted with black
cloth dye. (You could use
black paint, but the dye works
better.) A fabric dye called
Rit Dye is available at large
fabric, craft, or grocery stores.

Attach the tail
to the pants with
needle and thread.

(Directions for the
tail are shown below.)

Black socks make the feet.
You can just wear socks, or
if they are big enough,
put them on over your shoes.

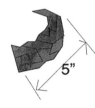

5"

Take three strips of any kind of
fabric. Cut strips 2 to 3 inches wide
by 15 inches long. Cut two white strips and
one black strip. Twist the three fabrics
together and tie them in a knot. Cut the pieces
of fabric beyond the knot in thin strips
to form the end of the tail.

Take aluminum foil and
crinkle it up tightly to form
the shape of a horn, about
5 to 6 inches from base to tip.
Make two horns. Next,
take masking tape and
cover the aluminum
foil with the tape. Make
two flaps of the masking
tape on both sides
of the horn. Attach
bobby pins to the flaps
to hold the horns
on the head.

Twist the ends together and sew
them in place. Now you are ready to sew
the tail onto the pants.

Figure 1

The Farmer Finds His True Friends

A play with music for very young people

Characters

- The farmer, Patrick
- His wife, Sara
- The horse, Beauty
- The mice (as many as possible: Spanish-speakers preferable)
- The cat
- The dog, Faithful
- The cow
- The pig
- The chicken
- The customer, Jake McClean
- Narrator (optional)

> *Note:* At the end of the Spanish version of this play there is a text, in bilingual form, which can be used to introduce each scene if this is wanted by the director, or if there is an extra actor available.

SCENE 1

(The cat, sitting in the middle of the stage, grooms himself with great care. One by one, the mice, in a teasing mood, come and stand behind him in a semicircle. The mice sing "Yo tengo un gato" while the cat looks at them sideways, thinking. When the song is finished, the cat finally jumps at the mice, who scatter fearfully, but at the same time they giggle from the fun they've had teasing the cat. The song may be sung by everyone at once or by a soloist and chorus.)

Soloist: *Yo tengo un gato,*

Chorus: ¡Miau-miau!

Soloist: *Con un rabo largo,*

Chorus: ¡Miau-miau!

Soloist: *Que es muy goloso,*

Chorus: ¡Miau-miau!

Soloist: *Y está muy gordo,*

Chorus: ¡Miau-miau!

(The farmer enters, carrying tools, which he slowly puts away.)

Farmer: Whew! A farmer has a long day. But it's worth it. What beautiful animals! And strong! I'm a great farmer, if I do say so myself!

(He sits on a stool, tired.)

Farmer: For example, the horse.

(The horse enters, strong and full of grace.)

Farmer: What a wonderful head and full mane! And the way he walks! What dignity!

(The horse exits. The cat comes in, licking his whiskers.)

Farmer: And the cat! The best mouser in the county! Just look at him.

(The cat exits. The dog comes in, sniffing everywhere. He looks ferocious and ready to attack, but he is gentle with the farmer.)

Farmer: And my dog! He would defend the farm even if it cost him his life! Come here, Faithful!

(The dog goes to the farmer, gently rubs against his legs, and then goes away, sniffing and ready to attack. The cow enters.)

Farmer: And what about the cow! She is a sweetie. She gives us the best milk in the whole county. Yum, yum!

(The farmer licks his moustache, thinking of the milk. The cow exits and the pig enters.)

Farmer: And the pig . . . We haven't tasted him yet, but my grandmother used to tell me when I was a boy that well-behaved pigs make good sausages. And he is a very well-behaved pig. *(He pats the pig.)* Piggy-piggy! Nice piggy!

(The pig exits, and in comes the chicken.)

Farmer: But how can I forget the chicken and the fat eggs that she gives us to cook our Sunday brunch omelettes with cheese!

(He rubs his belly while the chicken crosses in front of him and exits.)

Farmer: That reminds me. It's time for supper. Sara is waiting for me!

(The farmer rises and exits, full of self-satisfaction.)

SCENE 2

(In the dining room, Sara, the farmer's wife, is setting the table for supper. Her husband comes in, gives her a kiss on the cheek, and then both sit down to supper. The wife serves, and both eat.)

Farmer: The food is very good, Sara.

Sara: Thank you, Pat. But isn't the food always good?

Farmer: *(Eating a lot.)* It certainly is.

Sara: I do my best.

Farmer: *(Thoughtful.)* You know, Sara, I've been thinking. We have a stable full of very nice animals.

Sara: Yes—wonderful animals.

Farmer: I bet they're worth a lot of money. If I were to sell the horse . . .

Sara: *(Horrified.)* Sell the horse!?

(The cat walks in, approaches Sara.)

Farmer: Excuse me, but I am talking . . . If I were to sell the horse . . .

(Disgusted, Sara ignores Pat and pays attention to the cat. She gives him something to eat. The cat eats slowly, listening attentively.)

Farmer: . . . I bet you that I would get a good price for it. And if I were to sell the cow . . .

(Sara is about to say something, but eats instead, her head lowered.)

Farmer: . . . I would have enough money to buy milk in the store for the rest of my life.

Sara: Your life! What about mine?

Farmer: Yours too, sweetheart. In short, if I were to sell the animals, we could retire and move to Florida.

Sara: And what would we do there?

Farmer: Nothing. Enjoy the sunshine.

Sara: *(Weeping.)* Oh, I would miss my animals! They are so beautiful and friendly! In fact, they are my best friends!

Farmer: Yes, they are very nice, Sara. But after all, they are just animals. Dry your tears, and go to make some coffee.

(Sara leaves without a word, drying her tears. The cat stays where he is, listening. The farmer picks up the phone and dials a number. After a few rings, a voice answers, that of Jake McClean.)

Jake: *(Offstage.)* Howdy, who is this?

Farmer: Jake, this is your neighbor, Patrick MacDonald. I want to know whether you're still interested in buying animals for your farm.

Jake: I sure am, Pat. Do you want to sell some?

Farmer: That's why I'm calling.

Jake: Well, now, how about meeting tomorrow morning at ten o'clock at your place? I want to see the animals before I buy.

Farmer: That's fair! Please come over for coffee and cookies. My Sara is a great cook, you know.

Jake: I love cookies! Until tomorrow morning at ten, Pat.

Farmer: Good night, Jake.

(The farmer hangs up the phone and rubs his hands in delight, as if the deal were already done. The cat, without making a noise, leaves the room.)

SCENE 3

(In the barn, all the animals are asleep. The cat enters and starts making a lot of noise, meowing and pawing at the walls.)

Horse: *(Awakening in a bad mood.)* What's all this?

Cow: Yeah! That's what I say!

Chicken: *(With contempt.)* It's the cat again. Who else!

Cat: Sssshhhhhhhhhhhhhhhhh! Don't make a sound!

Pig: Why . . .

(The cat covers the pig's mouth with its paw.)

Cat: I have news, and it is not good.

(All the animals, fully awake now, sit surrounding the cat, looking worried.)

Cat: The farmer wants to sell us.

All: Sell us?!

Cat: Yes.

Cow: Why?

Cat: To retire and move to Florida.

Dog: To whom will he sell us?

Cat: To Jake McClean!

(They all gasp in horror.)

Pig: Oh, no! He'll starve us!

Dog: I'll never get another bath again.

Cat: He's coming tomorrow morning at ten to look at us.

Horse: He will buy us, for sure. We are the best.

Dog: We need a plan.

Cow: Exactly.

Cat: I think Sara will help.

(They sit in a circle, their heads together. They whisper for a few moments, then they put their arms around each other's shoulders, in a show of friendship.)

All the animals: *(In a loud whisper.)* Until tomorrow at ten!

(They all go back to sleep except the cat, who goes back to the house.)

SCENE 4

(On the porch at Pat MacDonald's house, Pat and Jake are sitting, a little table between them, with tea and cookies.)

Jake: Where are the animals, Pat?

Farmer: My wife has gone to fetch them. Here, have a cookie. Sara is a wonderful cook.

Jake: *(Happy at the thought of eating, Jake picks up a cookie.)* Chocolate chip! I love them.

(Jake takes a bite of the cookie and almost chokes. Very politely, he looks the other way, takes the bite out of his mouth, and puts it in his pocket.)

Jake: *(Aside.)* A good cook! That cookie almost killed me!

Farmer: What did you say?

Jake: N-nothing. I was just wondering what I am going to get my wife for Christmas.

Farmer: Christmas? But it's May!

Jake: I . . . I like to do things early. Say, may I take the rest of the cookie home? It's delicious!

Farmer: Take it home? *(Puzzled.)* Sure. Take this napkin.

Jake: Thank you . . . Now, where are the animals?

Farmer: *(Looking to the right.)* Here they come!

(Sara appears stage right with the animals. She is not sad anymore, but grinning. The horse enters first and stops in the middle of the stage. His walk is clumsy.)

Farmer: Here is the horse! The finest in the county! His name is Beauty.

Jake: Come here, Beauty.

(The horse approaches Jake, stumbling.)

Jake: What is this? Is this a horse or half a horse?

(The horse has only one ear, no tail, etc.)

Farmer: *(Eyes big in disbelief, embarrassed.)* I . . . I . . . Horse, go and get dressed!

(Still walking clumsily, the horse moves toward stage left.)

Horse: *(Aside, to audience.)* Isn't it great what you can do with costumes? Hee-haw! *(He starts to exit, but comes back.)* The way I see it, half a horse is better than no horse at all! Hee-haw!

(Walking clumsily again, the horse exits.)

Jake: And here comes the cat! Nice cat. Here, trap this little mouse for me, kitty!

(Jake takes a mouse out of his pocket and throws it toward the cat, who screams and runs out, stage left.)

Cat: A mouse! Agggghhhhhhhhhhh!

Jake: *(Giggling.)* The best mouser in the county, eh, Pat? Ha ha ha! Let's see the pig.

(The pig walks slowly toward the two men.)

Farmer: *(Afraid.)* He is . . . very sweet.

(The pig gets his paws on Jake's dish, grabs all the cookies he can, grins, runs around Jake, giggles, and runs off stage left. Both Jake and the farmer grab their seats, scared.)

Jake: *(Relaxing after the pig scare.)* So, the pig is sweet and Sara is a good c—

Farmer: What?

Jake: Nothing, I was talking to myself. The Christmas thing, you know.

Farmer: *(Very nervous.)* You're a very good husband. Here comes the chicken! We make the best omelettes . . .

(The chicken runs onstage, pursued by Sara. The chicken holds a big chunk of cheese omelette in her beak, which Sara is trying to recover. They run around for a while. Pat is worried and Jake grins. The chicken and Sara eventually run off stage left.)

Jake: *(With a mean grin.)* I'll bet you the eggs taste good in the omelette. My wife . . . But wait, here comes the dog.

Farmer: *(Soothing.)* We call him Faithful. He is a great watchdog—and very clean.

Jake: Good, because I hate spending money on soap for dogs.

(Faithful comes in. He is filthy. He rubs against Jake's legs over and over. Jake covers his nose and tries to move his legs to see if the dog will go away, but he won't. Pat is beside himself with rage but cannot say a word. Jake finally manages to get up, trying to avoid the dog.)

Jake: Grrrreat animals. I must go.

Farmer: But what . . . about . . . buying? And look, here's the cow!

(The cow is about to enter, covering her mouth with her hoof to hide her laughter.)

Jake: Ah, yes, the cow! If she's like the others! I . . . I'll call . . . when . . . I . . . talk . . . to my wife.

(Runs offstage.)

Farmer: *(Running after him with the wrapped cookie.)* Your cookie! *(Pat scratches his head, puzzled.)* Hmm! I guess Jake doesn't like the animals. They do look different today. Very different. Well, I can't retire to Florida, so I'll eat the cookie.

(He takes a bite, almost chokes, and rushes off in a rage.)

Farmer: Sara! Sara! Where are you? Sara!

(Exits stage right. Sara and all the animals, happy now, enter from stage left. Sara has a huge tray of cookies in her hand. They all smile.)

Sara: The real cookies!

All the animals: *(Each picking up a cookie and lifting them to toast.)* To Sara, the best cook in the county!

Sara: *(Lifting a cookie, standing in the middle of the group.)* To all my animals!

(The farmer reenters, watching. After a moment, Sara sees him.)

Sara: Here, Pat, have a cookie.

(The farmer approaches her slowly. He carefully picks up a cookie, examines it, and smells it.)

Farmer: Do I dare?

Sara: Pat, you know I'm a very good cook.

(Farmer bites carefully, chews, and smiles.)

Farmer: Well, I guess I have learned a lesson in love.

(Everyone eats the cookies. They sing "Yo tengo un gato" again, "Old MacDonald Had a Farm," or another song about animals. The mice appear again, as in the beginning, and as they start their teasing, the cat chases them offstage. The rest go on eating cookies.)

THE END

Yo tengo un gato

SOLO
Yo tengo un gato,

CHORUS
¡Miau-miau!

SOLO
Con un rabo largo,

CHORUS
¡Miau-miau!

SOLO
Que es muy goloso,

CHORUS
¡Miau-miau!

SOLO
Y está muy gordo.

EVERYONE
¡Miau-miau!

Words by Resurrección Espinosa
Music by Charles Frink

Allegro ma non troppo

Yo ten-go un ga-to ¡Mi - au! ¡Mi - au! Con

un ra-bo lar-go, ¡Mi - au! ¡Mi - au! Que

es muy go-lo-so ¡Mi - au! ¡Mi - au! Y es-

meno mosso ... *a tempo*

tá muy gor-do. ¡Mi - au! ¡Mi - au!

NOTE: The piece may be sung a cappella or with accompaniment by guitar or keyboard—preferably playing only the chords. A flute may play the melody with the voices. Any louder instrument will probably spoil the effect.

El granjero descubre a sus verdaderos amigos

Una obra para actores y bailarines jóvenes, con música

Personajes

- El granjero, Patricio MacDonald
- Su esposa, Sara
- El caballo, Belleza
- Los ratones
- El gato
- El perro, Fiel
- La vaca
- El cerdo
- La gallina
- El cliente, Joaquín McClean
- Narrador/a (opcional)

> (*Nota:* Si se decide usar un narrador/a, al final de la obra se encontrará una introducción bilingüe que se debe de hacer al principio de cada escena. Esto ayuda al público a comprender el argumento mejor.)

ESCENA 1

(Estamos en la granja de Patricio MacDonald. En la mitad del patio, el gato se limpia con mucho cuidado. Los ratones, uno a uno, entran y se sientan detrás del gato, formando un semicírculo. El gato está muy serio, mientras que los ratones se burlan de él con movimientos que pretenden imitar lo que el gato hace. De pronto, los ratones, que tienen un cantante solista, empiezan a cantar, mientras el gato los mira de reojo.)

Ratón solista: Yo tengo un gato,

Coro de ratones: ¡Miau, miau!

Ratón solista: Con un rabo largo,

Coro de ratones: ¡Miau, miau!

Ratón solista: Que es muy goloso,

Coro de ratones: ¡Miau, miau!

Ratón solista: Y está muy gordo.

Todos los ratones: ¡Miau, miau!

(Tan pronto como termina la canción, el gato se vuelve hacia los ratones, con la intención de comérselos. Los ratones se desbandan y se esconden donde pueden, entre miedosos y divertidos. El granjero aparece con sus instrumentos de trabajo, y los deja en su sitio con mucho cuidado.)

> **Granjero:** ¡Uf! El día es largo para un granjero. Pero merece la pena. ¡Qué bellos animales! ¡Y fuertes! Soy un gran granjero, aunque lo diga yo.

(Se sienta en una silla, cansado.)

> **Granjero:** ¡Qué animales! Por ejemplo, el caballo.

(El caballo entra, fuerte y lleno de gracia.)

> **Granjero:** ¡Qué bella cabeza tiene, con esa crin tan sana! ¡Y cómo camina! ¡Qué dignidad!

(El caballo sale del escenario. Entra el gato, lamiéndose los bigotes.)

> **Granjero:** ¡Y el gato! El mejor cazador de ratones en todo el condado. Ahí lo tienen.

(El gato sale. Se acerca el perro, oliéndolo todo, con apariencia feroz, listo para el ataque. Pero se porta muy cariñoso con el granjero.)

> **Granjero:** ¡Y mi perro! Defendería la granja aunque le costara la vida. ¡Ven aquí, Fiel!

(El perro se acerca a Patricio y restriega el cuerpo contra la pierna del granjero, y entonces se va, con la misma expresión con la que entró: feroz y listo para atacar. La vaca se acerca.)

> **Granjero:** ¿Y qué no podría decir yo de la vaca? Es muy dulce. Nos da la mejor leche del condado. ¡Ñam, ñam!

(El granjero se lame el bigote, pensando en la leche tan deliciosa que da la vaca. La vaca sale y entra el cerdo.)

> **Granjero:** ¡Y el cerdo! No lo hemos probado todavía, pero mi abuela siempre nos decía cuando yo era niño que de cerditos bien educados se hacen buenas salchichas. Y él es un cerdo bien educado. *(Patricio da unas palmaditas cariñosas al cerdo.)* ¡Cerdito, cerdito! Precioso cerdito.

(El cerdo se va, y entra la gallina.)

> **Granjero:** ¡Y no me puedo olvidar de la gallina y de los huevos tan gordos que nos deja para que nos hagamos tortillas con queso para los desayunos de los domingos!

(El granjero se acaricia el estómago, mientras la gallina cruza el escenario muy orgullosa y se va.)

> **Granjero:** Lo que me recuerda que es la hora de la cena. ¡Sara me está esperando!

(Satisfecho de su granja, el granjero se levanta y sale.)

ESCENA 2

(El comedor. Sara, la esposa, está poniendo la mesa. Su esposo entra. Le da un beso en la mejilla, y los dos se sientan a cenar. La esposa sirve la comida, y los dos comen.)

Granjero: La comida está muy buena, Sara.

Sara: Como siempre, Patricio.

Granjero: *(Comiendo mucho.)* Es verdad.

Sara: Gracias.

Granjero: *(Pensativo.)* ¿Sabes, Sara? Tenemos un establo lleno de buenos animales.

Sara: Lo sé, Patricio. Lo he visto.

Granjero: *(Pensativo, como si estuviera hablando consigo mismo.)* Apuesto a que valen un montón de dinero. Si yo vendiera el caballo . . .

Sara: *(Horrorizada.)* ¿Vender el caballo?

(El gato entra, muy silencioso, y se sienta cerca de Sara.)

Granjero: Perdón, que estoy hablando. Si vendiera el caballo . . .

(Enfadada, Sara le presta atención al gato. Le da comida. El gato come lentamente, escuchando con mucha atención.)

Granjero: . . . apuesto a que me pagarían un buen precio por él. Y si vendiera la vaca...

(Sara está a punto de decir algo, pero lo piensa mejor y sigue comiendo, con la cabeza baja.)

Granjero: . . . tendría bastante dinero para comprar leche en la tienda el resto de mi vida.

Sara: ¡Tu vida! Y la mía, ¿qué?

Granjero: La tuya también, mi amor. En resumen, si vendiera los animales, nos podríamos jubilar e irnos a vivir a Florida.

Sara: ¿Y qué haríamos allí?

Granjero: Nada. Gozar del sol.

Sara: *(Llorando.)* ¡Ay, extrañaría tanto a mis animales! ¡Son tan cariñosos y lindos! De hecho, son mis mejores amigos.

Granjero: Son buenos, Sara. Pero, después de todo, son sólo animales. Sécate las lágrimas, y vete a hacer café.

(Sara sale sin decir nada, secándose las lágrimas. El gato se queda donde está, escuchando. El granjero se levanta, descuelga el teléfono y marca un número. El teléfono suena tres veces y una voz responde, la de Joaquín McClean.)

Joaquín: *(Entre bastidores.)* ¿Dígame? ¿Qién habla?

> **Granjero:** Joaquín, soy tu vecino Patricio MacDonald. Quiero saber si todavía estás interesado en comprar animales para tu granja.
>
> **Joaquín:** Por supuesto, Patricio. ¿Vas a vender alguno?
>
> **Granjero:** Por eso llamo.
>
> **Joaquín:** ¿Qué te parece si nos vemos mañana en tu granja a las diez? Quiero ver los animales antes de comprarlos.
>
> **Granjero:** Me parece bien. Por favor, vente a tomar una taza de café y galletas de chocolate. Sabes que mi Sara es una gran cocinera.
>
> **Joaquín:** Hasta mañana a las diez, Patricio. Me encantan las galletas de chocolate.
>
> **Granjero:** Buenas noches, Joaquín.

(El granjero cuelga el teléfono, se restriega las manos muy contento, como si ya hubiera hecho negocio. El gato, sin hacer ruido, sale de la habitación.)

ESCENA 3

(El establo. Todos los animales duermen. El gato entra y empieza a hacer ruido, maullando y arañando las paredes. Los otros animales se despiertan de mal humor.)

> **Caballo:** *(De muy mal humor.)* ¿Qué pasa?
>
> **Vaca:** Sí, ¡eso es lo que a mí me gustaría saber!
>
> **Gallina:** *(Con desprecio.)* Es el gato otra vez. ¡Quién iba a ser!
>
> **Gato:** ¡Chitón! ¡No hagáis ningún ruido!
>
> **Cerdo:** ¿Por . . .

(El gato cubre la boca del cerdo con su garra.)

> **Gato:** Traigo noticias, y no son buenas.

(Los animales, completamente despiertos ahora, rodean al gato, preocupados.)

> **Gato:** El granjero nos quiere vender.
>
> **Todos:** ¿Vendernos!?
>
> **Gato:** Sí.
>
> **Vaca:** ¿Por qué?
>
> **Gato:** Para jubilarse y mudarse a Florida.
>
> **Perro:** ¿A quién nos va a vender?
>
> **Gato:** A Joaquín McClean.

(Los animales se quedan boquiabiertos, horrorizados.)

> **Cerdo:** ¡Oh, no! ¡Nos matará de hambre!
>
> **Perro:** No me bañarán otra vez en mi vida.
>
> **Gato:** Viene mañana a las diez a vernos.

Caballo: Nos comprará, seguro. Somos los mejores.

Perro: Necesitamos un plan.

Vaca: Exactamente.

Gato: Creo que Sara nos ayudará.

(Se sientan en un círculo con las cabezas muy juntas. Hablan en voz baja por unos segundos y echan los brazos alrededor de los hombros de los compañeros en señal de amistad.)

Todos los animales: *(En un murmullo audible.)* ¡Hasta mañana a las diez!

(Todos se echan a dormir otra vez, menos el gato, que vuelve a la casa.)

ESCENA 4

(El porche de la casa del granjero. Patricio y Joaquín están sentados frente a una pequeña mesa, sobre la que hay galletas y café.)

Joaquín: ¿Dónde están los animales, Patricio?

Granjero: Mi esposa ha ido a buscarlos. Anda, cómete una galleta. Sara es una gran cocinera.

Joaquín: *(Contento con la idea de comer, toma una galleta.)* ¡Galletas de chocolate! Me encantan.

(Joaquín le da un bocado a la galleta y casi se atraganta. Con mucha educación, se vuelve en dirección contraria a la que está Patricio, se saca la galleta de la boca y la pone en el bolsillo.)

Joaquín: *(Aparte.)* ¡Una buena cocinera! Si por pocas me mata la galletita esta.

Granjero: ¿Dijiste algo?

Joaquín: N-nada. Me estaba preguntando en voz alta qué es lo que le voy a comprar a mi esposa para Navidad.

Granjero: ¿Para Navidad? ¡Pero si estamos en mayo!

Joaquín: M-me gusta hacer las cosas con tiempo. Dime, ¿me puedo llevar el resto de la galleta a mi casa? ¡Está deliciosa!

Granjero: *(Extrañado.)* Por supuesto. Toma esta servilleta.

Joaquín: Gracias . . . ¿Dónde están los animales?

Granjero: *(Mirando a su derecha.)* ¡Aquí vienen!

(Sara aparece a la derecha del escenario con los animales. Parece muy feliz, y sonríe. El caballo entra primero, se para en el centro del escenario. Camina torpemente.)

Granjero: ¡Aquí está el caballo! El mejor del condado. Se llama Belleza.

Joaquín: Ven aquí, Belleza.

(El caballo se acerca a Joaquín, dando tropezones a cada paso.)

Joaquín: ¿Qué es esto? ¿Un caballo, o medio caballo?

(El caballo sólo tiene una oreja y no lleva rabo.)

Granjero: *(Los ojos muy abiertos, como si no pudiera creer lo que ve.)* Yo, yo . . . ¡Caballo, vete a vestirte!

(Sin dejar de caminar con torpeza y tropezando mucho, el caballo se dirige a la izquierda del escenario.)

Caballo: *(Al público.)* ¿No es fabuloso lo que uno puede hacer con disfraces? ¡Ja-ja! *(Empieza a andar hacia la salida, pero se vuelve.)* Lo que yo digo es que medio caballo es mejor que ninguno. ¡Ja-ja!

(El caballo se va, caminando torpemente. Los dos granjeros lo han estado mirando: Joaquín con ironía, y Patricio con asombro.)

Joaquín: ¡Y aquí viene el gato! Muy lindo. A ver, atrapa este ratoncillo, gatito.

(Joaquín se saca un ratoncillo del bolsillo y lo echa cerca del gato, que grita y sale corriendo del escenario.)

Gato: ¡Un ratón! ¡Ayyyyyyyyyyyyyyyyyyy!

Joaquín: *(Riendo entre dientes.)* El mejor cazador de ratones de todo el condado, ¿eh, Patricio? ¡Ja-ja-ja! Vamos a ver el cerdo.

(El cerdo camina lentamente hacia los dos hombres.)

Granjero: *(Con miedo.)* Es . . . muy dulce.

(El cerdo pone las patas dentro del plato de Joaquín, se lleva toda las galletas, se ríe, corre alrededor de la silla de Joaquín, se ríe más, y sale del escenario por la izquierda. Los dos hombres, agarrados a sus sillas, se quedan petrificados.)

Joaquín: *(Relajándose después de la salida del cerdo.)* Así que el cerdo es dulce y Sara—

Granjero: ¿Qué?

Joaquín: Nada, estaba hablándome a mí mismo. Lo de Navidad, ya sabes.

Granjero: *(Muy nervioso.)* Eres un buen esposo. ¡Aquí viene la gallina! Hacemos las tortillas más buenas . . .

(La gallina empieza a correr por el escenario, perseguida por Sara. El animal lleva en la boca un trozo grande de tortilla de queso, que Sara está intentando recuperar. Hacen esto por un rato, mientras Joaquín sonríe con burla y Patricio está más y más preocupado. La gallina y Sara salen del escenario por la izquierda, como los otros animales.)

Joaquín: *(Malicioso.)* Seguro que los huevos están buenos en la tortilla. Mi esposa . . . Pero mira, aquí viene el perro.

Granjero: *(Aplacador.)* Lo llamamos Fiel. Es un gran perro guardián. Y muy limpio.

Joaquín: Me alegra, porque odio gastar dinero en jabón para perros.

(Fiel entra. Está muy sucio. Se restriega contra la pierna de Joaquín una y otra vez. Joaquín se cubre la nariz y trata de mover la pierna para ver si el perro se va, pero sin conseguirlo. Patricio está furioso, pero no puede decir palabra. Joaquín logra levantarse por fin, en su intento de evitar el perro.)

Joaquín: Prrrrre-ciosos animales. Debo irme.

Granjero: Pero ¿y . . . qué pasa . . . con la compra? ¡Mira, aquí viene la vaca!

(La vaca está a punto de entrar, cubriéndose la boca para evitar que se le note la risa.)

Joaquín: ¡Ah, sí, la vaca! Si es como los otros . . . Yo te llamaré . . . cuando . . . cuando hable con mi esposa.

(Sale corriendo por la derecha.)

Granjero: *(Va corriendo detrás de Joaquín, con la galleta liada en la servilleta.)* ¡La galleta! *(Se para y se rasca la cabeza, sin saber qué hacer.)* ¡Ummmmmm! Me parece que a Joaquín no le gustan los animales. La verdad es que parecen diferentes hoy. Muy diferentes. Bueno, no me puedo retirar a Florida, así que me comeré la galleta.

(Le da un bocado a la galleta y casi se ahoga. Cruza el escenario corriendo, lleno de rabia.)

Granjero: ¡Sara! ¡Saraaaaaa! ¿Dónde estás, Sara?

(Sale por la derecha. Sara y los animales, arreglados y felices, entran por la izquierda. Sara lleva en la mano una gran bandeja de galletas. Todos sonríen.)

Sara: ¡Las galletas de verdad!

Todos los animales: *(Tomando una galleta cada uno.)* ¡A Sara, la mejor cocinera del condado!

Sara: *(Levanta una galleta, de pie en medio del grupo.)* ¡A todos mis animales!

(El granjero entra, mira la escena. De pronto, Sara lo ve.)

Sara: Ven, Patricio. Toma una galleta.

(El granjero se acerca lentamente, toma una galleta con cuidado, la examina, la huele.)

Granjero: ¿Me atrevo?

Sara: Patricio, sabes que soy muy buena cocinera.

(El granjero le da un bocado, mastica, sonríe.)

Granjero: Creo que he aprendido una lección sobre el amor.

(Todos comen galletas. Cantan "Yo tengo un gato" otra vez, "Old MacDonald Had a Farm," u otra canción sobre animales. Los ratones aparecen como al principio y empiezan a imitar al gato, que los ve, corre tras ellos, y gato y ratones desaparecen mientras los demás terminan las galletas.)

FIN

NARRADOR(A) BILINGÜE/BILINGUAL NARRATOR

Narrador(a) se acerca al público al principio de cada escena, antes de que salgan los actores. Cuando haya terminado, se sienta en una silla a la derecha del escenario. El/la narrador(a) puede tener en la mano una copia de la obra para ayudar a los actores en caso de que se pierdan.

The narrator approaches the audience at the beginning of each scene, before the actors come out. When he or she has finished speaking, the narrator may sit on a chair by either side of the stage. The narrator can also act as a prompter to help actors if they need it.

Escena 1/Scene 1

Narradora: Señoras y señores, estamos en la granja del señor Patricio Mac-Donald, de su esposa Sara, y de todos sus animales. El trabajo ha terminado, pero eso no quiere decir que la vida se pare aquí. ¡Es a la hora de la cena cuando la acción empieza!

Narrator: Ladies and gentlemen, we are at the farm of Pat MacDonald, his wife Sara, and all their animals. The day's work has ended, but that doesn't mean that life has stopped. It's at dinnertime when the action starts!

Escena 2/Scene 2

Narradora: Ahora vamos a ver lo buena cocinera que Sara es, y lo calculadores que pueden ser los hombres algunas veces. ¡Ah!, pero si hay un buen gato en la casa, nada cambiará, y la vida seguirá tan feliz como siempre.

Narrator: We are going to see now what a good cook Sara is—and how calculating men can be sometimes. Ah, but if there is a good cat in the house, nothing will change, and things will go on as happily as ever.

Escena 3/Scene 3

Narradora: Pero, ¿cómo? ¿Cómo va a seguir la vida tan bien como antes? Con los planes que tiene el granjero, las cosas no se ven muy bien para los pobres animales. Pero veamos lo que pasa en el establo.

Narrator: But, how? How is life going to continue as well as before? With the plans that the farmer has, things do not look good for the poor animals. But let's see what's happening in the barn.

Escena 4/Scene 4

Narradora: Son las diez de la mañana del día siguiente. El vecino, Joaquín McClean, está comiendo galletas con Patricio mientras llegan los animales que quiere comprar. ¡Dios mío! ¿Qué les espera a los pobres animales?

Narrator: It is ten in the morning of the following day. The neighbor, Jake McClean, is about to eat cookies with Pat while they wait for the animals that Jake wants to buy. Heavens! What's in store for the poor animals?

Nota: Al final de la obra, invita al público a comer galletas.

Note: At the end of the play, invite the audience to eat cookies.

VOCABULARY–VOCABULARIO

Nouns–Nombres

barn: *establo*
costume: *disfraz*
county: *condado*
mane: *crin*
sausage: *salchicha*
tool: *herramienta*
whisper: *murmullo*

Adjectives–Adjetivos

embarrassed: *avergonzado, incómodo, molesto*
faithful: *fiel*
full: *lleno, completo*
mouser: *cazador de ratones*
sweet: *dulce, cariñoso*

Verbs–Verbos

to giggle: *reirse con una risilla tonta*
to groom oneself: *cuidarse, arreglarse, ponerse guapo*
to look sideways: *mirar de reojo*
to scatter: *dispersar, desparramar*
to starve: *matar o morir de hambre*
to tease: *molestar, tomar el pelo a alguien, jorobar*

The Princess Is Sad

La princesa está triste

Bird

(Directions for making the beak are shown below.)

Attach a few feathers to the head held in place with clips or bobby pins.

Wear a matching turtleneck with tights or sweatpants. Color depends on the bird. Red, blue, green, etc.

For the wings, take a piece of material, such as felt, about 2 yards long, and cut the feathers as shown. Sew to the sleeves and back of a turtleneck. Use a color that matches closely, or contrasts nicely, with the turtleneck.

Orange socks for the feet.

Tie enough string through both sides of beak to tie at the back of the head.

First fold here.

Place holes in both sides of the beak.

FOLD   FOLD

For the beak take a piece of orange construction paper that measures 5 1/2 by 4 inches. Make the first fold, as shown. Next, paint the nostrils, and fold both sides under.

Tape the two corners together.

Tape here

Figure 2

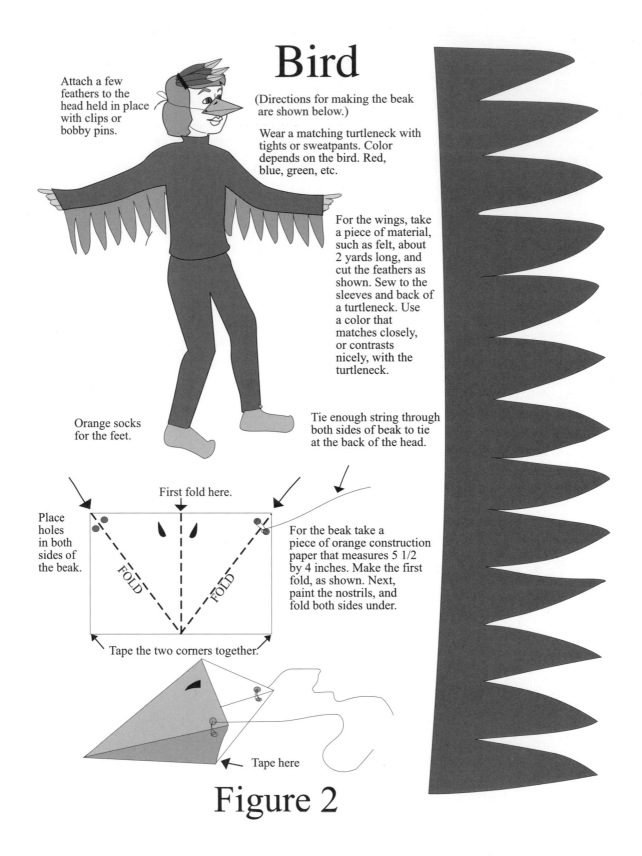

The Princess Is Sad

INTRODUCTION TO *THE PRINCESS IS SAD*

(Read by the Narrator.)

Welcome to *The Princess Is Sad,* a bilingual play for young people. The play starts in the living room of the palace, where the friends of the Princess are trying to make her feel better because she is very sad. What is the reason for her sadness? If you pay attention to what happens, you will know.

We hope that you like the performance. We have worked very hard making the scenery and learning how to act.

The characters are the Princess, the Page, the Dog, the Bird, the Centipede, the Cloud, the Tree, the Rose, the Teacher/Witch, the Palace Musicians, and the Narrator.

If you want to ask us questions when we are finished, please do so. And be attentive—we need silence to tell the story of the sad Princess and her friends.

Thank you.

Characters

- The Princess
- The Page
- The Bird
- The Centipede
- The Dog
- The Teacher/Witch
- The Rose
- The Tree
- The Cloud
- The Narrator

SCENE 1

(A room in the palace.)

Narrator: The Princess is very sad and walks around sighing, not knowing what to do with herself. Her attendants try to cheer her up, without success.

Page: The Princess is sad.

Dog: Sad. Very, very sad.

Bird: I wonder what's bothering her.

(The friends look at their audience, asking for help.)

Narrator: If anyone in the audience knows what's the matter with the Princess, please raise your hand.

Page: She is pale.

Dog: She has circles under her eyes.

Bird: She's upset.

Page: Her color is gone.

Dog: She's disconsolate.

Bird: Without speech and without a voice.

Page: I wonder what's bugging the Princess?

Bird & Dog: *(To the audience.)* Do you know?

Page: Does her head hurt?

(The Princess shakes her head. The Bird and the Dog look at the audience. Nobody knows the answer.)

Narrator and Audience: NOOOOO!

Page: Maybe her belly hurts.

(The Princess shakes her head. The Bird and the Dog look at the audience.)

Narrator and Audience: NOOOOOOOOOOO!

(The Princess starts crying and leaves. The Centipede comes in.)

Centipede: I know what's wrong with the Princess. Her heart aches.

Everybody: Her heart?

Page: Impossible!

Dog: That's what I say: impossible! The Princess has everything!

Bird: And, besides, she has friends: us!

Everybody: *(To the Centipede.)* IMPOSSIBLE!

Centipede: *(Turns its back on them, self-important.)* Well, that's up to you. If you don't believe me, good-bye.

Everybody: Wait! Did you say . . . did you say that her heart aches? And, why?

Centipede: You know how much the Princess loves to walk in the garden every morning and talk to the flowers, don't you?

Everybody: Of course we know! Of course we know!

(They all go to the garden.)

Rose: *(Very coquettish.)* Soy una rosa muy preciosa.

Tree: Y yo soy un árbol muy alto.

Cloud: Y yo soy una nube que sale y que entra, pero que por lo general vive aquí.

Bird: Oh, my! What's this?

Dog: I don't understand a word!

Page: (*Thoughtful.*) They certainly speak a very strange language.

Centipede: What has happened, I believe, is that the garden is bewitched.

Everyone: (*Trembling.*) Bewitched! Who . . . who h-h-h-as d-done it?

Centipede: I don't know. The best thing will be for each one of us to take a different direction and investigate.

(They separate.)

SCENE 2

(The palace's basement.)

Narrator: The Teacher/Witch is in the palace's basement. In a big pot, she is cooking letters-and-words soup.

Teacher/Witch:

Hokus-pokus!
Eeny-meeny!
¡Ostras-tortas!
Lizard-wizard!
¡Maison-liason!

Ha ha-ha-ha-ha-ha-ha-ha-ha-ha-ha! What a wonderful letters-and-words soup I'm cooking for myself! The letters-and-words soup is much more tasty than the just-letters soup! It is whisker-licking-good! Deeeliciouuusss! And as soon as I learn more, I'll make sentence soup, paragraph soup, poem soup, story soup, and even novel soup. And in as many languages as I want—that's my ambition. Let's see how my Italian sounds today: (*Sings.*) "Tralalalalalalala, *arrivederci, bambina,* tralalalalalalala." Ay, ay, ay! I don't know how to do rhymes in Italian yet. Let me see . . . where's the dictionary. . . .

(The Bird comes down the basement stairs, looks at what's going on, and is very afraid.)

Narrator: The Bird has just come down the stairs and discovered the Teacher/Witch. He is terrified!

Teacher/Witch: Ha-ha-ha-ha-ha-ha-ha-ha-ha-ha! With all the language study I'm doing, soon I'll be the wisest woman in the world—apart from being the most beautiful, of course—and afterward I'll be the most powerful. I'll show that stuck-up girl, the Princess! She didn't want to study Spanish because she said that she didn't need to, because she is the Princess. And so her father sent me here, to the basement. For a long time, I wept. Here, all by myself, I wept and wept. And so, just to see if I could forget my sadness, I started to read. And then I stopped crying. I realized that learning Spanish, French, or Italian is something I like to do very much. At first, it helped me to pass the time. Then, I realized that saying words in another language is like singing. And it was then that I conceived my vengeance. My terrible, total, turbulent, tormenting vengeance. With the knowledge I have from being a teacher, plus two or three magic words, I'm going to force the whole kingdom to speak another language. They will speak the language I want them to speak, whenever I want, because I want them to. In other words, they are going to be bewitched. The garden is already done. Let's see what's left: his Majesty the King, the Dog, the Page, the Bird . . . Hmmm . . . And then, when everything is bewitched, let's see what the Princess has to say . . . She who has everything, who knows eveything. Ha-ha-ha-ha-ha-ha-ha-ha! *Arrivederci!* Good-bye! *¡Adiós!*

Narrator: While the Teacher looks up a word in the dictionary, the Bird, who has seen everything, leaves, trembling.

SCENE 3

(The Bird goes in search of his friends.)

Narrator: The Bird tells his friends what he has seen. Everyone thinks hard to decide whether anything can be done.

Bird: So that's what the teacher said. What can we do?

Page: I have it! We could kidnap the Teacher.

Dog: And what would we do with her?

Page: I don't know . . . We could lock her up in the basement!

Bird: She is already in the basement.

Page: That's true.

Dog: Maybe, maybe . . .

Bird: *(To the public.)* Any idea? *¿Tenéis alguna idea?* Ahhhggggggggg!

Centipede: Easy, now. There is only one solution. We can go to the Teacher to tell her that we want her to be *our* teacher. It is possible that she feels wounded because the Princess rejected her. Besides, I would like to learn languages. I have always wanted to go to Greece, and I can't because I don't know the language.

Page: Learn languages! That's a lot of work.

Centipede: A lot of work? And how do you spend your time, jumping around?

Page: *¡Y yo que sé!* Ahhhgggggggggggggggggggg!

(They tremble and look around, huddled together.)

SCENE 4

(The basement.)

Narrator: The four friends arrive in the basement, smiling nervously. I think that they are afraid.

Everybody: Teacher!

Teacher/Witch: *(On the defensive.)* You want to fool me! Who are you?

Everybody: Your new and humble students.

Teacher/Witch: Ha-ha-ha-ha-ha-ha-ha! They think they can fool me! What do you want? Quick! Tell me before I confound your tongues forever!

Page: Teacher, I want to learn Spanish!

Dog: So do I!

Bird: And me too!

Centipede: We know that you are the best teacher around here. And here we are.

Everybody: ¡Sí!

(All the friends agree to the Centipede's words. When they try to say "Yes," they say "Sí," and tremble again.)

Teacher/Witch: And how will you pay me if I agree to teach you?

Page: With our friendship.

Dog: And hot chocolate after each lesson.

Bird: And a birthday cake.

Teacher/Witch: You have convinced me. Let's start: *¡A, B, C: Una, dos y tres— A, B, C: Una, dos y tres!*

(They say what the Teacher tells them. Then, they all sing to the tune of "Clementine.")

Everybody:
In the dungeon of the castle,
Brewing multilingual stew,
Five good friends work hard together
But they know they're one too few:
Oh, my princess! *¡Oh, Princesa!*
How we wish that you were here!
If you taste the stew we're cooking
You'll make sense
Of all you hear!

SCENE 5

(In the garden. The Princess sits next to the Rose, the Tree, and the Cloud.)

Narrator: The Princess is trying to be happy again in her garden, as before. But it is impossible.

Princess: What a fresh-smelling Rose!

Rose: *Soy una Rosa muy preciosa.*

(The Princess weeps disconsolately.)

Princess: I am so unhappy! I am so alone in the world! I cannot even talk to the flowers in my garden anymore! What shall I do?

(The four friends enter.)

Page: Hi, Princess.

Princess: *(Weeps.)* Hi.

Dog: Why are you so sad?

Princess: Ay! Something terrible has happened! Someone has bewitched the garden, and the flowers do not understand me!

Bird: Let's see what's going on here!

Centipede: Yes, let's see. *¡Hola, Rosa!*

Rose: *Hola, amigo. ¡Qué día tan bueno hace, y qué voz tan bella tienes!*

Centipede: *Gracias.*

Bird: *(To the Rose.) Eres muy preciosa y, además, hueles muy bien.*

Tree: *¡Oh, qué conversación tan interesante! ¡Señorita Nube, señorita Nube, venga aquí con nosotros!*

Princess: I don't get it! How is it that you understand and I don't?

Page: Princess, what happened is that we go to school.

Dog: Yes, we all go to school. We go because we think that one good thing we can do with our time is to learn how to communicate with others.

Princess: To school. And why should I go to school if I am the Princess?

Bird: Well, if you want to talk to the flowers in your garden . . .

Centipede: And if you want to understand what we are saying . . .

Princess: I will prohibit everyone from speaking that silly language!

Page: You cannot prohibit the flowers from doing anything. They are free.

Bird: Nor can you prohibit the hearts of your friends from caring about you.

Dog: Unless you don't want to have any friends.

Princess: What an unhappy girl am I! Everyone has abandoned me!

Centipede: Today, we'll learn a song in school. Do you want to come along?

Everyone: *(To the Princess.)* Yes, come! Yes, yes, yes!

Princess: But . . . but . . . I am the Princess! I don't have to do this!

Centipede: That's right. You don't have to. We're not saying you have to. But you'll be so lonely by yourself!

Narrator: The Princess thinks for a little while about what her friends tell her, dries her tears, holds their hands, and off they go to school together, quite happy.

Princess: I just don't want to miss the singing. Let's go!

(The friends arrive in the basement; when the Teacher sees the Princess, she is not happy.)

Teacher: Well! Look who's here!

Princess: Teacher . . . Would you . . . could you . . . forgive me?

Teacher: Forgive you? When I think of how I've suffered here, in this basement! *(Softens after thinking a while.)* But then, I have learned a lot, and I have wonderful pupils now!

Centipede: And when we all think of what day it is!

Everyone: Yes! Yes! Yes!

Teacher: Of course! Yes, Princess, I forgive you. Imagine, I have not even forgotten that it is your birthday.

Narrator: The Teacher and the Princess hug. They are happy to be together again. The friends bring in a birthday cake for the Princess, and the garden comes in to join in the celebration.

Everybody: *(Singing.)*

> *Cumpleaños feliz,*
> *cumpleaños feliz,*
> *mi querida Princesa,*
> *cumpleaños feliz.*

Princess: *(To her friends.)* ¡Gracias! *(To the public.)* ¿Nos acompañáis?

Narrator: Now everyone, the actors and the audience, are invited to sing one last song to celebrate the fact that the Princess is happy again, with her teacher, her friends . . . and the flowers in her garden, who speak a language that the Princess can understand. Now, if something similar to what happened to the Princess ever happens to you, you know what to do. But let's sing one last song:

> Do you speak English?
> Do you speak English?
> Let me hear your Yes or No
> Because your teacher,
> Because your teacher,
> Does not mind your *acento.*

(To the tune of "La Cucaracha.")

THE END

La princesa está triste

INTRODUCCIÓN A LA PRINCESA ESTÁ TRISTE

(Leída por el Narrador o la Narradora.)

Bienvenidos a *La princesa está triste,* una obra de teatro para jóvenes. La obra empieza en la sala de estar del palacio, donde los amigos de la Princesa están intentando hacerla sentirse mejor, porque está muy triste. ¿Cuál es la razón de su tristeza? Si pones atención a lo que pasa, lo sabrás.

Esperamos que te guste la función. Hemos trabajado mucho construyendo el escenario y aprendiendo a actuar.

Los personajes son: la Princesa, el Paje, el Perro, el Pájaro, el Ciempiés, la Nube, el Árbol, la Rosa, la Maestra/Bruja, los Músicos de Palacio, y el Narrador o la Narradora.

Si quieres hacernos preguntas cuando terminemos, ¡adelante! Y presta atención. Necesitamos silencio para contar la historia de la Princesa triste y sus amigos.

Personajes

- La Princesa
- El Paje
- El Pájaro
- El Ciempiés
- El Perro
- La Bruja/ Maestra
- La Rosa
- El Árbol
- La Nube
- El Narrador (o la Narradora)

> *(Nota:* el monólogo de la Maestra es algo más largo en la versión española que en la inglesa. Las dos versiones funcionan bien, pero todo depende del nivel de los actores. La versión española es la original, pero se puede condensar si se desea.)

ESCENA 1

(Una habitación del palacio.)

Narrador: La Princesa está muy triste, y camina de aquí para allá sin saber qué hacer, suspirando. Sus ayudantes tratan de animarla, sin éxito.

Paje: La Princesa está triste.

Perro: Muy triste. Tristísima.

Pájaro: ¿Qué tendrá la Princesa?

(Miran a los niños que están viendo esta obra, pidiéndoles ayuda.)

Narrador: Si alguien en el público sabe lo que le pasa a la Princesa, que levante la mano, por favor.

Paje: Está pálida.

Perro: Ojerosa.

Pájaro: Toda descompuesta.

Paje: Perdida la color.

Perro: Como desconsolada.

Pájaro: Sin habla y sin voz.

Paje: ¿Qué tendrá la Princesa?

Perro y Pájaro: *(A los niños.)* ¿Lo sabéis vosotros?

Paje: ¿Le duele la cabeza?

(La Princesa niega con la cabeza. El Perro y el Pájaro miran a los niños. Nadie sabe la respuesta.)

Narrador y público: ¡NOOOOOOO!

Paje: ¿Le dolerá la barriga quizás?

(La Princesa niega con la cabeza. El Perro y el Pájaro miran a los niños. Todos dicen "NO". La Princesa rompe a llorar y se va corriendo. Entra el Ciempiés.)

Ciempiés: Yo sé lo que le duele a la Princesa. A la Princesa le duele el corazón.

Todos: ¿El corazón?

Paje: ¡Imposible!

Perro: Eso mismo: ¡imposible! La Princesa tiene de todo.

Pájaro: Y, además, tiene amigos: nosotros.

Todos: *(Al Ciempiés.)* ¡IMPOSIBLE!

Ciempiés: *(Les vuelve la espalda con autosuficiencia.)* Bueno, allá vosotros. Si no me creéis, adiós.

Todos: ¡Espera! Dices . . . ¿Dices que le duele el corazón? Y, ¿por qué?

Ciempiés: Vosotros sabéis lo que le gusta a la Princesa pasear por el jardín cada mañana y hablar con las flores.

Todos: Hombre, claro que lo sabemos. ¡No lo vamos a saber!

(Se van al jardín.)

Rosa: *(Muy coqueta.) I am a very pretty rose.*

Árbol: *And I'm a very tall tree.*

Nube: *And I am a cloud which comes in and goes out, but which mainly lives here.*

Pájaro: ¡Dios mío! ¿Qué es esto?

Perro: No entiendo nada de lo que dicen.

Paje: (*Pensativo.*) Ciertamente, hablan una lengua extraña.

Ciempiés: Lo que pasa es que el jardín está hechizado.

Todos: (*Temblando.*) ¡Hechizadooooo! ¡Qui-én lo-lo-lo ha he-he-choooo¡?

Ciempiés: No lo sé. Lo mejor será que cada uno tome su camino y vaya a investigar.

(Se separan.)

ESCENA 2

(El sótano del palacio.)

Narrador: La Bruja-Maestra está en el sótano de palacio. En una caldera enorme, está cocinando sopa de letras y palabras.

Bruja-Maestra:

Hokus-pokus!
Eeny-meeny!
¡Ostras-tortas!
Lizard-wizard!
¡Maison-liason!

¡Jejejejejejejejejejejejejejejejejejejejejeje! ¡Qué sopa de letras y palabras me estoy haciendo! La sopa de palabras y letras está mucho más rica que la de letras a solas. ¡Está para chuparse los dedos! Rrrrrrrrrrrrrrrriquíííííísima. Y en cuanto sepa más, haré sopa de frases, de párrafos, de poemas, de cuentos, y hasta de novelas. Y en tantos idiomas como me dé la gana: ésa es mi ambición. *Let's see how my Italian is today.* (*Canta.*) "Tralalalalalala, *arrivederci, bambina,* tralalalalalalalalala." ¡Ay, si no sé rimar en Italiano! A ver, a ver, el diccionario . . .

(El Pájaro acaba de descubrir a la Bruja-Maestra. La observa escondido y lleno de terror.)

Narrador: El Pájaro ha bajado por las escaleras y ha descubierto a la Bruja-Maestra. ¡Está aterrorizado!

Bruja-Maestra: ¡Jejejejejejejejejejejejejejejejejejejejeje! Con todo este estudio de lenguas que estoy haciendo, pronto seré la mujer más sabia del mundo—además de ser la más guapa, por supuesto—y después llegaré a ser la más poderosa. Ya le daré una lección a esa niña presumida, la Pincesa. Porque yo, *because I-I-I*, Rosa Reyes (*Rose Kings in English*), antigua maestra de la niña Princesa y despreciada por ella, no me voy a quedar con los brazos cruzados mientras la niña me deja a un lado como si fuera una planta seca. ¡Después de trabajar y de hacer tanto por ella! Me decía, "Maestra, ¿cuál es el resultado de sumar dos y dos?", y yo le decía, "Cuatro, mi Princesa bella". Entonces, iba y le decía a su papá que ella ya sabía matemáticas. Y yo, como la quería, pues me lo callaba todo.

Y, claro, el día llegó en que había que empezar a aprender inglés. Y la niña Princesa dice que para qué va a gastar ella el tiempo en llamar a la ventana *window* o a la mano *hand* cuando ella ya sabe ventana y mano, y que eso es suficiente. Y cuando le expliqué que hay otras gentes en otros países que hablan así, la niña Princesa va y se ríe y dice que vaya con las tonterías que digo, que esas cosas son invenciones mías. Y que para qué quiere ella aprender nada, siendo Princesa, y que ella lo único que quiere hacer es jugar. Y va y le dice al señor Rey, su papá, que ella ya lo ha aprendido todo y no me necesita más. Y el papá, que estaba ocupado escuchando la orquesta de palacio, dice que muy bien, y sin más va y me despide. Me dieron una habitación en el sótano, y cada día me mandan la comida. Ni más ni menos. Durante segundos, y minutos, y horas, y días, y semanas, e incluso meses, lloré. Aquí, yo solita, lloré y lloré. Así que para ver si me olvidaba de mis penas, me puse a leer. Y ahí terminé de llorar. Me dí cuenta que aprender inglés, francés o italiano es una actividad que me gusta mucho. Al principio me ayudaba a pasar el tiempo. Luego me dí cuenta que el decir palabras en otro idioma era como cantar una canción. Y entonces se me ocurrió mi venganza. Mi terrible, tétrica, total, taimada, todopoderosa, turbia venganza. Con mis conocimientos de maestra y alguna que otra palabra mágica, voy a hacer que todo el reino hable otra lengua. Babel va a ser un juego de niños comparado con esto. Hablarán la lengua que yo quiera, cuando yo quiera, porque yo quiero. Que van a estar hechizados, vamos. El jardín ya está hecho. Vamos a ver lo que queda: el señor Rey, el Perro, el Paje, el Pajarito . . . Vamos a ver . . . Y entonces, cuando todo esté hechizado, a ver lo que dice la niña Princesa, la que lo sabe todo, la que lo tiene todo. ¡Jejejejejejejejejeje! *¡Arrivederci!* ¡Adiós! *Good-bye!*

Narrador: Mientras que la Bruja-Maestra busca una palabra en el diccionario, el Pájaro, que lo ha visto todo, se va temblando.

ESCENA 3

(El Pájaro va en busca de sus amigos.)

Narrador: El Pájaro le dice a sus amigos lo que ha visto. Todos empiezan a pensar para ver si hay algo que se pueda hacer.

Pájaro: Así que eso es lo que dijo la Maestra. ¿Qué podemos hacer?

Paje: ¡Ya lo tengo! Podríamos secuestrar a la Maestra.

Perro: ¿Qué haremos con ella?

Paje: Pues, no sé . . . ¡La podríamos encerrar en el sótano!

Pájaro: ¡Pero si ya está en el sótano!

Paje: Es verdad.

Perro: Quizás, quizás . . .

Pájaro: *(A los niños.)* ¿Alguna idea? Any ideas? Ahhhhhhhhhhhhhhhhhhhhhhhhh!

Ciempiés: Tranquilos, tranquilos. Hay sólo una solución. Podemos ir a la Maestra y decirle que queremos que sea nuestra maestra. Es muy posible que esté herida por haber sido rechazada. Además, me gustaría aprender idiomas porque siempre he tenido la ilusión de visitar Grecia, pero no puedo ir porque no sé griego.

Paje: ¡Aprender idiomas!? Eso es mucho trabajo.

Ciempiés: ¿Mucho trabajo? ¿Y en qué pasas el tiempo, dando saltos?

Paje: *I don't know! Ahhhhhhhhhhhhhhhhhhhhhhhhhhhhhh!*

(Todos se echan a temblar. Miran a su alrededor, cogidos de la mano.)

ESCENA 4

(Llegan al sótano.)

Narrador: Los cuatro amigos llegan al sótano, sonriendo nerviosamente. Creo que tienen miedo.

Todos: ¡Maestra!

Bruja-Maestra: *(Defensiva.)* ¡Me queréis engañar! ¿Quiénes sois?

Todos: Vuestros nuevos y humildes estudiantes.

Bruja-Maestra: ¡Jejejejejeje! Se creen que me van a engañar a mí. ¿Qué queréis? ¡Rápido! ¡Decidlo antes de que confunda vuestras lenguas para siempre!

Paje: Maestra, yo quiero aprender inglés.

Perro: ¡Y yo!

Pájaro: Y yo también.

Ciempiés: Y yo. Sabemos que usted es la mejor maestra que hay por aquí, así que aquí estamos.

(Todos están de acuerdo. Cuando van a decir "sí", todos dicen "yes", y se ponen a temblar otra vez.)

Bruja-Maestra: ¿Y qué me dáis si os enseño?

Paje: Nuestra amistad.

Perro: Y chocolate caliente después de cada lección.

Pájaro: Y un pastel de cumpleaños.

Bruja-Maestra: ¡Me habéis convencido! Vamos a empezar: *A, B, C: one-two-three!*

(Repiten, en inglés, lo que la Maestra les enseña; después, todos cantan.)

Todos:

> *In the dungeon of the castle*
> *Brewing multilingual stew,*
> *Five good friends work hard together*

But they know they're one too few!
Oh, my Princess! ¡Oh, Princesa!
How we wish that you were here!
If you taste the stew we're cooking
You'll make sense
Of all you hear!
(*Esta canción se canta con la melodía de "Clementine".*)

ESCENA 5

(*En el jardín. La Princesa se sienta al lado de la Rosa, el Árbol y la Nube.*)

Narrador: La Princesa está intentando ser feliz en su jardín otra vez, como antes. Pero es imposible.

Princesa: ¡Qué Rosa tan fresca y olorosa!

Rosa: *I'm a very pretty Rose.*

(*La Princesa llora con desconsuelo.*)

Princesa: ¡Qué desgraciada soy! ¡Qué solita estoy en el mundo! Ya no puedo ni hablar con las flores de mi jardín. ¿Qué voy a hacer ahora?

(*Entran los cuatro amigos.*)

Paje: Hola, Princesa.

Princesa: (*Llorando.*) Hola.

Perro: ¿Por qué estás tan triste?

Princesa: ¡Ay! ¡Algo terrible ha pasado! Alguien ha hechizado el jardín, y las flores ya no me entienden.

Pájaro: A ver qué es lo que pasa.

Ciempiés: Sí, a ver: *Hi, Rose!*

Rosa: *Hi, friend. What a wonderful day, and what a wonderful voice you have!*

Ciempiés: *Thank you.*

Pájaro: (*A la Rosa.*) *Not only are you pretty, but you smell nice too.*

Árbol: *Ohhhhhhhhhh, what a wonderful conversation! Miss Cloud, Miss Cloud, come and join us!*

Princesa: No entiendo. ¿Cómo es que vosotros entendéis y yo no?

Paje: Princesa, es que nosotros vamos a la escuela.

Perro: Sí, todos. Porque hemos pensado que una cosa buena que podemos hacer con nuestro tiempo es aprender a entendernos con los demás.

Princesa: A la escuela. ¿Para qué quiero yo ir a la escuela, si soy Princesa?

Pájaro: Pues si quieres hablar con las flores de tu jardín . . .

Ciempiés: Y si quieres entender lo que nosotros hablamos . . .

Princesa: ¡Prohibiré que habléis esa lengua estúpida!

Paje: A las flores no les puedes prohibir nada.

Pájaro: Y al corazón de los amigos tampoco les puedes prohibir nada.

Perro: A menos que no quieras tener amigos.

Princesa: ¡Ay, qué desgraciada soy! ¡Todos me abandonan!

Ciempiés: Hoy vamos a aprender una canción en la escuela. ¿Vienes?

Todos: *(A la Princesa.)* ¡Sí, sí, ven!

Princesa: Pero . . . pero . . . ¡soy la Princesa! ¡Yo no tengo por qué hacer esto!

Ciempiés: Cierto. No tienes que hacerlo, ni nosotros insistimos en que lo hagas. ¡Pero te vas a quedar tan sola!

Narrador: La Princesa piensa por un rato sobre lo que sus amigos le han dicho, se seca las lágrimas, los toma de la mano, y se van juntos a la escuela, muy felices.

Princesa: Bueno, no me quiero perder las canciones. ¡Vamos!

(Llegan al sótano. Cuando la Maestra ve a la Princesa, no está feliz.)

Maestra: ¡Mira quién está aquí!

Princesa: *(A la Maestra.)* ¿Me perdonas, Maestra? ¿Puedes perdonarme?

Maestra: ¿Perdonarte? ¡Cuando pienso en lo que he sufrido en este sótano. . .! *(Se suaviza después de unos momentos.)* Claro, que también he aprendido mucho, y tengo unos estudiantes magníficos.

Ciempiés: ¡Y no nos hemos olvidado del día que es!

Todos: ¡Síííí!

Maestra: Claro que te perdono, Princesa. Imagínate, ni siquiera me he olvidado que es el día de tu cumpleaños.

Narrador: La Maestra y la Princesa se abrazan. Están felices de estar juntas otra vez. Los amigos traen un pastel de cumpleaños para la Princesa, y el jardín entra para participar en la fiesta. Todos cantan "Cumpleaños feliz" en inglés.

Princesa: *(A todos, después de la canción.) Thank you. (A los niños que han estado viendo esta obra.) Will you join us, too?*

Narrador: Ahora invitamos a todos, a los actores y al público, a que canten otra canción, la última, para celebrar el que la Princesa esté feliz otra vez con su maestra, sus amigos . . . y las flores de su jardín, que hablan una lengua que la Princesa puede entender. Y si algo parecido a lo que le pasó a la Princesa te pasa a ti, ya sabes lo que hacer. Y aquí está la última canción. ¡A cantar!

Do you speak English?
Do you speak English?
Let me hear your Yes or No,

Because your teacher,
Because your teacher,
Does not mind your *acento*.

(Con la melodía de "La cucaracha".)

FIN

NOTE: La versión española de esta obra se imprime aquí con permiso de University Press of America. (The Spanish version of this work, "La princesa está triste," is reprinted from *El Gaucho Vegetariano and Other Plays for Students of Spanish* by Resurrección Espinosa, 1994, with the permission of the University Press of America.)

VOCABULARY–VOCABULARIO

Nouns–Nombres

basement: *sótano*
belly: *barriga*
centipede: *ciempiés*
Greek: *griego*
hurt: *herida, dolor*
witch: *bruja*

Adjectives–Adjetivos

disconsolate: *desconsolado*
flirtatious: *coqueta*
foolish remarks: *tonterías*
having circles under the eyes: *ojeroso*
rejected: *rechazado*
unhappy: *infeliz*

Verbs–Verbos

to bewitch: *hechizar*
to have a headache: *dolerle a uno la cabeza*
to hide: *esconder*
to miss: *perder, extrañar, echar de menos*
to sigh: *suspirar*
to smell: *oler*
to trick: *engañar*

Clothes Do Not Make the Man

El hábito no hace al monje

Clown and Performer

The clown should be dressed in bright crayon colors like red, yellow, orange, green, and turquoise.

The performer should be dressed in black with a white face and white gloves and shoes.

(Directions for the hat are below.)

Face should be painted to look like a clown.

Borrow a big, colorful shirt from your big brother or sister or your parents. The color should be bright.

Hold the cuffs with an elastic.

Belt the top with a bright colored scarf.

Wear fancy tights or leotards, either a print or a very bright color.

You can use face paint to paint the face white and add a tear. Paint on round, pink cheeks.

HAT: Take a square of posterboard or construction paper that measures 8 1/2 by 8 1/2 inches. Choose a bright color.

 Find the center of the square and cut a straight line to the center.

 Then cut the corners off to round out the square.

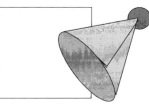 Take one side where it was cut, and place it over the other side until hat shape is right for you. Tape in place. Glue on a pompom.

Figure 3

Clothes Do Not Make the Man

A play for young people of all ages, but especially for singers, athletes, jugglers, and buffoons.

Characters

- The King
- The Prince/Camel
- Advisors 1, 2, and 3
- Buffoon
- Pantomime
- Royal Messenger
- Grocer
- Vagabond
- Little Old Lady
- Young Carpenter
- Old Carpenter
- Juggler
- Gymnasts
- Singers (optional)

> *Note:* The actors may change what happens at the party. If there are no singers, perhaps actors can read a poem instead. If there are not enough older students to portray Buffoon and Pantomime, the play can be done without those parts; cut scene 2 and perform the birthday party with the activities that young actors are able to perform—a dance, a song, some athletics, and so forth. But the message at the end should remain the same: the Prince returns, and there is reconciliation between him and his father.

SCENE 1

(The main hall of the palace. The King has assembled his Advisors to prepare a party for the Prince's birthday. The King is not in a good mood, and the Advisors are serious and somewhat afraid.)

King: We must concentrate and think!

Advisor 1: We must think!

Advisor 2: And concentrate!

Advisor 3: Seriously!

King: *(Upset with Advisor 3.)* Ahem! I haven't said *that* yet, although I will.

Advisor 3: Please forgive me, Your Majesty.

King: You are forgiven—this time! *(Speaking with much emphasis, as if what he is saying were very important.)* Now, we must concentrate and think very seriously!

Advisor 1: We must think!

Advisor 2: And concentrate!

Advisor 3: Very seriously!

(The three Advisors, who have imitated the King's speech, imitate now his posture. Each of them now has his right hand on his forehead, which is wrinkled; half-closed eyes are fixed on the floor. Suddenly, from stage right, the Prince enters. He is a crazy-looking young man, dressed in the latest "punk" fashion or something similar. The King is horrified. Advisors 1 and 2 imitate the King's reaction, but Advisor 3 sympathizes with the Prince.)

King: What did you put on your hair? You look terrible!

Prince: It's coconut oil. The latest fashion!

King: Wash it off right now!

Prince: I am this Kingdom's Prince, and I do what I please!

King: *(Furious, but trying to control himself.)* With whose permission?

Prince: With my own. He-he-he-he-he!

(The King opens his eyes very wide in disbelief but doesn't say anything. His hands tremble with rage. Advisor 3 smiles on the sly, so that the King won't see him.)

Prince: Ah, I forgot! I came to tell you that your favorite horse, Café-café, has a broken leg.

King: Café-café has a broken leg!? *(About to cry.)* And how . . . how . . . did it happen?

Prince: Well, it just happened. He-he! I was riding him, and he . . .

King: *(Stands up, furious.)* You rode Café-café! I prohibited that!

Prince: *(Sarcastic.)* Everything you prohibit is wonderful! Good-bye!

King: Where are you going?

Prince: I am going to ride my bicycle with my friends!

King: I prohibited that also!

Prince: I know. Bye!

King: Wait! We are making preparations for your birthday party!

Prince: *(Cruelly.)* Well, you can invite all the old folks in the kingdom. I won't show up.

El hábito no hace al monje 43

(The King and Advisors 1 and 2 are shocked, not able to believe what they have just heard. The Prince leaves and, after a few moments, the king sits down and the meeting continues.)

King: Advisor 1! Prepare the menu for the banquet!

(Advisor 1 gets his pad and pencil and starts writing.)

King: Advisor 2! Write the guest list!

(Advisor 2 imitates Advisor 1.)

King: Advisor 3! Arrange the entertainment program! Select the best artists!

(Advisor 3 does the same as the other two, but slowly and a bit casually.)

Advisor 3: _(With irony in his voice.)_ And the artists, must I chose them from among those liked by the old?

(The King gets up, furious.)

King: I told you to select the best artists!

(The King stomps out of the room, leaving the three men working. Advisor 3 trembles visibly, and now the other two smile at him with condescension.)

SCENE 2

(Buffoon and Pantomime are in the garden, rehearsing their routine as Court entertainers. Pantomime speaks only when he or she is out of character. They try a few movements, which they intend to be funny but which are not so at this point in their rehearsal. The entertainers need more practice, or a better idea.)

Buffoon: Afterward, I raise my arms and shout, as if I were scared, and the people . . . the people . . . do not laugh.

(Pantomime looks at Buffoon, but says nothing.)

Buffoon: _(Sits down, depressed.)_ I am not funny.

Pantomime: Do not get depressed, Buffoon. Your work always turns out to be very good.

(They are comforting each other when the Prince enters, combing his hair and putting on a leather jacket over his princely robes before going out with his friends. The Prince stops and looks at the two artists, and explodes with derisive laughter. Buffoon and Pantomime stand up in front of their Prince, in silence.)

Prince: You are still dressed up like babies?

Buffoon: _(Sad.)_ I regret that my Prince does not like my suit.

Prince: How old are you? Two, three years?

Buffoon: I am older than my Prince.

Prince: You are? Well, you look as if you were born without brains. Buy yourself a new suit! Bye! I am leaving for the modern world. He-he-he-he-he!

(Buffoon and Pantomime, who have lowered their heads as a sign of respect for the Prince, raise them again as soon as he leaves. They are sad and sit down on the floor.)

Buffoon: Do you know why our work is so difficult?

Pantomime: Why?

Buffoon: Because there is no happiness in our lives. The King is always in a bad mood, and the Prince does not respect anyone.

Pantomime: You are right, Buffoon. Yes.

Buffoon: *(Gets up, very determined.)* I am right, and I have an idea, too! Come with me!

(Buffoon exits in a hurry, and Pantomime follows.)

SCENE 3

(The town square. The citizens come and go, shopping, talking to one another, sitting on a bench, and so forth. The Royal Messenger arrives, carrying a huge rolled piece of paper under his arm. He stands in the middle of the stage, in the center of the group of people, very solemn and professional. When they see the Messenger, the people become afraid.)

Royal Messenger: Ladies and Gentlemen of this Kingdom! Tomorrow, and lasting the whole day long, there will be a celebration in honor of the Prince's birthday. The finest food will be served, and the best actors will delight young and old with their performances. The party starts at ten in the morning. Everyone is invited! By order of His Majesty the King!

(The people tremble when they hear the words "By order of His Majesty the King!" The Royal Messenger wraps up his paper, puts it under his arm, and leaves without another word. The people, who had gathered in a semicircle around the messenger, remain that way to discuss the party.)

Grocer: A party in the Palace! But they have bought nothing from me!

Vagabond: Money is the only thing that concerns you. If you don't profit, you are not interested.

Grocer: Look who's talking! A vagabond, who lives on respectable's people charity.

Vagabond: It is better to beg than to steal.

Grocer: Are you calling me a thief?

Vagabond: *(Pleased that he has enraged the other and with false innocence.)* Come now—would I do such a thing?

(The grocer, enraged, approaches the vagabond. A little old woman separates them.)

Old Lady: Peace! Tomorrow is the Prince's birthday, and the King has invited us to the party. It is our duty to be there.

Young Carpenter: I am not going. The King is always in a bad mood, and the Prince is a jerk.

Old Carpenter: *(Worried.)* This Kingdom is a mess. It cannot be repaired.

Vagabond: I am going to the party. *(Caressing his belly while his face shows gluttony.)* I have not eaten in three days.

Old Lady: It is not true! I gave you breakfast this morning.

Vagabond: True, true. The hard life of a vagabond is beginning to take its toll—I am losing my memory.

Old Carpenter: So, are we going or not? If we don't go, the King will be in a horrible mood for a whole year.

Young Carpenter: Are we going to go to a party only because we are afraid of the King?

Grocer: In this Kingdom, there is no longer a good reason to do anything.

Vagabond: My stomach has a great reason, he-he!

Old Lady: *(Looking at the vagabond with contempt.)* And I have a wonderful reason to go to the party—to visit my friends, the artists.

Old Carpenter: That's a great idea! I'll be there.

Young Carpenter: Not a bad idea, not bad at all. An artist is like a carpenter—he's always creating something.

Old Lady: Until tomorrow!

(The old lady leaves. The carpenters measure something along the wall, write down numbers in their notebooks, and leave.)

Vagabond: *(To the grocer, who does not look at him and is busy with a crate of fruit.)* How could I have forgotten my favorite artists, Buffoon and Pantomime!

Grocer: *(He turns his back on the vagabond, moves his wares away, and talks to himself.)* Well, the King's servants haven't bought anything from me for the party. But I suppose I have to go. If I don't, business will get even worse.

(The grocer exits, leaving the vagabond alone on the stage. He looks around to make sure that he is alone. He addresses the audience, downstage.)

Vagabond: I don't want anyone to know it, but I am not forgetful. I have a great memory! However, when the time comes to eat, it is wise to help those who have fed you to forget.

(He smiles to himself, winks at the audience, and leaves.)

SCENE 4

(The main hall of the Palace has been decorated for the party. The King's chair is placed between center stage and stage right. There is a smaller chair for the Prince just to the left of the King's. There are chairs for the advisors to the left of these two. The King and the three advisors enter and sit down. The Royal Messenger enters next and stands close to the King on his right. Grouped on stage right, there are the chairs for the citizens invited to the party.)

King: *(Looking sadly at the Prince's chair, which is empty, and then at his advisors.)* Let the party begin!

Advisor 1: *(To Advisor 2.)* Let the party begin!

Advisor 2: *(To Advisor 3.)* Let the party begin!

Advisor 3: *(To the Messenger.)* Let the party begin!

Messenger: *(Looking to stage right.)* Let the guests enter the hall!

(The citizens enter and occupy the chairs prepared for them. The Messenger plays the role of Master of Ceremonies, announcing each artist who appears on stage.)

Messenger: Ladies and gentlemen! We start the festivities in honor of . . . in honor of . . . *(He looks at the empty chair next to the King's, and then to the King, who motions for him to continue.)* . . . in honor of the Prince's birthday, with the famous singer The Pearl of the Caribbean!

(Everyone applauds. The singer, dressed in an exotic costume, sings a passionate love song. If there are actors who want to sing, they can be the chorus. The name of the group can be changed if desired. The song chosen must be one that the actors are familiar with and enjoy singing, and it is received with great success.)

Messenger: *(Carried away by the music.)* What rhythm, ladies and gentlemen! Whaaaaat rhythm! We hope—or, at least, I hope—to hear that song again. And now we welcome the famous juggler Juan Más-y-Más.

(Now that there is a party atmosphere, everyone applauds with great enthusiasm. Even the King and his advisors are almost happy—with the exception of Advisor 3, who regrets the others' happiness. The juggler enters, dressed in very bright colors. He presents his act using balls, apples, oranges, and so forth. He addresses the King, then the court, then the guests.)

Guests: Higher, higher, higher! Más-y-Más, Más-y-Más, Más-y-Más!

(The juggler, happy because of his success, starts throwing the fruit high in the air and gives it to the guests.)

Vagabond: *(Eating one of the fruits.)* The best apple that I have eaten in my life!

Old Lady: Really? Let me try one. I grow loads of apples, as you well know!

Vagabond: I remember them, and I am grateful. They are very good, also.

Old Lady: *(She starts eating one of the Juggler's apples while looking at the artist, who is now saying good-bye. The old lady expresses delight and nudges the vagabond with her elbow while winking at him.)* Delicious! Even better than mine, I must admit.

(The vagabond winks back at her. They all applaud the Juggler's departure, who leaves still throwing things in the air. The Messenger, also eating an apple, gets ready to introduce the gymnasts.)

Grocer: *(Aside.)* If things go on like this, I am ruined. Apples, delicious and *free*. And now, what else?

Messenger: These apples taste like magic!

Old Lady: They are magic! If even I can admit they are better than mine . . . that's magic!

Messenger: Thank you for your generosity, lady. And now, we introduce the most daring gymnasts! And that's their name: The Most Daring. Welcome!

(Everyone applauds. The gymnasts enter, wearing colorful suits, although they must wear something that identifies them as members of a team. They enter with great order, salute their audience, and start their performance. The public should feel free to applaud frequently, although the athletes should be allowed plenty of time to do their work without interruptions.)

Old Carpenter: Perfect!

Young Carpenter: Repeat it! Do that number again! What agility!

(The athletes return to their original position to leave the stage, and the King looks at the Prince's empty chair. His face shows sadness, but he is not angry anymore.)

King: I wish that the Prince were here! He would enjoy this a lot!

(The gymnasts exit, accompanied by the applause of the audience.)

Messenger: What a party! It's great! We should have a party more often.

King: *(Suddenly angry.)* Do not comment on how you feel. Your job is to announce the entertainers!

(The guests and advisors become sad again and look at the King with a little bit of fear—all, except Advisor 3, who grins on the sly. Pantomime enters, looking very serious, dragging a camel with a rope. The camel wears sun glasses. Pantomime looks around herself, thinks, makes the camel sit down stage left, and exits. The camel stays where it has been placed, and soon Pantomime reenters, bent under the burden of an imaginary weight. She puts the weight on the floor, looks at the camel, and starts building something that represents a house for the camel—all imaginary. But all her movements should communicate rigidity in her feelings and thoughts, and that she is not allowing enough room for the camel to be able to get in. Buffoon enters, in a very good mood.)

Buffoon: What is this!? A camel!!!

(Pantomime signals that it is her camel.)

Buffoon: *Your* camel! Well, that makes it even more interesting.

(Pantomime continues building the house, steadily, and with very rigid movements.)

Buffoon: *(To the camel.)* Could you lend me one of your humps, or whatever they are called?

(The camel nods, delighted. He looks around, as if he's having a lot of fun and wants to share it, especially when Buffoon puts on one of the camel's humps and pretends to be a camel.)

Buffoon: To be a camel looks like a lot of fun! Do I look beautiful?

(The camel laughs at Buffoon, who parades around the stage pretending to be the animal. Pantomime continues building the camel's house.)

Buffoon: Yes, I would like to be a camel. It would be fun.

(Buffoon returns the hump to the camel, and sits down next to him. The camel is delighted with his new friend.)

Buffoon: But if I were a camel, I would die of thirst. And I love lemonade! No, my friend. The best thing is for me to continue being Buffoon and for you to continue being a camel. The world is more beautiful when one is just what one is.

(The camel agrees, and there is silence for a while. Pantomime continues building, without changing her expression. Then, Buffoon looks at Pantomime.)

Buffoon: What are you building? A planter for flowers?

(Pantomime stops what she is doing, and looks at Buffoon. Pantomime says "no" with her head, and points at the camel, and mimes that what she is building is for the camel to sleep in.)

Buffoon: *(Does not understand, and gets up, afraid.)* A tomb for your camel?

(Pantomime laughs—silently—for the first time, and shakes her head. Now Pantomime looks less rigid, looks at the work which she has been doing, and decides that it is finished. She takes the camel's rope and brings him to the new building, into which she tries to put him. The camel obeys with great difficulty, puts his head inside, but he really cannot get in because the space is too small. The camel turns to look at Pantomime, his face full of pain: the space is too small for him, and Pantomime does not understand it. Buffoon observes, not believing what he sees.)

Buffoon: Pantomime, what you want your camel to do is impossible.

(Pantomime, very rigid and serious, pushes Buffoon aside and tries to put the camel in again. Those invited to the party are very attentive to what is going on. Some know that what Pantomime is trying to do is impossible.)

Old Carpenter: The house is too small for the camel!

Buffoon: *(Very nervous because Pantomime does not seem to hear.)* Pantomime, the carpenter says that the house is not big enough for the camel.

(Pantomime does not pay attention and pushes the camel again.)

Camel: *(Crying.)* Buah-buah-buaaaaahhhhh!

Buffoon: The poor camel! He cannot breathe in there!

Vagabond: He has enough space, and he is only an animal. He'll get used to sleeping in there.

Camel: Buah-buah-buaaaaahhhhhhhhhh!

Buffoon: *(Addressing the audience, desperate.)* Help! Help! Is there a good heart to take pity on the poor camel?

(There is silence among the spectators, who look around to see if anyone will say something. Suddenly, the King stands up, very upset.)

King: *(To Pantomime.)* Leave the poor camel alone. Can't you see that he cannot get in there?

(Pantomime obeys the King, and the camel, free now, speaks to the King.)

Camel: Thank you, my King. You have saved me from the hands of an owner who is blind to my needs.

(Everyone, and specially the King, are taken aback by the camel's words—especially because the voice is familiar to them.)

Camel: *(To Buffoon.)* Buffoon, you have just shown me that if we all use our authority to create good conditions, instead of doing things just to show how powerful or important we are, the world would be a happy place.

Buffoon: *(Pretending to doubt for a moment what the camel says.)* Are you sure? I love to have power, and to let the world know it!

Camel: I am sure of that, Buffoon.

(The camel starts taking off his costume—the humps, the glasses, and so forth. Everyone sees that the camel is actually the Prince.)

Prince: *(To Buffoon.)* Before I met you, I used my power to make everyone unhappy—especially myself. But the duty of a prince is to make his people happy. Otherwise, he does not deserve to wear the prince's clothes. Because . . .

(The Prince, Buffoon, and Pantomime hold hands and speak to the audience, all three at the same time.)

Prince, Buffoon, and Pantomime: Because clothes don't make the man!

King: *(To the Prince.)* Son, what a great birthday party you have prepared! I understand what you are saying: I have been smothering you with my demands. I will try to listen to you, because I also have to become worthy of wearing the royal clothes. Please, come and sit next to me.

Prince: *(He wears just his prince's clothes, and sits next to the King.)* We must thank Buffoon and Pantomime, Father. It was their idea.

King: Is that true?

Buffoon: *(In a comic mood.)* Your Majesty, we—

Pantomime: *(Getting a little bit in front of Buffoon.)* I shall explain.

Buffoon: Your role is never to talk.

Pantomime: That depends, because it was I who gave you the answer that—

Buffoon: But it was I who was complaining about not being funny enough and—

Pantomime: What you would like to do is—

Buffoon: I am guessing what you want to say, and I do not want the audience to—

(The audience starts laughing at the silly couple, and the laughter is accompanied by applause and whistles.)

Buffoon and Pantomime: *(Holding hands and saluting the audience.)* And the duty of two comics is, when they have told their story, to get out of the way so that others may entertain.

(Buffoon and Pantomime leave, saying good-bye in a very exaggerated way. The rest of the artists enter again, and the singer sings another song to finish the party. Buffoon and Pantomime sit with the audience.)

THE END

El hábito no hace al monje

Una obra para jóvenes de todas las edades, especialmente para cantantes, atletas, malabaristas y bufones.

Personajes

- El Rey
- El Príncipe/Camello
- Consejeros 1, 2, 3
- Bufón
- Pantomima
- Mensajero Real
- Comerciante
- Vagabundo
- Viejecita
- Carpintero joven
- Carpintero viejo
- Malabarista
- Gimnastas
- Cantante (opcional)

Nota: Invitamos a los actores a que se tomen la libertad de cambiar lo que sea necesario. Si no hay malabaristas o cantantes, pueden incluir bailarines, poetas, guitarristas, etc. Si no hay bastantes actores participando de los grados superiores, la obra se puede hacer sin Bufón y Pantomima. Se corta escena 2, y la fiesta de cumpleaños se hace solamente con los músicos y gimnastas que haya. Pero el mensaje de la obra debe permanecer, que es la reconciliación entre padre e hijo.

ESCENA 1

(En la sala de palacio, donde el Rey está reunido con su corte para decidir los detalles de la fiesta de cumpleaños del Príncipe. El Rey no está de buen humor, y los Consejeros están muy serios y algo asustados.)

Rey: ¡Hay que pensar con concentración!

Consejero 1: ¡Hay que pensar!

Consejero 2: ¡Con concentración!

MONTROSE LIBRARY DISTRICT
320 So. 2nd St.
Montrose, CO 81401

Consejero 3: ¡Y con seriedad!

Rey: *(Disgustado con Consejero 3.)* ¡Ejem! Eso todavía no lo he dicho, aunque lo diré.

Consejero 3: Perdón, su Majestad.

Rey: Estás perdonado. *(Con mucho énfasis, como si lo que está diciendo fuera muy importante.)* ¡Hay que pensar con mucha concentración, y con seriedad!

Consejero 1: ¡Hay que pensar!

Consejero 2: ¡Con mucha concentración!

Consejero 3: ¡Y con seriedad!

(Los tres Consejeros, que han imitado la manera de hablar del Rey, imitan ahora su postura: los cuatro tienen la mano derecha en la frente, el ceño fruncido, los ojos en el suelo o medio cerrados, pensando muy seriamente. De pronto, por la derecha del escenario, entra el Príncipe - un joven alocado, vestido a la última moda, que puede ser el estilo "punk" u otro similar. El Rey lo mira horrorizado. Los Consejeros 1 y 2 imitan al Rey, pero el 3 parece simpatizar con el Príncipe.)

Rey: ¿Qué llevas en el pelo? Estás feísimo.

Príncipe: Es aceite de coco. ¡La última moda!

Rey: ¡Lávate ahora mismo!

Príncipe: Soy el Príncipe de este reino, y hago lo que quiero.

Rey: *(Furioso, pero intentando controlarse frente a sus Consejeros.)* ¿Con qué permiso?

Príncipe: Con el mío. ¡Ji-ji-ji!

(El Rey abre mucho los ojos, las manos le tiemblan, pero no dice nada. Consejero 3 sonríe sin que el Rey lo vea.)

Príncipe: ¡Ah! Vengo a decirte que tu caballo favorito, Café-café, se rompió una pata.

Rey: ¡Café-café tiene una pata rota! *(A punto de llorar.)* ¿Y cómo. . . , cómo . . . ?

Príncipe: Comiendo. ¡Ji-ji! Me monté, y él—

Rey: *(Se levanta, furioso.)* ¡Te montaste en Café-café! ¡Te lo tengo prohibido!

Príncipe: *(Con sarcasmo.)* Todo lo que me prohíbes es maravilloso. ¡Adiós!

Rey: ¿A dónde vas?

Príncipe: A montar en motocicleta con mis amigos.

Rey: ¡Eso también está prohibido!

Príncipe: Lo sé. ¡Adiós!

Rey: ¡Espera! Estamos preparando tu fiesta de cumpleaños.

Príncipe: *(Muy cruel.)* ¡Pues invita a los viejos del reino! Yo no vengo.

(El Rey y los Consejeros, excepto el número 3, no se pueden creer lo que han visto. El Prínicpe se va y, después de unos momentos, el Rey se sienta y la reunión continúa.)

Rey: ¡Consejero 1! ¡Prepara el menú para el banquete!

(Consejero 1 saca papel y lápiz, y se prepara para escribir.)

Rey: ¡Consejero 2! ¡Escribe la lista de los invitados!

(Consejero 2 saca papel y lápiz y, muy serio, imita al Consejero 1.)

Rey: ¡Consejero 3! ¡Organiza la lista de los artistas!

(Consejero 3 empieza a hacer lo mismo que los otros, aunque más lentamente y con menos respeto.)

Consejero 3: *(Con algo de ironía en la voz.)* Y los artistas, ¿deben ser los que les gustan a los viejos?

(El Rey se levanta, furioso.)

Rey: ¡Te dije que organizaras la lista de los artistas!

(El Rey se va, dejando a los tres Consejeros trabajando, y al número tres temblando también. Es ahora que los Consejeros 1 y 2 sonríen al número 3 con ironía.)

ESCENA 2

(Bufón y Pantomima están en el jardín, ensayando su rutina para entretener a la corte. Pantomima sólo habla cuando no está en su papel de artista. Están haciendo algunos movimientos que pretenden ser graciosos pero todavía no lo son: necesitan mucho trabajo, o una mejor idea.)

Bufón: Y después, levanto los brazos y grito, como si estuviera asustado, y la gente . . . la gente . . . no se ríe.

(Pantomima mira a Bufón, pero no dice nada.)

Bufón: *(Se sienta, deprimido.)* ¡No soy gracioso!

Pantomima: No te deprimas, Bufón. Tu trabajo es muy bueno.

(Están así, consolándose, cuando entra el Príncipe arreglándose el pelo y poniéndose una chaqueta de piel sobre su traje de príncipe antes de salir a la calle. El Príncipe mira a los dos artistas, se para frente a ellos, y se echa a reír con desdén. Bufón y Pantomima se levantan del suelo.)

Príncipe: ¿Todavía estáis vestidos así, de bebés?

Bufón: *(Triste.)* Siento que a mi Príncipe no le guste mi traje.

Príncipe: ¿Cuántos años tienes, dos o tres?

Bufón: Soy mayor que mi Príncipe.

Príncipe: ¿Sí? ¡Pues parece como si hubieras nacido sin cerebro! ¡Cómprate un traje nuevo! Adiós, me voy al mundo moderno. ¡Ji-ji-ji!

(Pantomima y Bufón han bajado la cabeza en señal de respeto al Príncipe. Cuando se va, ellos levantan la cabeza, entristecidos, y se sientan otra vez en el suelo sin saber qué hacer.)

Bufón: ¿Sabes por qué es difícil nuestro trabajo?

Pantomima: ¿Por qué?

Bufón: Porque no tenemos felicidad en nuestras vidas. El Rey está siempre de mal humor, y el Príncipe no respeta a nadie.

Pantomima: Tienes razón, Bufón. Mucha razón.

Bufón: *(Se levanta de pronto, animado por una idea.)* ¡Tengo razón, y tengo una idea! ¡Ven!

(Bufón sale corriendo y Pantomima lo sigue.)

ESCENA 3

(En la plaza de la ciudad, los ciudadanos van de compras, están sentados en el jardín público, etc. El Mensajero Real llega con un papel enrollado bajo el brazo, y se sitúa en medio de la gente, muy serio y profesional. La gente, al ver al Mensajero de palacio, se pone seria y muestra miedo.)

Mensajero Real: ¡Damas y caballeros del Reino! Mañana durante todo el día se celebrarán festividades en honor del cumpleaños del Príncipe heredero. Habrá mucha comida, y las actuaciones de los mejores artistas deleitarán a grandes y a pequeños. La fiesta empieza a las diez. ¡Todos están invitados! ¡Orden del Rey!

(La gente tiembla cuando se oyen las palabras "¡Orden del Rey!" El Mensajero pone su rollo de papel bajo el brazo, y se va sin decir más. La gente, que se había agrupado en un semicírculo, se queda como estaba para hablar sobre la fiesta.)

Comerciante: ¡Una fiesta en palacio! Pues a mí no me han comprado nada.

Vagabundo: A ti, lo único que te interesa es el dinero. Si tú no ganas, ¡nada!

Comerciante: ¡Mira quién habla! Un vagabundo que vive de la gente respetable.

Vagabundo: ¡Es mejor pedir que robar!

Comerciante: ¡Me llamas ladrón!?

Vagabundo: *(Divirtiéndose con su crueldad.)* ¿Yooooooooo?

(El comerciante, muy enfadado, se aproxima al vagabundo. Una viejecita los separa.)

Viejecita: ¡Silencio! Mañana es el cumpleaños del Príncipe, y el Rey nos ha invitado a la fiesta. Es nuestro deber asistir.

Carpintero Joven: Yo no voy. El Rey está siempre de mal humor, y el Príncipe es un estúpido.

Carpintero Viejo: *(Preocupado.)* ¡Este Reino es un lío! No se puede arreglar.

Vagabundo: Yo voy a la fiesta. *(Se acaricia la barriga, glotón.)* No he comido en tres días.

Viejecita: ¡No es verdad! Te invité a desayunar esta mañana.

Vagabundo: Verdad, verdad. La dura vida de vagabundo me hace perder la memoria.

Carpintero Viejo: Bueno, ¿vamos a la fiesta o no? Si no vamos, el Rey va a estar de muy mal humor por un año entero.

Carpintero Joven: ¿Vamos a ir a una fiesta porque tenemos miedo del Rey?

Comerciante: ¡En este Reino ya no hay una buena razón para hacer nada!

Vagabundo: Mi estómago tiene una razón buenísima, ¡ji-ji!

Viejecita: *(Mirando al vagabundo con desprecio.)* ¡Y yo tengo una razón superbuena para ir a la fiesta! Vamos a ir a visitar a nuestros amigos los artistas.

Carpintero Viejo: ¡Una idea maravillosa! Allí estaré.

Carpintero Joven: No está mal la idea, no está mal. Total, un artista es como un carpintero: siempre está arreglando algo.

Viejecita: ¡Hasta mañana!

(La viejecita se va. Los carpinteros empiezan a medir algo, toman notas, y luego se van.)

Vagabundo: *(Al comerciante, que casi no lo escucha.)* ¡Cómo es que se me habían olvidado mis artistas favoritos, Butón y Pantomima!

Comerciante: La dura vida de vagabundo te está haciendo desmemoriado. *(Se va, hablando consigo mismo.)* Palacio no me ha comprado nada para la fiesta, pero tengo que ir. Si no, el negocio irá de mal en peor.

(El vagabundo es el único que queda en la plaza. Mira a su alrededor para estar seguro que está solo.)

Vagabundo: No quiero que nadie lo sepa, pero no soy desmemoriado. ¡Tengo buena memoria! Pero uno nunca sabe, a la hora de comer, si a la gente le gusta que recuerdes o que no.

(Se sonríe con picardía y sale.)

ESCENA 4

(En la sala de palacio, arreglada para la fiesta. Hacia centro-derecha del escenario, está el trono del Rey, y un sillón más pequeño para el Príncipe. El Rey entra, seguido de sus Consejeros, que se sientan en sillas detrás del Rey. De pie, al lado, está el Mensajero Real.)

Rey: *(Mira la silla vacía del Prícipe y se vuelve a sus consejeros.)* ¡Que empiece la fiesta!

Consejero 1: *(A Consejero 2.)* ¡Que empiece la fiesta!

Consejero 2: *(A Consejero 3.)* ¡Que empiece la fiesta!

Consejero 3: *(Al Mensajero.)* ¡Que empiece la fiesta!

Mensajero Real: *(Mira hacia fuera.)* ¡Que entren los invitados! ¡La fiesta va a empezar!

(Entran los ciudadanos, y se sientan en sillas que se han puesto a la derecha del escenario. El Mensajero hace de Maestro de Ceremonias, anunciando a cada artista que aparece en el escenario.)

Mensajero Real: ¡Damas y caballeros! Damos comienzo a las festividades en honor del . . . , en honor del . . . , *(Mira la silla vacía, y luego al Rey, que lo anima impacientemente a que termine.)* . . . en honor del Príncipe heredero, con la actuación del famoso cantante La Perla del Caribe.

(Todos aplauden. El cantante o la cantante, vestido-a muy exóticamente, canta una canción de amor con mucha pasión. Si hay más actores que quieran actuar de acompañantes o de coro, pueden hacerlo. La actuación tiene gran éxito. El nombre del cantante se puede cambiar si se desea, y la canción elegida debe ser una que los jóvenes actores puedan cantar con facilidad.)

Mensajero Real: *(Entusiasmado por la música.)* ¡Qué ritmo, damas y caballeros! ¡Qué ritmo! Esperamos, o por lo menos yo espero, oir esa canción otra vez. Y ahora damos la bienvenida al famoso malabarista Juan Más-y-Más.

(Grandes aplausos, ahora más entusiastas que antes porque ya hay atmósfera de fiesta. Hasta el Rey está algo más animado, y por tanto sus Consejeros lo están también - con la excepción del número 3, que se alegra más de la tristeza de los otros que de su alegría. Entra el malabarista, vestido con ropas muy brillantes. Hace juegos de manos con naranjas, limones, pelotas, etc. Muy ágil y siempre dirigiendo su arte al Rey y luego al pueblo, tira las frutas cada vez más alto.)

Público: ¡Más, más, más, más . . . !

(Recibe mucho aplauso. Juan Más-y Más regala manzanas y otras frutas al público.)

Vagabundo: *(Comiendo una de las manzanas.)* ¡La mejor manzana que he comido en mi vida!

Viejecita: ¡Desagradecido! Te he dado tantas manzanas de mi jardín . . .

Vagabundo: Las recuerdo. También son buenas. Pero en cosas de amor no hay nada como el que uno tiene en las manos.

Viejecita: ¡Desagradecido! *(Mueve la cabeza en señal de desprecio, y muerde una de las manzanas del malabarista, que está preparándose para despedirse. Inmediatamente, su expresión cambia: está encantada, y le da al vagabundo con el codo en señal de complicidad.)* ¡Buenísima! Mejor que las mías.

(El vagabundo le guiña un ojo. Todos aplauden la marcha del malabarista, que se va como si todavía estuviera en el escenario, haciendo malabarismos. El Mensajero, comiendo una manzana, se prepara para introducir a los gimnastas.)

Comerciante: *(Aparte.)* Si las cosas siguen así, estoy en la ruina. Manzanas buenas y gratis. Y después, ¿qué más vendrá?

Mensajero Real: ¡Estas manzanas saben a magia!

Viejecita: ¡Son magia! Si puedo aceptar que son mejor que las mías . . . , eso es cosa de magia.

Mensajero Real: Gracias por su generosidad, señora. Y ahora, ¡los gimnastas más atrevidos! Y así se llaman: Los Más Atrevidos. ¡Adelante!

(Aplausos de todo el mundo. Entran los gimnastas vestidos con sus trajes de ejercicio, aunque todos deben de llevar algún color o dibujo que los identifique como miembros de un equipo. Entran con mucha gracia y orden, saludan, y empiezan sus números: saltos, ejercicios de agilidad, juegos con aros y cuerdas, etc. Aplausos frecuentes: elegir el mejor momento, porque los atletas deben de tener la oportunidad de saludar sin perder su concentración.)

Carpintero Viejo: ¡Perfecto!

Carpintero Joven: ¡Otra vez! ¡Repitan ese número! ¡Qué agilidad!

(Los atletas están ya poniéndose en el mismo orden en que entraron para despedirse, cuando el Rey mira el asiento vacío del Príncipe. De pronto, su cara expresa tristeza, no enfado ni impaciencia - sólo tristeza.)

Rey: ¡Ojalá el Príncipe estuviera aquí! Le gustaría esto, le gustaría mucho.

(Pero Los Más Atrevidos ya se van, seguidos por aplausos cada vez más fuertes y entusiastas.)

Mensajero Real: ¡Qué fiesta, qué fiesta! Deberíamos de tener cumpleaños con más frecuencia.

Rey: *(Muy tiránico de repente.)* ¡No hagas comentarios! ¡Tu trabajo es anunciar!

Mensajero Real: *(Triste y frío ahora.)* Sí, su Majestad. Y ahora, un número dramático a cargo de Bufón y Pantomima.

(La atmósfera ha cambiado: todos en el público están serios y miran al Rey con miedo. El único que parece divertirse es el Consejero 3, que sonríe con malicia a escondidas. Pantomima entra, muy seria, tirando de la cuerda de la que va atado un camello, que lleva gafas de sol. Pantomima mira a su alrededor, piensa, deja al camello sentado a un lado del escenario, y sale. Entra muy lentamente, doblada bajo el peso de algo imaginario que lleva en los hombros. Pone su peso en el suelo, mira al camello, y se pone a construir algo que representa una casa para el camello. Pero todos sus movimientos nos deben de decir que su actitud es muy rígida, y que no va a haber bastante espacio para el camello en lo que construye. Entra Bufón, de buen humor.)

Bufón: ¡Qué es esto!? ¡Un camello!

(Pantomima le dice por señas que es suyo.)

Bufón: ¡Tu camello! Vaya, eso lo hace más interesante.

(Pantomima sigue construyendo: diligentemente, pero muy rígida.)

Bufón: *(Al camello.)* ¿Me prestas una de tus chepas, o joroba, o giba? Como se llame.

(El camello dice que sí con la cabeza, encantado. Mira a todos lados, y se ríe cuando Bufón se pone una de sus gibas, imitándolo.)

Bufón: ¡Qué divertido, ser un camello! ¿Me veo guapo?

(El camello se ríe del Bufón, que se pasea por el escenario imitando al animal. Pantomima sigue construyendo la casa para el camello.)

Bufón: Sí, me gustaría ser un camello. Sería divertido. *(Bufón le devuelve la giba al camello, y se sienta a su lado. El camello está encantado con su nuevo amigo.)* Pero me moriría de sed. ¡Con lo que a mí me gusta la limonada! No, amigo: lo mejor es que yo siga siendo Bufón, y tú un camello. El mundo es más bonito cuando cada uno es lo que es.

(El camello parece estar de acuerdo, y así están sentados juntos un rato. Pantomima no deja de trabajar en su construcción, sin cambiar de expresión. De pronto, Bufón mira a Pantomima.)

Bufón: ¿Qué es eso? ¿Un plantador para poner flores?

(Pantomima se para y lo mira. Dice que no con la cabeza, y señala al camello, a la vez que indica que es para dormir.)

Bufón: *(No comprende, se levanta asustado.)* ¿Una tumba para tu camello?

(Pantomima se ríe por primera vez, y dice que no otra vez. Ahora Pantomima está algo menos rígida, y da por terminada su obra. Mira la construcción desde varios ángulos, y parece estar satisfecha. Se acerca al camello, lo toma por la rienda y lo lleva a la nueva construcción, donde intenta meterlo. El camello obedece con gran dificultad, mete la cabeza, pero se vuelve, la cara llena de dolor: el espacio es muy pequeño. Bufón observa, asombrado.)

Bufón: Pantomima, lo que quieres que tu camello haga es imposible.

(Pantomima, muy rígida y seria, aparta a Bufón con una mano e intenta meter al camello en la casilla otra vez. Los invitados a la fiesta están muy atentos, intentando comprender qué pasa. Los carpinteros se miran, dicen que no con la cabeza.)

Carpintero Viejo: La casilla es muy pequeña para el camello.

Bufón: *(Nervioso ante la indiferencia de Pantomima.)* ¿Ves? El carpintero dice que no es bastante grande para el camello.

(Pantomima no hace caso, empuja al camello.)

Camello: Buá-buá-buá . . .

Bufón: ¡Que se va a axfisiar! ¡El pobre camello!

Vagabundo: Es sólo un animal. Tiene bastante espacio. Ya se acostumbrará a dormir ahí.

Camello: Buá-buá-buá . . .

Bufón: *(Dramático, dirigiéndose al público.)* ¡Ayuda, ayuda! ¡Un corazón bondadoso que se apiade del pobre camello!

(Silencio tenso entre los espectadores, que miran a su alrededor a ver quién va a decir algo. De pronto, el Rey se pone de pie, muy agitado.)

Rey: ¡Deja al pobre camello! ¿No ves que no cabe?

(Pantomima obedece, y el camello, libre, se va hacia el Rey y le habla.)

Camello: Gracias, Rey. Me has salvado de las manos de una dueña insensible a mis necesidades.

(Todos, y especialmente el Rey, se quedan un poco extrañados por las palabras del camello —sobre todo porque la voz les resulta familiar.)

Camello: *(A Bufón.)* Bufón, me acabas de demostrar que si cada uno usamos la autoridad que tenemos para crear buenas condiciones, en vez imponer nuestra voluntad a lo loco, el mundo sería feliz.

Bufón: *(Pensativo, pero de broma.)* ¿Estás seguro, camello? A mí gusta tener poder, ¡y que el mundo lo sepa!

Camello: Estoy segurísimo, Bufón. *(Empieza a quitarse el disfraz de camello para revelar debajo el traje de príncipe.)* Antes de conocerte, yo usaba mi poder para hacer infeliz a todo el mundo, especialmente a mí mismo. Pero el deber de un príncipe es el de hacer feliz a su gente. Si no, no se merece este traje. Porque . . .

(Príncipe, Bufón, y Pantomima se cogen de las manos y le hablan directamente al asombrado público, en coro.)

Príncipe, Bufón, y Pantomima: ¡Porque el hábito no hace al monje!

Rey: *(Al Príncipe.)* Hijo, ¡qué gran fiesta de cumpleaños has preparado! Comprendo lo que dices: te he estado axfisiando con mis demandas. Yo también tengo que ser digno de mi traje de rey. Ven y siéntate a mi lado.

Príncipe: *(Ya sin disfraz, se sienta al lado del Rey.)* Tenemos que agradecérselo a Bufón y Pantomima, Padre. Fue idea suya.

Rey: ¿Es verdad?

Bufón: Verá, su Majestad . . .

Pantomima: Yo explico.

Bufón: Lo tuyo no es hablar.

Pantomima: Eso depende, porque fui yo quien te hice la pregunta que—

Bufón: Pero fui yo el que no era gracioso y—

Pantomima: Lo que tú quieres hacer es—

Bufón: Te estoy adivinando el pensamiento y no quiero que el pú—

(El público empieza a aplaudir y a silbar muy alto.)

Bufón y Pantomima: *(Saludando al público.)* Y el deber de unos cómicos es, cuando hayan contado su historia, salirse del escenario para que otros diviertan al público.

(Se van, saludando muy extravagantemente. El resto de los artistas entran, y los cantantes cantan otra canción para terminar la fiesta—a la que asisten Bufón y Pantomima.)

FIN

VOCABULARY–VOCABULARIO

Nouns–Nombres

audience: *público*
demand: *exigencia, demanda*
entertainer: *artista, actor*
hump: *joroba, jiba*
rhythm: *ritmo*
robe: *túnica, hábito*

Adjectives–Adjetivos

daring: *atrevido*
forgetful: *desmemoriado*
kind: *bondadoso*
retarded: *retardado*
scared: *asustado*

Verbs–Verbos

to die of thirst: *morirse de sed*
to juggle: *hacer juegos de manos o juegos malabares*
to lend: *prestar*
to smother: *axfisiar*
to take pity on someone: *apiadarse de alguien*

Cinderella in Modern Times

Cenicienta en tiempos modernos

Limousine

Take a piece of paperboard 5 to 6 feet long. You can also use a styrofoam board. Cut out the outline of the limousine and then cut out the windows. Paint it to look like a limousine. You can make the tires separately and glue them on, or make them part of the overall piece. Cut straps of a heavy fabric such as denim and glue to the inside of the limousine for the two people sitting inside to use as handles.

Two people sit on chairs behind the limousine and hold the handles that are attached to the inside of the limousine.

Figure 4

Cinderella in Modern Times

Characters

- Cinderella
- Father
- Stepmother
- Molly
- Polly
- Governor
- Governor's son
- Narrator
- Mother's voice
- Chauffeur

> *Note:* Some young actresses like to modernize names. Some have changed Cinderella's name to Cindy, and the stepsisters have become Sara and Tara. Please feel free to do the same.

SCENE 1

(The living room of a contemporary home. Cinderella, a girl of about nine, sits at the desk, writing. She is concentrated and calm. Once in a while, she looks at a photograph—that of her mother, who has died.)

Narrator: This is what Cinderella does every night. She writes in her diary, but it is a letter that she writes. And to whom? Listen . . . .

Cinderella: "Dear Mother: I spent the whole day waiting for this hour, when I can be alone with you. I know that you are with me always, but during the day, I have to do other things so I am not completely with you, as I like to be. It is seven-thirty in the evening. Father and I have eaten supper. We had pizza, and it was good. But I miss your suppers, you know, the nice soups and the custard with cream. And your smile, I miss your smile. That's why I have your picture here, so that I will never forget it. Do you eat good suppers in Heaven? I hope so, because sometimes I worry that the food there is not as good as your cooking. I had a good day in school. Do you remember my friend Laura? We are in dance class together, and we are practicing something very, very beautiful—"

(Father enters the room. He is not cold, but he is in a hurry and wants to finish what he has to say quickly. He sits on a chair next to his daughter. Cinderella listens.)

Father: Hi, Cinderella.

Cinderella: Hi, Father. Thank you for buying pizza for supper tonight. It was good. I am writing to—

Father: Cinderella, I have news for you. You see, since Mother died—

Cinderella: I am writing to her now. She likes to know that we are well.

Father: *(Sighs, a bit impatient.)* That's . . . nice, Cinderella. Very nice. But I have been thinking that we need someone . . . another . . . mother to help us cook supper.

Cinderella: *(Does not understand, waits a little before speaking.)* Another mother? We already have one.

Father: *(Gets up, speaks in a hurry.)* A new mother will be coming to live with us very soon. She will be nice to you, and I hope that you will be nice to her. She has two daughters who will be like sisters to you, and you won't be lonely.

Cinderella: I am not lonely!

Father: *(Bending and kissing his daughter.)* Good night, Cinderella. I must go to bed because I have to get up early to go to work.

(Father turns to go, and does not look back when Cinderella talks to him.)

Cinderella: *(Upset.)* But Father!

(Father has left, and Cinderella is alone with her Mother's picture.)

Cinderella: *(Looks at the picture on the desk for a while and then takes it in her hands.)* I don't want anybody to take your place, Mother. But I do not want to disobey Father. What should I do?

(A voice is heard, Mother's voice. It's calm and sweet, and Cinderella is not afraid because she has heard the voice before.)

Mother's Voice: Don't be sad, Cinderella. You knew this would happen one day.

Cinderella: *(Very sad.)* Yes, but I don't want you to go away.

Mother's Voice: I will be always with you. Do what Father says you must do, and write to me every night, as always. Life goes on, Cinderella, and we must accept what happens.

Cinderella: But what if—?

Mother's Voice: The only way to be prepared for what will happen is to be calm and strong. Good night, Cinderella, go to sleep. You know I love you. Forever.

(Cinderella thinks of what Mother has said, kisses the picture, closes the diary, and gets up to leave.)

Cinderella: Good night, Mother. I love you, too. Forever.

(Cinderella is about to leave the room, but stops and picks up the picture and the diary. She takes them with her.)

SCENE 2

(The living room. Cinderella enters with her schoolbooks inside her bag. She freezes while the Narrator explains what is happening.)

Narrator: Cinderella has just arrived home from school. She is ready to do what she does every day. But a big surprise awaits her!

(Cinderella puts her schoolbag on the living room table and her jacket on the back of a chair. Someone comes into the room and addresses Cinderella in a bossy manner.)

Stepmother: Don't leave your jacket on the chair! Pick up that bag at once!

Cinderella: *(Astonished. Responds with difficulty.)* Excuse me?

Stepmother: Do as I say!

Narrator: Cinderella does not understand what is going on. The two stepsisters come out to help their mother. Here they come!

(Two graceless girls enter, dressed in a pretentious manner and who do not appear very friendly. They look at Cinderella with contempt.)

Molly: Hiiiii! Didn't you hear mother ordering you not to put your jacket on the chair?

Polly: And didn't she tell you to take the bag away from the table?

Cinderella: Yes . . . I mean . . . Why? That's the way that I have always done it and I—

Stepmother: Well, things have changed.

Molly: They certainly have.

Polly: And you better understand that!

Stepmother: By the way, I am the lady of the house. Please call me Mrs. at all times.

Molly: I am Molly, and I like to have my things just so!

Polly: And I am Polly; you have just heard what is good for you.

Cinderella: Where is my father?

Stepmother: My husband will be home for supper, and I want the house to be clean when he arrives.

Molly: Where do you eat supper, usually?

Cinderella: Where? Well, at the dining room table.

Polly: Sorry, child. It is too small.

Molly: Yes, yes. Too small.

(The stepmother and her daughters look at each other, delighted by the idea of excluding Cinderella even from her own table.)

Stepmother: Molly and Polly are quite right, child. You will have to eat by yourself in the kitchen.

Cinderella: But . . . why?

Molly: You must learn to be obedient and never ask questions.

Polly: That's right. Go on! Clean up! Move!

Stepmother: I cannot believe the manners of that child! Humph!

Molly: Humph!

Polly: Humph!

Narrator: And with those last words, the stepmother and her two daughters leave poor Cinderella to herself. At first, she just sits, sad and tired. Then, she has a thought!

Cinderella: *(Takes her mother's picture out of her schoolbag.)* Hi, Mother. What do I do now?

Mother's Voice: Be patient, Cinderella. Everything will be all right. Put your things in your room and eat your supper in the kitchen. And write me a letter tonight.

Cinderella: Of course I'll write you a letter! But . . .

Mother's Voice: Everything will be all right, Cinderella.

(Cinderella kisses her Mother's portrait and puts it in her bag. She leaves the room.)

SCENE 3

(The stepmother and her daughters in the living room. The television is on, and they are polishing their nails, doing their hair in front of the mirror, and so forth. Even with all that, they look a fright, and seem to be unhappier than ever.)

Narrator: This is the way Cinderella's stepmother and her daughters spend their days. Listen!

Stepmother: This room looks messy, but not messy enough. Let's give Cinderella something to do when she comes home from school.

(The three of them laugh and throw something on the floor.)

Molly: I need a new color for my nails.

Polly: And I need a new ribbon for my hair.

(Just then, Cinderella comes home from school. She has not even taken her schoolbag off her shoulders when she finds herself surrounded by the stepmother and her daughters.)

Stepmother: Cinderella, you must clean this room at once! What a bad housekeeper you are!

Molly: Cinderella, you must go to the beauty shop at once and buy me some new nail polish!

Polly: Cinderella, I need a new ribbon for my hair at once!

Cinderella: How can I do all that at once? I can only do one thing at a time.

Stepmother, Molly, Polly: *That* is *your* problem!

(They leave the room, in the order in which they speak, their noses up and their mouths pursed in disgust. Cinderella is desperate. Just then, her father enters the house.)

Cinderella: Father, I am so happy to see you! But I don't know what . . .

Father: And I am happy to see you, Cinderella. But I must leave very soon. I don't have time to talk now.

Cinderella: Why not? Why is it that we don't spend time with each other anymore?

Father: *(Evasive.)* I know, but . . . I have to work more hours to make more money.

Cinderella: Father, you must help me. Your new wife and her daughters order me around as if I were a servant. I can't do enough to satisfy them.

Father: Do your best. They are your family now, and you must learn to get along with them. This is their house too. I have to go, Cinderella.

Cinderella: But, Father!

Narrator: Father has gone. Cinderella is desperate. She thinks about her Mother, takes her picture out of her bag, kisses her, tries to do her best to follow her advice . . .

Mother's Voice: Be strong, Cinderella.

SCENE 4

(The stepmother comes into the living room with a letter in her hand. She seems pleased with the news it bears. The two daughters follow and stand on either side of their mother, looking at the letter. While the stepmother reads the letter aloud, Cinderella comes into the room and listens, keeping her distance.)

Stepmother: Listen to this, girls! It is a letter from the community center, and it is signed by the director and by the Governor!

Molly and Polly: Oooooohhhhhhhhhhhhhhhh!

Molly: How important! Do they mention our names?

Stepmother: Yes. *All* of our names.

(The three look behind them, in the direction of Cinderella. Their faces show disgust. Cinderella doesn't move, but stands there listening.)

Molly: We don't have to take her with us.

Polly: We can say that she's sick.

Cinderella: *(Coming forward and facing them.)* You don't need to lie on my account, Polly. Especially since I intend to participate in the Governor's Neighborhood Talent Show.

Stepmother: Who gives you permission?

Cinderella: The Governor. It was announced at school. All children can take part.

Stepmother: Oh . . . well . . .

Molly: Humph!

Polly: Humph!

Stepmother: Just make sure that you don't tell anyone about this conversation!

(The three new members of the family exit, leaving Cinderella by herself. She takes out of her jacket her Mother's picture, looks at it, and smiles.)

Mother's Voice: Well done, Cinderella. Now, get ready!

SCENE 5

(The Governor's Neighborhood Talent Show. He is in the center of the stage, accompanied by his son, a handsome young man named Charles. This is a great night, when all the talented young people are there to show off their skills. Cinderella and her family arrive when the contest has already started. The two sisters and Cinderella stand by the governor's right. His son is to his left. The stepmother and Father enter and sit on chairs near Charles, facing the stage where the talent show is happening.)

Governor: Now, have we seen and heard all the participants?

Charles: I think there's one family that arrived a little late.

Father: Yes, sir. It was my fault.

Governor: No problem. Who's first?

Polly: *(Stepping forward.)* I am!

Governor: Very well . . . Polly, isn't it?

Polly: Yes, Mister Governor.

Governor: And what is the talent that you have developed to deal with a challenge in life?

Polly: *(Takes her makeup case out and opens it.)* I'll show you. With this *(a lipstick)*, I paint my lips like this. And with this *(nail polish)*, I paint my nails like that. In short, I make myself beautiful, and that is *my* talent.

(Charles and the Governor look at each other, a bit puzzled. They continue.)

Governor: Thank you, Polly. Very . . . very interesting. And the next is . . . Molly.

Molly: *(Stepping forward.)* Yes, Mister Governor.

Governor: And what is your talent, Molly?

Molly: My thing is my hair. *(She opens her beauty bag, and out come ribbons of all colors.)* I have blue ribbons and pink ribbons and golden ribbons for the holidays, and white ribbons for bad-hair days. That does it for me. And, if I ever want another one, I just send Cinderella to the store to get it for me.

Governor: You what?

Molly: *(Covering her mouth with her hand, suddenly aware of what she has said.)* Oh, I was not supposed to say that!

(The stepmother points a menacing finger at Cinderella, while Father hangs his head, ashamed.)

Governor: *(Clears his throat.)* Ahem! Well, and who is our next . . . participant?

Cinderella: I am, sir. My name is Cinderella.

Governor: *(Sounding tired and disappointed.)* Yes, I have it in the list. And what is the . . . talent . . . that you want to . . . share with us?

Cinderella: I would like to tell a story.

(The Governor and his son nod. The stepmother and her daughters become very tense.)

Cinderella: *(Using mime to illustrate her story, since she doesn't have any objects in her hands nor any furniture around her.)* Once upon a time, there was a girl who lived happily with her mother and father in a nice little house. Then, one day, the mother died, leaving the girl and the father alone. But, although they missed mother, they went on with their lives. The girl went to school, and every night she wrote a letter to her mother. Father took care of supper, and life was not that bad after all. Then, everything changed. The father married again, and the new wife brought home her own daughters. The girl wrote her mother about it, and got the message that one must accept change. And life changed at home. The girl was treated like a servant, ordered to pick up the trash that the others threw around, to go to the store for nail polish when she had to do her homework . . . There was never a kind word from anyone, and the father was always away working, to make more money —always, more than ever. So the girl kept writing to her mother, who sent the message that the only way to be happy when life brings us bad experiences is to be strong and calm and patient. And the girl learned from her mother, and her life has been happy, because she has kept her heart clean.

Governor and Charles: *(Clapping, enthusiastic.)* What a beautiful story! Did you think it up yourself?

Cinderella: I didn't have to, sir. I am the girl in the story.

Stepmother: *(Standing up in a huff.)* You were warned not to say anything, you stupid girl!

Governor: Cinderella, you have shown that you have the ability to deal with the challenges of life. I believe that this is the most important talent to develop.

(Father grabs the stepmother to get her to sit down.)

Charles: If it is all right with you, Father, I would love to invite Cinderella to come with me to the concert of the Diamond Sisters.

Governor: All right with me, Son? I think she's great! She wins the contest.

Narrator: Well, you saw and heard what happened. And do you think that the three new members of the family are ashamed? Let's see.

Molly: She wins! Why not me?

Polly: Yeah! What's special about her?

Stepmother: She isn't worth that much.

(And the three women walk out: first the stepmother, then Molly, and then Polly, their noses up in the air, and very upset. Father walks up to Cinderella, tears in his eyes.)

Father: That's a great story that you told, Cinderella. Mother would be proud of you.

Cinderella: Thank you, Father. I know she is proud. My heart tells me so.

(They embrace.)

Father: Have a good time at the Diamond Sisters' concert. I'll be waiting for you when you get home. Probably we can have some late-night pizza. From now on, we'll spend more time together.

Cinderella: Let's do that, Father. I love you.

(Charles and the Governor, who have been waiting, lead Cinderella to their limousine. The driver opens the door for them.)

Chauffeur: This is your car tonight. I am your driver. Please, come in.

Narrator: And now, if you have a story to tell, stand up and tell us. We don't have tickets to the Diamond Sisters' concert, but we may give you a better gift—our appreciation for a good story well told, which is not a small thing!

THE END

Cenicienta en tiempos modernos

Personajes

- Cenicienta
- Padre
- Madrastra
- Mili
- Pili
- Gobernador
- Hijo del Gobernador (Carlos)
- Narrador/a
- Voz de la madre
- Chófer

ESCENA 1

(La sala de estar de una casa contemporánea. Cenicienta, una niña de nueve años, está sentada frente a un escritorio, escribiendo. Está concentrada y tranquila, y de vez en cuando mira una fotografía—la de su madre, que ha muerto.)

Narrador: Esto es lo que Cenicienta hace cada noche: escribe en su diario, pero lo que escribe es una carta. Y, ¿a quién? Escuchad . . .

Cenicienta: "Querida madre: me pasé todo el día esperando este momento para poder estar sola contigo. Sé que estás siempre conmigo, pero durante el día tengo que hacer otras cosas y no estoy completamente contigo, como me gusta estar. Son las siete y media de la noche. Padre y yo hemos cenado. Comimos pizza, y estaba muy buena. Pero extraño tus cenas, ¿sabes?, las buenas sopas y el flan con crema. Y tu sonrisa; extraño tu sonrisa, y por eso tengo tu foto aquí para no olvidarla nunca. ¿Comes buenas comidas en el cielo? Espero que sí, porque a veces me preocupa que la comida allí no sea tan buena como cuando tú cocinabas. Pasé un buen día en la escuela. ¿Te acuerdas de mi amiga Laura? Estamos juntas en la clase de baile, y estamos practicando algo muy bello".

(Padre entra en la habitación. No se porta con frialdad, pero tiene prisa y quiere terminar lo que tiene que decir rápidamente. Se sienta en una silla al lado de su hija. Cenicienta escucha.)

Padre: Hola, Cenicienta.

Cenicienta: Hola, padre. Gracias por comprar pizza esta noche para la cena. Estaba muy buena. Estoy escribiéndole a—

Padre: Cenicienta, tengo noticias que darte. Verás, desde que madre murió—

Cenicienta: Le estoy escribiendo ahora; le gusta saber que estamos bien.

Padre: *(Suspira, algo impaciente.)* Es . . . está muy bien, Cenicienta. Muy bien. Pero he estado pensando que necesitamos a alguien . . . otra . . . madre que nos ayude a hacer la cena.

Cenicienta: *(No comprende y espera un poco antes de responder.)* ¿Otra madre? Ya tenemos una.

Padre: *(Se levanta y habla rápidamente.)* Una madre nueva vendrá muy pronto a vivir con nosotros. Te tratará bien, y espero que tú la trates bien también. Tiene dos hijas que serán como hermanas; así no estarás sola.

Cenicienta: ¡Pero si no estoy sola!

Padre: *(Besa a su hija.)* Buenas noches, Cenicienta. Me voy a la cama porque me tengo que levantar temprano para ir a trabajar.

(Padre se da la vuelta y no mira a su hija cuando ella le habla.)

Cenicienta: *(Turbada.)* Pero, ¡padre!

(Padre se ha ido, y Cenicienta se queda sola con la foto de su madre.)

Cenicienta: *(Toma la foto en la mano y la mira por un rato.)* No quiero que nadie ocupe tu puesto, madre. Pero no quiero desobedecer a padre. ¿Qué puedo hacer?

(Se oye una voz, la de madre. Es dulce y tranquila, y Cenicienta no tiene miedo porque la ha oído antes.)

Voz de Madre: No te entristezcas, Cenicienta. Sabías que esto iba a pasar un día.

Cenicienta: Sí, pero no quiero que te vayas.

Voz de Madre: Siempre estaré contigo. Haz lo que padre te diga, y escríbeme todas las noches, como siempre. La vida sigue, y debemos de aceptar lo que pase.

Cenicienta: ¿Pero y si—?

Voz de Madre: La única manera de estar preparados para lo que la vida nos traiga es siendo fuertes y estando tranquilos. Buenas noches, Cenicienta. Vete a dormir. Sabes que te quiero, y te querré siempre.

(Cenicienta piensa por un rato en las palabras de su madre, besa la foto, cierra el diario, y se levanta para irse.)

Cenicienta: Buenas noches, madre. Yo también te quiero a ti, y te querré siempre.

(Recoge el diario y la foto, y se las lleva.)

ESCENA 2

(En la sala de estar otra vez. Cenicienta entra con su cartera de la escuela llena de libros, y se queda inmóvil mientras que el narrador explica lo que pasa.)

Narrador: Cenicienta acaba de llegar de la escuela. Está lista para hacer lo que hace cada día, pero una gran sorpresa la aguarda.

(Cenicienta pone su cartera en la mesa y la chaqueta en la espalda de una silla, cuando una mujer entra y le habla de una manera mandona.)

Madrastra: ¡No te dejes la chaqueta en la silla! ¡Recoge esa cartera inmediatamente!

Cenicienta: *(Sorprendida, responde con dificultad.)* ¿Perdón?

Madrastra: ¡Haz lo que te digo!

Narrador: Cenicienta no comprende lo que pasa. Así que las dos hermanastras acuden en ayuda de su madre. ¡Aquí vienen!

(Dos muchachas desgarbadas entran, vestidas de una forma pretenciosa, y muy desagradables. Miran a Cenicienta con desprecio.)

Mili: ¡Holaaaaaa! ¿No oíste que madre te mandó que no pusieras la chaqueta sobre la silla?

Pili: ¿Y no te dijo que quitaras la cartera de encima de la mesa?

Cenicienta: Sí . . . , quiero decir . . . ¿Por qué? Así es como he hecho las cosas siempre y yo—

Madrastra: Bueno, las cosas han cambiado.

Mili: Es cierto que han cambiado.

Pili: ¡Y espero que lo entiendas!

Madrastra: A propósito, soy la señora de la casa. Por favor, llámame Señora siempre.

Mili: Yo soy Mili, y a mí me gusta tener mis cosas a mi manera.

Pili: Y yo soy Pili, y tú acabas de oír lo que es bueno para ti.

Cenicienta: ¿Dónde está mi padre?

Madrastra: Mi esposo estará aquí para cenar, y quiero que la casa esté limpia cuando llegue.

Mili: ¿Dónde te comes tu cena?

Cenicienta: ¿Dónde? Pues en la mesa del comedor.

Pili: Lo siento, nena. Es demasiado pequeña.

Mili: Sí, sí. Demasiado pequeña.

(Los tres nuevos miembros de la familia se miran entre sí, muy felices con la idea de excluir a Cenicienta de su propia mesa.)

Madrastra: Pili y Mili tienen razón, nena. Tendrás que comer tú sola en la cocina.

Cenicienta: Pero, ¿por qué?

Mili: Debes de aprender a ser obediente y NUNCA hacer preguntas.

Pili: Exactamente. ¡Hala! ¡A limpiar! ¡Muévete!

Madrastra: ¡Los modales de esa niña! ¡No me lo puedo creer! ¡Bah!

Mili: ¡Bah!

Pili: ¡Bah!

Narrador: Y con esas palabras, la madrastra y sus dos hijas dejan sola a la pobre Cenicienta. Se sienta, cansada. Entonces, ¡tiene una idea!

Cenicienta: *(Saca la foto de su madre de la cartera.)* Hola, madre. ¿Qué debo de hacer ahora?

Voz de Madre: Ten paciencia, Cenicienta. Todo acabará bien. Pon tus cosas en tu habitación y come tu cena en la cocina. Y escríbeme una carta esta noche.

Cenicienta: ¡Claro que te escribiré! Pero . . .

Voz de Madre: Todo saldrá bien, Cenicienta.

(Cenicienta besa la foto de su madre y la pone en la cartera. Sale de la habitación.)

ESCENA 3

(La madrastra y hermanastras en la sala de estar. Tienen la televisión encendida, están pintándose las uñas, peinándose frente a un espejo, etc. Incluso así, se ven feísimas, y están más infelices que nunca.)

Narrador: De esta manera la madrastra y hermanastras de Cenicienta pasan los días. ¡Escuchad!

Madrastra: La habitación está sucia, pero no lo suficiente. Vamos a darle a Cenicienta algo que hacer cuando vuelva de la escuela.

(Las tres se ríen y tiran cosas en el suelo.)

Mili: Necesito un nuevo color para mis uñas.

Pili: Y yo necesito un lazo nuevo para mi pelo.

(Cenicienta llega de la escuela en este momento. Ni siquiera le ha dado tiempo a quitarse la cartera del hombro, cuando se encuentra rodeada por las tres mujeres.)

Madrastra: Cenicienta, ¡debes de limpiar esta habitación ahora mismo! ¡Eres un ama de casa terrible!

Mili: Cenicienta, tienes que ir a al salón de belleza a comprarme un bote de pintauñas nuevo. ¡Ya mismo!

Pili: Cenicienta, ¡necesito un lazo nuevo para el pelo ahora mismo!

Cenicienta: ¿Cómo puedo hacer tantas cosas ahora mismo? Sólo puedo hacer las cosas de una en una.

Madrastra, Mili, y Pili: ¡*Eso* es *tu* problema!

(Y las tres salen de la habitación, en el orden en que hablaron, con las narices en el aire y en los labios una mueca de disgusto. Cenicienta está desesperada. En ese momento, su padre entra en la casa.)

Cenicienta: Padre, ¡qué alegría de verte! Pero no sé qué—

Padre: Yo también estoy contento de verte, Cenicienta. Pero tengo que irme pronto. No tengo tiempo para hablar ahora.

Cenicienta: ¿Por qué no? ¿Por qué no pasamos tiempo juntos ya?

Padre: *(Evasivo.)* Lo sé, pero . . . tengo que trabajar más horas para ganar más dinero.

Cenicienta: Padre, tienes que ayudarme. Tu nueva esposa y sus hijas me tratan como si fuera una sirvienta. Nada de lo que hago las satisface.

Padre: Haz lo que puedas. Son tu familia ahora, y debes de aprender a llevarte bien con ellas. Ésta es su casa también. Me tengo que ir, Cenicienta.

Cenicienta: Pero, ¡padre!

Narrador: Padre ya se ha ido. Cenicienta está desesperada. Piensa en su madre, saca la foto de su cartera, la besa, e intenta hacer todo lo posible por seguir su consejo . . .

Voz de Madre: Sé fuerte, Cenicienta.

ESCENA 4

(La madrastra entra en la sala de estar con una carta en la mano. Parece estar muy contenta con las noticias que trae. Las dos hijas la siguen, y se paran una a cada lado, mirando la carta. Mientras que la madrastra lee la carta en voz alta, Cenicienta entra en la sala y escucha, a cierta distancia.)

Madrastra: ¡Escuchad, chicas! ¡Es una carta del Centro de la Vecindad, y está firmada por el director y por el Gobernador!

Pili y Mili: ¡Oooooooohhhhhhhhhhhhhhhhhhhhhh!

Mili: ¡Qué importante! ¿Menciona nuestros nombres?

Madrastra: Sí. Todos nuestros nombres.

(Las tres miran hacia atrás, en dirección de Cenicienta. Sus expresiones muestran descontento. Cenicienta no se mueve, sino que se queda allí, escuchando.)

Mili: No tenemos por qué llevarla con nosotros.

Pili: Podemos decir que está enferma.

Cenicienta: *(Adelantándose y poniéndose enfrente de ellas.)* No tienes por qué mentir por mi causa, Pili. Sobre todo, porque tengo la intención de participar en el Concurso de Talento de la Vecindad del gobernador.

Madrastra: ¿Quién te da permiso?

Cenicienta: El Gobernador. Ha sido anunciado en la escuela. Todos los chicos pueden participar.

Madrastra: ¡Ah, bueno!

Mili: ¡Bah!

Pili: ¡Bah!

Madrastra: Pero mucho cuidado con contarle a nadie esta conversación.

(Los tres nuevos miembros de la familia se van, dejando sola a Cenicienta. Saca de su cartera la foto de su madre, la mira y sonríe.)

Voz de Madre: Bien hecho, Cenicienta. Y ahora, ¡a prepararte!

ESCENA 5

(El Concurso de Talento en el Centro de la Vecindad, patrocinado por el Gobernador. El salón debe de estar decorado para la ocasión, y el gobernador y su hijo, un joven muy elegante llamado Carlos, están sentados en la mitad del escenario. Ésta es la gran noche, cuando todos los jóvenes están reunidos para mostrar sus talentos. Cenicienta y su familia llegan cuando la función ya ha empezado. Las dos hermanas y Cenicienta se ponen a la derecha del Gobernador. El hijo está a la izquierda. La madrastra y el padre entran y se sientan en sillas al lado de Carlos, mirando a la parte del escenario donde los jóvenes participan en el concurso.)

Gobernador: Bueno, ¿hemos visto y oído a todos los concursantes?

Carlos: Creo que hay una familia que llegó un poco tarde.

Padre: Sí, señor. Fue culpa mía.

Gobernador: No se preocupe. ¿Quién va primero?

Pili: *(Tomando un paso adelante.)* ¡Yo!

Gobernador: Muy bien . . . Pili, ¿no?

Pili: Sí, señor Gobernador.

Gobernador: ¿Y cuál es el talento que has desarrollado para hacerle frente a los retos de la vida?

Pili: *(Saca su bolsa de maquillaje y la abre.)* Se lo enseñaré. Con esto *(una barra de pintalabios)* me pinto los labios así. Y con esto *(pintauñas)* me pinto las uñas de esta manera. En resumen, me pongo guapa, y ése es mi talento.

(Charles y el Gobernador intercambian miradas, algo confusos. Continúan.)

Gobernador: Gracias, Pili. Muy . . . muy interesante. Y la próxima es . . . Mili.

Mili: *(Tomando un paso adelante.)* Sí, señor Gobernador.

Gobernador: ¿Y cuál es tu talento, Mili?

Mili: Lo mío es el pelo. *(Abre sa bolsa, y de ella salen lazos y lazos de todos los colores.)* Tengo lazos azules, y lazos color rosa, y lazos dorados para las fiestas, y lazos blancos para días tontos. Y eso es todo. Y si en algún momento quiero otro, mando a Cenicienta a la tienda a que me lo compre.

Gobernador: Tú, ¿qué?

Mili: *(Se cubre la boca con la mano, dándose cuenta de pronto de lo que ha dicho.)* ¡Oh, no debería de haberlo dicho!

(La madrastra apunta un dedo amenazador en dirección de Cenicienta, mientras que el padre baja la cabeza, avergonzado.)

Gobernador: *(Se aclara la garganta.)* ¡Ajem! Bueno, y ¿quién es nuestra próxima . . . concursante?

Cenicienta: Yo, señor. Me llamo Cenicienta.

Gobernador: *(La voz llena de cansancio y desilusión.)* Sí, lo tengo en la lista. ¿Y cuál es el . . . talento . . . que quieres compartir . . . con nosotros?

Cenicienta: Me gustaría contar una historia.

(El Gobernador y su hijo asienten con la cabeza. La madrastra y sus hijas se ponen muy tensas.)

Cenicienta: *(Usa movimientos para ilustrar su historia, pues no tiene obejetos a mano.)* Érase una vez una jovencita que vivía muy feliz con su madre y su padre en una linda casita. Entonces, un día, la madre murió, dejando al padre y a la niña solos. Pero aunque echaban de menos a la madre, ellos siguieron viviendo. La niña iba a la escuela y cada noche escribía una carta a su madre. Padre se encargaba de la cena, y la vida realmente no iba mal. Entonces, todo cambió. El padre se casó otra vez, y la nueva esposa trajo a casa a sus propias hijas. La niña le escribió a su madre contándole lo que pasaba, y la madre le respondió que uno debe de aceptar los cambios. Y la vida cambió en la casa. A la niña la trataban como si fuera una sirvienta; le mandaban que recogiera la basura que los otros tiraban, y que fuera a la tienda a por pintaunas cuando tenía que hacer su tarea . . . Nunca recibía una palabra amable de nadie, y el padre estaba siempre fuera trabajando para ganar más dinero - siempre más, más que antes. Así que la joven le escribía a su madre, que le mandaba mensajes diciendo que la única manera de ser feliz cuando la vida nos trae malas experiencias es ser fuerte, estar tranquila y tener paciencia. Y la joven aprendió de su madre, y su vida ha sido feliz porque ha mantenido su corazón limpio.

Gobernador y Carlos: *(Aplaudiendo con entusiasmo.)* ¡Qué historia tan bonita! ¿Te la has inventado tú?

Cenicienta: No he tenido que inventar nada, señor. Yo soy la joven de la historia.

Madrastra: *(Poniéndose de pie con mucho enfado.)* ¡Te dije que no contaras nada, estúpida!

Gobernador: Cenicienta, nos has enseñado que tienes la habilidad de hacerle frente a los retos de la vida. Pienso que es el talento más importante que uno puede desarrollar.

(Padre toma a la madrastra del brazo y la fuerza a que se siente.)

Carlos: Si te parece bien, padre, me gustaría invitar a Cenicienta a que viniera conmigo al concierto de las Hermanas Diamante.

Gobernador: ¿Que si me parece bien, hijo? ¡Es fabulosa! Ella gana el concurso.

Narrador: Bueno, ya vísteis y oísteis lo que pasó. ¿Y creéis que los tres nuevos miembros de la familia están avergonzados? Veamos.

Mili: ¡Ella gana! ¿Y por qué no yo?

Pili: ¡Eso! ¿Qué tiene ella tan especial?

Madrastra: No vale tanto.

(Y las tres se marchan, en el orden en que hablaron, con las narices en el aire y muy enfadadas. El padre se acerca a Cenicienta, con los ojos llenos de lágrimas.)

Padre: ¡Qué gran historia la que nos contaste, Cenicienta! Madre estaría orgullosa de ti.

Cenicienta: Gracias, padre. Sé que está orgullosa porque mi corazón me lo dice.

(Se abrazan.)

Padre: Diviértete en el concierto de las Hermanas Diamante. Te estaré esperando cuando llegues a casa. A lo mejor podemos comernos una pizza, aunque sea tarde. De hoy en adelante, pasaremos más tiempo juntos.

Cenicienta: Me encantaría, padre. Te quiero.

(Carlos y el Gobernador, que han estado esperando, acompañan a Cenicienta a la limosina. El chófer les abre la puerta.)

Chófer: Éste es su automóvil para esta noche, y yo soy su chófer. Por favor, entren.

Narrador: Y ahora, si tienes una historia que contar, levántate y cuéntanosla. No tenemos entradas para el concierto de las Hermanas Diamante, pero a lo mejor te damos un regalo mejor: ¡nuestra apreciación por una historia bien contada, que no es poco!

FIN

VOCABULARY–VOCABULARIO

Nouns–Nombres

challenge: *reto*
heart: *corazón*
ribbon: *lazo, cinta*
stepmother: *madrastra*
stepsister: *hermanastra*
trash: *basura*

Adjectives–Adjetivos

calm: *tranquilo*
dirty: *sucio*
happy: *feliz*
patient: *paciente*
pretty: *lindo*
sick: *enfermo*

Verbs–Verbos

to be ashamed: *estar avergonzado*
to be someone's fault: *ser la culpa de alguien*
to be strong: *ser fuerte*
to get up: *levantarse*
to lie: *mentir*

El Bully

El valentón

The Funky Gazette!

Once again, the Broad Street Players impressed the Funky Gazette staff. They tackled the complex issue facing kids today, BULLIES! The story takes place mainly in a classroom setting; but ventures out to the immediate community surrounding the school. My partner and right- hand man Kenny Ramirez, handled the tuff interviews and covered the background scene involving this play. He discovered, after speaking with Neville Beckford(stage – manager) that all was not well with the preparation of the play. "The actors have an easier job then the stage personnel...Actors don't have to think hard", were the words spoken from Neville. His assistant Joseph Mota added, " We want to get paid dinero, not comida.." Through all the smoke behind the scenes, the Broad Street Players still came out with another banger! With the returned talent of Rummy(the princess from the earlier play) and a strong supporting cast; Me and my amigo Kenny give "El Bully" TWO THUMBS UP & a pinky toe...Good Job Y'all...

Figure 5

(Review of the play, written by children and a counselor at ¡City Arts! for Youth in Providence, Rhode Island, in the summer of 1999.)

El Bully

A bilingual interactive play for young people, ages 8 to 12

Characters

- Emilia
- Richard (Dick)
- Teacher (Mrs. Senterfeet)
- Elaine
- María
- Joshua
- José
- A few extra students for playground and hall.

> *Note:* This play takes place in a school and is concerned with the origins and effects of hierarchies in personal relations. Before the play is performed, it would be a good idea to prepare both actors and the audience to discuss the characters and the story. Is Dick, in some way or ways, superior to Emilia? What kind of life experiences, in your opinion, produce a person like Dick? Why is it that no one speaks up at first? Do you think that the teacher should have behaved differently? What would you do in a similar situation? The jump-rope song included in the play comes from Spain, is sung in a sing-song-type melody, and can be substituted with any other with which the actors are familiar or with some simple song in Spanish that the actors can master without difficulty.

SCENE 1

(A classroom. There is a new student, seated, whom the teacher is about to introduce to the class. Students look at her in a welcoming way.)

Teacher: Hi, class! I want to introduce a new student, Emilia.

All: Hi, Emilia!

Dick: *(In a high, shrill voice.)* Welcome, Emilia.

Emilia: Thank you. *Gracias.*

Teacher: *¡Gracias!* Thank you for reminding me, Emilia. Class, Emilia's first language is Spanish, although she speaks English very well.

María: *(Raising her hand excitedly.)* *¡Y yo!* I also speak Spanish.

Teacher: I know, María. And you are helpful in teaching us some words. But we all speak English in class.

María: *(Sad.)* Yes, Mrs. Senterfeet.

José: *(As if to himself, frustrated.)* I never say anything.

Teacher: José, did you say something?

José: *(Unpleasantly.)* No. I was talking to myself.

Teacher: All right. Now, we are all going to introduce ourselves to Emilia. Say something about yourself that you would like Emilia to know, something nice. Let me start. Emilia, I am your teacher, Mrs. Senterfeet. I love my class, my two dogs, and my little boy, Jim. I hope that you will be happy here. Elaine, please.

Elaine: I am Elaine . . . *(Speaking quickly and nervously.)* I like books, I ride a bicycle, I play softball, I—

Teacher: Thank you, Elaine. That's good enough. You'll have time later on to tell her more about yourself. María?

María: *Hola,* Emilia. Welcome.

(María and Emilia smile at each other and wave across the room. Teacher motions to Joshua.)

Joshua: I'm Joshua, Josh to my friends. I am a computer geek. If you want to learn to use a computer, ask me.

Teacher: That's so nice of you, Josh! José?

José: I am José. Have nothing to say.

Teacher: All right, José. You'll talk enough later. Richard, it's your turn.

(Richard has a nervous, disturbed face. His eyes are wide open, and he wears his baseball cap backward.)

Dick: Dick, to my friends. Please, call me Dick. I am se-serious, we'll be friends. Ni-nice meeting you. You'll like it here. We-we-we make a Christmas tree and ha-have a party too.

Teacher: That's right, Richard. We do have a nice party for Christmas, don't we? Thank you all. Emily, welcome to our class. And now, Math Time Made Fun! Get your paper and pencil ready. Ready? Think of a number . . . Multiply that number by two . . . To that, add two . . .

(All students write down instructions very quickly. Emilia gets lost soon and panics. She is about to raise her hand but doesn't do it. Dick notices and smiles unkindly. He is also lost. He raises his hand.)

Teacher: Richard, are you lost?

Dick: *(Mean, pointing at Emilia, loud.)* I'm not lost. She is!

Teacher: I am sorry, Emilia. Why didn't you say something?

Emilia: I didn't want to interrupt.

Teacher: That's not an interruption: it's part of the lesson. Just raise your hand when you need anything, dear. We continue. Now, divide the result in half . . . Subtract the original number that you thought of . . . And the answer is . . . ? Richard, what is the answer?

Dick: *(Deadpan.)* I don't have it.

Teacher: Did you get lost?

Dick: I didn't get lost. I think that we all lost our concentration when—

(He looks at Emilia. All are silent. Elaine raises hand.)

Teacher: Yes, Elaine.

Elaine: The answer is one.

All, except Dick: Yeah! That's what I got.

Teacher: *(A bit confused, looking at all the students.)* Hummm . . . Yes, that's correct. Well, now, class, time for recess. Enjoy!

(All get up. Richard makes lots of noise and behaves in a disorderly manner.)

SCENE 2

(Playground. The girls are on one side of the stage, playing jump rope. We do not hear them at the beginning. We hear the boys playing ball offstage. Suddenly, Dick shows up on stage, dishevelled and more disturbed than ever. His baseball hat is about to fall off. Boys' voices are heard offstage calling to him, mockingly.)

Voice 1: Hey, Dick, don't leave us!

(Laughter.)

Voice 2: We can't play without you!

(More laughter.)

Voice 3: Bring us the ball, pleeeeeease!

(More laughter. A ball is thrown in his direction, and Dick struggles, very clumsily, to regain his balance. He looks lost, very sad, his cap is about to fall from his head, and his shoulders are hunched over. There is now a period of silence and, while he recovers, the boys' voices disappear and the girls come to the middle of the stage. Emilia and María are singing a song in Spanish, "Soy la reina de los mares," to which they all jump rope. They need someone to hold the rope at one end, so they motion Dick to come closer, and when he does, they give one end of the rope to him. He accepts, and slowly his expression changes from being sad to feeling happy. While the girls sing and jump rope, Dick moves the rope and tries to imitate their singing. He only gets a few endings of lines. Other girls can add to dialogue by including brief comments, exclamations— "That's great!" "You do it so well!" and so on, but they should not interfere with dialogue or the singing.)

Emilia and María: *(Singing.)*

> *Soy la reina de los mares,*
> *ustedes lo van a ver,*
> *tiro mi pañuelo al suelo,*
> *y lo vuelvo a recoger.*
> *¡Pañuelito, pañuelito!*
> *¡Quién te pudiera tener,*
> *metidito en el bolsillo,*
> *como un barco de papel!*

Dick: . . . -ares . . . ver . . . elo . . .

(He jumps up and down, delighted.)

Dick: I like this much more than playing ball! I don't even care what the boys say! I am doing this during recess from now on!

María: Do you want to jump rope and I'll hold it for you?

Dick: Yeeeeh! This is great! I wish I knew the song, though. " . . . ares!" All I know!

All girls: *(They sing while Dick jumps rope. María and Elaine are holding it.)*

> *Soy la reina de los mares,*
> *ustedes lo van a ver,*
> *tiro mi pañuelo al suelo,*
> *y lo vuelvo a recoger.*
> *¡Pañuelito, pañuelito!*
> *¡Quién te pudiera tener,*
> *metidito en el bolsillo,*
> *como un barco de papel!*

Emilia: You jump rope better than many girls, Dick. I'll write out the song for you so that you can learn it at home.

Dick: *¡Gracias,* Emilia!

(Dick hugs Emilia clumsily. Emilia smiles, proud, a bit shy. The other girls are picking up the rope when the teacher shows up. Recess has ended, they all go toward classroom. The teacher appears at one side of the stage, welcoming her class. She has pencil, pad, and a smile.)

SCENE 3

(Ouside school, or in school corridor. Dick accompanies Emilia toward the bus stop. Both are carrying their books. Dick's attitude is that of an important individual, very big.)

Dick: It's nice that we have busses, although I personally don't need them. My mom comes to pick me up every day.

Emilia: I wish my father could pick me up, but he's at work now.

Dick: That's all right. This way, you make friends, practice your English and stuff. Besides, buses are very ecological.

Emilia: E-co-lo-gi-cal?

Dick: You don't know that word? It's when something—a product or an action—is planet friendly.

Emilia: Pla—?

Dick: I forgot that you haven't been in this school for long. We are more advanced than most, you know. And planet . . . But your bus is here! I'll see you tomorrow.

Emilia: *(Rushed, but manages to take a piece of paper out of her bag.)* I forgot to give you this. It's the song. We will sing it together tomorrow during recess. I have even illustrated it with drawings in color!

Dick: How nice! Bye, Emilia. Thanks!

Emilia: *¡Hasta mañana!*

Dick: *¡Has-ta-ma-nia-a-na!*

(Emilia leaves. Voices of other students are heard off stage, passing by in a hurry. Dick opens the piece of paper, looks at it for a long time, eyes wide open. Smiles, a strange smile, which is almost happy, but insecure. Carefully, he folds paper and puts it inside pocket.)

Dick: I think that Emilia is a nice girl. Yes, truly nice. *(Changes to a self-important tone.)* But she's not as advanced as we are.

SCENE 4

(A picnic table in the playground, during recess. Emilia is helping Elaine with homework. In the background, girls and boys are talking, holding a ball, rope, and so on. We don't hear them, and they should move very carefully so as not to take the attention away from the conversation.)

Emilia: Let's see if you can remember the names now. *(She points to her mouth.)*

Elaine: *Boca.*

(Emilia mimics eating.)

Elaine: *Comer.*

(Emilia mimes that she eats with her mouth.)

Elaine: *Tú comes boca.*

(Emilia laughs and writes "con" on a piece of paper, shows it to Elaine.)

Elaine: *(Laughs.) Tú comes con la boca.*

(Emilia points to Elaine.)

Elaine: *Yo como con la boca.*

(They both laugh and applaud. Elaine gets ready to leave with her books. Dick starts making himself visible. He comes forward very slowly. He looks angry at what he sees, jealous perhaps. He takes out of his pocket the piece of paper that Emilia gave him and is about to tear it up, but instead he crumbles it and puts it back in his pocket. He looks dangerous now.)

Emilia: You learn very fast.

Elaine: That's because you are a great teacher. I was so worried about the Spanish quiz, and now I am looking forward to it! How can I repay you?

Emilia: I am sure that you'll have a chance to repay me, but don't feel that you have to do it. That's not why I helped you. I believe that we should be good to one another, without expecting anything in return. I am just happy when I do a good action. My grandmother has taught me that.

Elaine: And do you believe in that? I mean, it's beautiful, but not everyone thinks that way. Many people expect something in return when they do someone else a favor.

Emilia: Yes, I believe that helping others and not expecting anything in return is good in itself. So I am happy today!

Elaine: That's great! I have to tell this to my mother. She'll love it. *Hasta mañana,* Emilia.

Emilia: *¡Hasta mañana, Elaine! y, ¡suerte con el examen de español!*

(Elaine leaves with her books. Emilia remains where she is, copying a drawing from a picture book onto a piece of paper. Dick approaches her slowly from behind and startles her.)

Dick: *(Very loud.)* Draw me if you can! Ha-ha-ha!

Emilia: *(Afraid, looking around quickly.)* Ah . . .

Dick: It's just me. Drawing again?

Emilia: Yes, well, copying this beautiful house here. I love drawing more than anything else in the whole world.

Dick: Did you do this? *(He takes the drawing with the song out of his pocket, smooths it out.)*

Emilia: *(Very pleased.)* Yes, I did!

Dick: *(With contempt, throwing the paper at her.)* Anyone can do this.

(Emilia's face falls. Dick grins, happy that he has hurt her.)

Dick: *(Very important.)* You should have seen the watercolors that the art teacher gave Mrs. Senterfeet for Christmas. Now, that's art. But you were not here for Christmas.

Emilia: *(After a pause.)* No, I was not here.

Dick: *(Leaning over.)* Let me see what you are doing. *(In an accusatory tone.)* So, copying directly from the book.

Emilia: I—

Dick: It doesn't matter what you say. I can see clearly what's going on here. And that drawing that you gave me—is that yours?

(The word drawing *is pronounced in such a way that Emilia gives a start. Every time Dick says "drawing," the same thing will happen. There is an accusation in Dick's tone that hurts Emilia.)*

Emilia: Yes, it is mine. I did it from imagination.

Dick: That drawing is yours, you're saying.

(Emilia starts at the word drawing. *She tries to leave.)*

Emilia: Yes. Excuse me, but I have to—

Dick: *(Puts a hand on her arm to stop her.)* Wait! You haven't taught me the song yet, like you promised.

Emilia: *(Hesitates.)* All right. Do you—are you taking Spanish?

Dick: I just bought a book of the most common expressions. Great stuff. My mom buys me everything.

Emilia: All right. I'll read it alone first, and then—

Dick: No need to. Let's just sing it.

Emilia: *(Singing from memory. Dick gets the paper back and looks at it.)*

> *Soy la reina de los mares,*
> *ustedes lo van a ver,*
> *tiro mi pañuelo al suelo,*
> *y lo vuelvo a recoger.*
> *¡Pañuelito, pañuelito!*
> *¡Quién te pudiera tener,*
> *metidito en el bolsillo,*
> *como un barco de papel!*

(Dick attempts to follow her, late and badly, tripping all over the place, singing just the last syllable. Emilia finishes the song.)

Dick: *(Pronouncing just a few of the last syllables.)*

> *. . . ares,*
> *. . . lo,*
> *. . . llo,*
> *. . . pel.*

Emilia: Now you know how it goes. Practice, and you can join us on the play-ground.

(Dick is taken aback by Emilia's show of strength and by his own clumsiness. She picks up her books and stands up. She even smiles.)

Emilia: Time to take the bus. Bye!

Dick: *(Sad.)* Bye, Emilia. *(Suddenly, he's the bully again.)* Ah! And those drawings . . . are not bad, even if they are not original.

(Emilia shudders at the mention of the drawings, which Dick enjoys. She picks her things up and leaves. Dick goes out giggling, his back shaking with pleasure. From now on, Dick's eyes should be very open and have a fixed quality, accompanied by a grin.)

SCENE 5

(Joshua, José, Elaine, María, and other girls from the playground. They are in the hallway. Joshua comes down the corridor with computer keyboard. Dick is waiting and approaches him with tiny steps. He motions him to come closer, whispers something in his ear with that same fixed grin. Joshua imitates the grin and leaves. José arrives. The same action from Dick follows, but José does not react. His face is very serious; Emilia comes along, and José looks away. Emilia looks hurt, and Dick grins unpleasantly. No one says a word. Emilia and José leave, not talking to each other. Dick shares his secret with María, who is not happy. She goes away in silence, as if ashamed of herself. The teacher comes along, Dick stops her.)

Dick: I hope we are going to draw today.

Teacher: Sure! In fact, I was thinking that we should do something fun today, you people have been working so hard with those quizzes! Yes, we'll draw.

(Teacher goes into classroom, where students are already seated, followed by Dick who is smiling with triumph.)

Teacher: Good morning, class! Isn't the weather beautiful? We are going to start the day with something fun. I know that you have been working extremely hard, especially with that Spanish quiz yesterday. *(The teacher pauses and looks at Emilia. Dick gloats and Joshua grins. María and José look down. Emilia senses that something is going on and looks around without understanding.)* Emilia, thank you for helping Elaine prepare for the test. She told me all about it! That was very nice of you. *(Elaine smiles, grateful, but she then looks around at Joshua and Dick, who are giggling. Elaine frowns a bit, confused.)* Emilia, I hope that you help Elaine again. We need more of that. *(More giggles from Joshua and Dick. The teacher stops to look at them severely. They stop making noises, but their expressions do not change. The teacher's tone is a bit bossy from now on, because she is confused also.)* Allright. And now, let's all take paper and pencil, and draw.

(Emilia's pen drops to the floor. Dick points at her, delighted.)

Teacher: Emilia, do you like drawing?

Emilia: *(After a pause.)* Yes.

Teacher: Well! Pick up your pencil and draw!

(After hesitating for a few seconds, trembling a little, Emilia picks up her pencil. Joshua and Dick can hardly contain their laughter.)

Teacher: O.K! Let's all draw, and . . . enjoy!

(The teacher glances at Dick and Joshua, who look down, afraid. Now the actors, except those who are asked to move or speak, freeze. The idea is to be able to move the audience's attention away from the physical world and concentrate on thoughts and feelings. This episode is to be done in a nonrealistic style. The teacher stops moving completely, and the action concentrates on the children. When they talk, they don't address anyone in particular—they may look at the audience. If there are lights, the focus should be on the one who speaks, while the rest of the class is in darkness.)

José: I never say anything. *¡Nada! ¡Nunca! ¿Para qué?* I am always pushed around when I ask what's going on, when I tell what I see and what I hear . . . I am not to be pushed around anymore, no way!

Joshua: Life is like a computer keyboard: punch the letter you want to get, that's all. Easy.

(Joshua looks at Emily, grins for a second, then goes back to his computer.)

Elaine: I wonder whether it's Dick picking on poor Emilia. It feels like it. I haven't heard yet, because I am her friend, and he knows I will speak up. So, I'll be the last one to find out. But I promise that if he is the one, I'll speak up this time. That jerk!

Dick: Ha-ha-ha-ha-ha! Hee-hee-hee-hee! School is so much fun! People all around waiting for me to bring the news, to spread the word! Fun, fun, fun! That's all there is to it!

Emilia: *¿Qué pasa?* What's going on? Something is making me sick. It's not . . . drawing, I like it very much. There is something going on, I feel it in my stomach. Like when they used to laugh at me in the other place, when I didn't know English well. It's the same. I wonder whether helping Elaine was a good thing to do. The teacher says it was, and the others laugh. They say one thing, and think another. I would like to talk to the teacher, but maybe that won't help me. What should I do?

María: It happened to me before, but I am not where I was anymore—down there. If I say anything, nobody will be my friend. But Emilia is so sweet! I feel really bad. No one cares.

(Only Emilia and the teacher move at first. Emilia gets up resolutely, although at first she's dizzy and her movements are unsteady. The teacher starts pacing right and left at the front of the room. Emilia approaches her; they talk. We do not hear what they say, but the teacher frowns while Emilia tries to explain what she feels is happening. The teacher's expression turns to one of frustration, and that's the end of the conversation. Emilia turns to her desk, sits down, freezes. The teacher looks at Dick, who gets up, goes up to her and they start talking. The teacher points at Emilia, and, while he talks, Dick's expression moves from fear to relief to the denial that he has any idea of what's going on. The other students pick up their drawings and leave the room, one by one, not looking at anybody. Dick goes by Emilia and laughs noiselessly. The teacher does not see this, because she has turned her back on the class after talking to Dick. After Dick laughs and sits at his desk, the teacher turns and confronts Emilia in an accusatory tone. Dick is delighted. If there are lights, a very red light should flood Emilia while the teacher talks to her.)

Teacher: Well, Emilia, you must be imagining things, because Dick says that he doesn't know what you are talking about.

Emilia: But he is . . . I know he's doing something.

Teacher: What.

Emilia: He's putting my drawings down, and for some reason he thinks that my helping Elaine was wrong.

Teacher: How do you know that?

Emilia: I just know . . . Every time he says the word drawing, it feels as if he's attacking what I do. He even said to me that my drawings were not original. I don't care what he thinks, I want him to stop it.

Teacher: Now, now, Emilia. Aren't you imagining things?

Emilia: No, I am not. And my classmates do not talk to me any longer. That's what truly hurts, not what Dick thinks or doesn't think!

Teacher: Well, they are too busy to talk.

(The teacher turns her back on Emilia.)

Dick: Ha-ha-ha! She thinks she's going to get somewhere by explaining. No, no, no. I win! Hee-hee.

(Emilia has heard this and gets very upset.)

> **Emilia:** He doesn't stop! I can't believe it!

> **Teacher:** *(Turning around.)* I don't see anything. Listen, Emilia, I think you're tired. You're new in this school, and you need more time to get used to how things are done here. Besides, it's time for you to get your bus. You don't want to be late.

(Both Emilia and Dick get up and face the audience, the teacher between them.)

> **Teacher:** *(As if talking to herself, addressing the audience.)* Obviously Emilia sees something that isn't happening. And there's so much school work to be done without this other stuff to take care of! Time to go home. Everything will be all right.

> **Emilia:** *(Addressing the audience also.)* I wonder why the teacher doesn't see what everybody sees. Or is it that she doesn't want to get involved? Who will help?

> **Dick:** *(Addressing the audience.)* I am safe. Now I pass around the rumor that she sees things. In no time, no one will want to be near her.

(Elaine and José enter, stand downstage facing the audience. Dick, Emilia, and the teacher turn their backs to the audience and stand still while the dialogue with the audience goes on.)

> **Elaine:** I am Elaine.

> **José:** And I am José.

> **Elaine:** We know how the play ends, because we are part of the story.

> **José:** In fact, because of us, the play has taken a turn right now—we hope for the better.

> **Elaine:** We would like to know what you think about a few things. For example, do you think that Dick will win?

(Elaine should wait to see whether anyone in the audience has an opinion, or even point at someone who may seem ready to participate. Teachers and parents could be asked beforehand to be ready to give an answer if the younger members of the audience are shy at first.)

> **José:** And what about Emilia? Has she done the right thing by speaking up, or should she just accept the situation and keep silent?

(Wait for feedback from the audience. If the actors want to comment on the audience's responses, they may do so, as long as they do not reveal how the story ends.)

> **Elaine:** Is the teacher acting correctly? Do you think that she's being fair towards all the students?

> **José:** What will all of us—the students—do? Or some of us?

(If the audience has anything to say, the actors should listen. Otherwise, José and Elaine will just introduce the next scene.)

> **José and Elaine:** Well, we are in scene six—the last one.

(They leave stage left.)

SCENE 6

(The teacher, Dick, and Emilia are in the same place where we last saw them, in front of the classroom, their backs turned to the audience. They now turn around, and the rest of the pupils—Elaine, María, José, Joshua, and the other students who were in the playground—come in with garlands to decorate the classroom, a tray with cookies, a bottle of juice, and so on. Everyone brings something for the party.)

Teacher: *(Surprised and delighted.)* My goodness! What's all this?

Elaine: We are having a party.

Teacher: A party? And what's the occasion?

(Most of the students prepare the room for the party. José and Elaine talk to the teacher. Dick looks unpleasantly surprised. Emilia looks happy.)

Elaine: The occasion is our being together. We want to have a party to celebrate that.

(Dick's eyes open wide with fear; he stumbles backward, and runs out of the room. The teacher looks at him leaving.)

Teacher: Dick! Aren't you staying for the party?

(Dick does not return. The other students, who have been serving juice until everyone has a glass, gather around.)

Elaine: I don't think that he will be here, although he is invited.

Teacher: Much mystery here. What's going on?

José: I will explain. I want to talk now, and I hope that I will never be silent again in a situation like this. Dick is a bully, a clever one, a new kind of bully.

(All nod. José goes on.)

José: Dick doesn't pick a fight even with the youngest boy, because he won't win. He is scared of being seen for what he is. But he is not afraid of abusing a little girl by passing on rumors about her. All he needs to win is our silence. Well, Elaine came to us and told us that if we allow Dick to get away with what he had done, we would lose Emilia's friendship. And then, someone else's. And then, someone else's, and so on. And one day, it would be my turn.

Teacher: That's very nice of you all. But I still don't know what he said.

Joshua: He came up to me in the hall, and told me that Emlia copies her drawings from a picture book all the time and that she was angry at Dick because he had discovered it and she wanted to fool us. So Dick told me that the thing to do was to say *drawing* in a put-down tone and then laugh. This will make her stop lying to us about those drawings.

Emilia: But I don't copy all my drawings.

Joshua: We know that. Sorry, Emilia.

María: To me, Dick said to stay away from Emilia because he had seen her helping Elaine, and there was something weird going on. I didn't want people whispering things about me when they saw me talking to Emilia.

Elaine: Well, that tells us something about the kind of boy he is. Don't worry, María.

María: I am not worried. I never believed him. But it is scary to think that you will be his next victim if you speak up.

Teacher: So Emilia was right: something was going on. Thank you, class, for helping to solve this mystery. But why didn't Dick stay for the party? He could have apologized, and everything would have been all right.

Elaine: Because he's guilty. He thought he had won because no one spoke up when Emilia was trying to tell you that she was suffering. Until he acknowledges what he did and asks for Emilia's forgiveness, he won't be able to face us.

Emilia: Thank you, class. Thank you, Elaine. How can I repay you?

Elaine: That's easy to answer: tomorrow I have a Spanish quiz!

(They laugh and continue with the party. José and Elaine take their former position close to the audience while the party goes on, noiselessly. They address the audience.)

José: Well, I guess there's a moral to this story.

Elaine: Or two, or three, or as many as there are points of view.

José: You're right, Elaine. Why don't we each say what the moral is for us?

Elaine: Sure! For me, what this story tells is that to be concerned only with what happens to me is not enough. What happens to other people also affects me.

José: That's good. What I want to point out is the fact that if you have done harm to someone and do not apologize, you won't be able to join the group, you won't be able to be at the party. So be careful what you do.

(José and Elaine take a bow, and one by one the rest of the cast joins them. The teacher now addresses the audience.)

Teacher: If we had time, I would like to do the play again—with the audience as actors. We would have a different play, a different ending. But we don't have the time. Why don't you try writing that play?

THE END

El valentón

Un drama interactivo y bilingüe para jóvenes de 8 a 12 años

Personajes

- Emily
- Ricardo (Rico)
- Maestra (Señora Zapata)
- Elena
- Mary
- Joselito
- Josh
- Varios estudiantes para el patio y el pasillo

Nota: Esta obra de teatro tiene lugar en una escuela, y trata de las razones y los efectos de jerarquías en las relaciones personales. Antes de que la obra sea presentada, sería una buena idea preparar a los actores y al público para hablar sobre los personajes y la historia. ¿Es Rico de alguna manera superior a Emily? ¿Qué tipo de experiencias personales, en tu opinión, produce una persona como Rico? ¿Por qué nadie dice nada al principio? ¿Piensas que la maestra se debería de haber portado de manera diferente? ¿Qué harías tú en una situación semejante? Me gustaría decir también que la canción que incluyo para saltar a la comba viene de España, pero aquí se debe de cantar una en inglés que los estudiantes conozcan bien.

ESCENA 1

(Un salón de clase. Hay una estudiante nueva, sentada, a quien la maestra va a presentar a la clase. Los otros estudiantes la miran amablemente.)

Maestra: ¡Hola, estudiantes! Me gustaría presentaros a una chica nueva, Emily.

Todos: ¡Hola, Emily!

Rico: *(En una voz alta y chillona.)* Bienvenida, Emily.

Emily: Gracias. *Thank you!*

Maestra: *Thank you!* Gracias por recordármelo, Emily. Estudiantes, el idioma nativo de Emily es el inglés, aunque habla español muy bien.

Mary: *(Levanta la mano con mucho entusiasmo.)* *Me too!* Yo también hablo inglés.

Maestra: Lo sé, Mary. Y nos ayudas mucho a aprender algunas palabras. Pero en clase todos hablamos español.

Mary: *(Triste.)* Sí, señora Zapata.

Josh: *(Hablando consigo mismo, fustrado.)* Yo nunca digo nada.

Maestra: ¿Dijiste algo, Josh?

Josh: *(Desagradable.)* No. Hablaba solo.

Maestra: Bueno. Vamos a presentarnos a Emily uno por uno. Decidle algo que queréis que ella sepa sobre vosotros, algo bonito. Voy a empezar yo. Emily, soy tu maestra, la señora Zapata. Me encanta mi clase, y amo a mis dos perros y a mi hijito Jaime. Espero que seas feliz aquí. Elena, por favor.

Elena: Me llamo Elena . . . *(Habla muy rápidamente.)* Me gustan los libros, monto en bicicleta, juego béisbol, y—

Maestra: Gracias, Elena. Es bastante. Tendrás tiempo después de contarle más cosas. ¿Mary?

Mary: Hi, Emily. Bienvenida.

(Mary y Emily se sonríen y saludan con la mano. La maestra mira a Joselito.)

Joselito: Soy José, Joselito para los amigos. Soy un forofo de las computadoras. Si quieres aprender a usar una computadora, dímelo.

Maestra: ¡Qué generoso eres, Joselito! ¿Josh?

Josh: Soy Josh. No tengo nada que decir.

Maestra: Está bien, Josh. Ya tendrás tiempo de hablar. Ricardo, te toca a ti.

(Ricardo está muy nervioso, con una cara trastornada. Los ojos, abiertos como platos, y la gorra de béisbol la lleva al revés.)

Rico: Rico para los amigos. Por favor, llámame Rico. De veras, se-se-seremos amigos. Me ale-legra conocerte. Te va a gustar esto. Ha-ha-hacemos un árbol de Navidad y u-u-una fi-fiesta también.

Maestra: Es verdad, Ricardo. Hacemos una linda fiesta para Navidad, ¿eh? Gracias a todos. Emily, bienvenida a nuestra clase. Y ahora, "¡las matemáticas son divertidas!" Tomad papel y lápiz. ¿Listos? Pensad en un número . . . Multiplicad el número por dos . . . Añadid dos al resultado . . .

(Los estudiantes escriben las instrucciones rápidamente. Emily se pierde pronto y le entra pánico. Va a levantar la mano, pero no lo hace. Rico lo nota y se sonríe con malicia. Él también está perdido, y levanta la mano.)

Maestra: Ricardo, ¿estás perdido?

Rico: *(Señalando a Emily con desprecio.)* Yo no estoy perdido. ¡Ella sí!

Maestra: Lo siento, Emily. ¿Por qué no me lo dijiste?

Emily: No quise interrumpir.

Maestra: No es una interrupción: es parte de la lección. Por favor, levanta la mano cuando necesites ayuda. Vamos a continuar. Ahora, dividid el resultado por dos . . . Restad el número en que pensásteis al principio . . . Y el resultado es . . . Ricardo, ¿cuál es el resultado?

Rico: *(Muy serio.)* No lo tengo.

Maestra: ¿Te perdiste?

Rico: Yo no. Creo que todos perdimos la concentración cuando . . .

(Rico mira a Emily. Silencio general. Elena levanta la mano.)

Maestra: ¿Sí, Elena?

Elena: La respuesta es uno.

Todos *(excepto Rico)*: ¡Sí! Eso es lo que yo tengo.

Maestra: *(Confundida, mira a los estudiantes.)* Ummm . . . Sí, es la respuesta correcta. Bueno, clase, es la hora del recreo. ¡A divertirse!

(Todos se levantan. Ricardo hace mucho ruido, moviéndose de una manera muy desordenada.)

ESCENA 2

(El patio. Las chicas están a la izquierda del escenario, saltando a la comba. No las oímos cuando comienza la escena. A los muchachos los oímos jugando a la pelota fuera del escenario. De repente, Rico aparece en el escenario, desarreglado y más confundido que lo hemos visto hasta ahora. Su gorra de béisbol está a punto de caérsele. Voces de muchachos se oyen fuera del escenario, llamándolo en tono burlón.)

Voz 1: ¡Eh, Rico, no nos dejes!

(Risas.)

Voz 2: ¡No podemos jugar sin ti!

(Más risas.)

Voz 3: ¡Tráenos la pelota, porrrr favorrrrrrr!

(Más risas. Tiran una pelota en su dirección, y Rico intenta con mucha dificultad mantener el equilibrio. Parece perdido, muy triste, su gorra está a punto de caérsele y tiene los hombros caídos. Hay ahora un período de silencio y, mientras se recupera, las voces de los muchachos se desvanecen y las chicas se mueven al centro del escenario. Emily y Mary cantan una canción para saltar a la comba, en inglés. Necesitan a otra persona para que mueva la cuerda a uno de los lados, le hacen señas a Rico para que la tome, y él lo hace. Al aceptar, su expresión cambia de tristeza a felicidad. Mientras que las chicas cantan y saltan, Rico mueve la cuerda y trata de cantar con ellas. Sólo le sale el final de algunas líneas de la canción. Otras chicas pueden contribuir a la escena con frases como "¡Fabuloso!" "¡Lo haces tan bien!" etc., pero no deben de interferir ni con la canción ni con el diálogo de los personajes.)

Emily y Mary: *(Aquí las actrices deben de cantar una canción que sepan bien, en inglés. Lo que sigue es una traducción de una canción española, para mostrar la manera de hacer la escena.)*

I'm the queen of the seas,
As you'll see.
I drop my kerchief on the ground,
And I pick it up.
Little, little kerchief!
Who could have you

Folded in my pocket,
Like a paper boat!

Rico: *. . . seas . . . see . . . boat.*

(Da saltitos, muy ilusionado.)

Rico: Me gusta esto más que jugar a la pelota. ¡Y no me importa lo que digan los muchachos! De aquí en adelante, esto es lo que voy hacer durante el recreo.

Mary: ¿Quieres saltar y yo muevo la comba?

Rico: ¡Síííííí! ¡Es fabuloso! ¡Y me gustaría tanto saber la canción! "*. . . see*" es todo lo que sé.

Todas las chicas: *(Cantan mientras Rico salta a la comba. Mary y Elena la mueven.)*

I'm the queen of the seas,
As you'll see.
I drop my kerchief on the ground,
And I pick it up.
Little, little kerchief!
Who could have you
Folded in my pocket,
Like a paper boat!

Emily: Saltas a la comba mejor que muchas chicas, Rico. Escribiré la canción para que te la aprendas en casa.

Rico: *Thank you, Emily!*

(Rico abraza a Emily con muy poca gracia. Emily sonríe, orgullosa y un poco tímida. Las otras chicas están recogiendo la cuerda cuando la maestra aparece. El recreo ha terminado, y todos se van a clase. La maestra se pone a un lado del escenario, sonriendo a sus estudiantes mientras entran en la clase, con papel y lápiz en la mano.)

ESCENA 3

(Fuera de la escuela, o en el pasillo. Rico acompaña a Emily a la parada del autobús. Los dos llevan sus libros bajo el brazo. La actitud de Rico es la de una persona que se cree ser muy importante, muy sobresaliente.)

Rico: Me alegra que tengamos autobuses, aunque yo personalmente no los necesite. Mi madre viene a por mí todos los días.

Emily: Ojalá y mi padre me pudiera recoger, pero está trabajando.

Rico: No te preocupes. De esta manera, te haces de amigos, practicas tu español, etcétera. Además, los autobuses son muy ecológicos.

Emily: ¿E-co-ló-gi-cos?

Rico: ¿No sabes esa palabra? Es cuando algo, un producto o una acción, no daña el planeta.

Emily: ¿El pla—?

Rico: Se me olvidaba que no llevas mucho tiempo en esta escuela. Estamos más avanzados que la mayoría, ¿sabes? Y el pla . . . ¡Tu autobús acaba de llegar! Hasta mañana.

Emily: *(Aunque con prisa, logra sacar una hoja de papel de su bolsa.)* Se me olvidó dártelo. Es la canción. La cantaremos juntos mañana en el patio. ¡Hasta la he ilustrado con un dibujo en color!

Rico: ¡Qué bonito! Hasta luego, Emily. Gracias.

Emily: *Until tomorrow!*

Rico: *Un-til-to-mo-rrow!*

(Emily se va. Las voces de otros estudiantes saliendo de la escuela se oyen fuera del escenario. Rico abre la hoja de papel, y la mira por mucho tiempo con los ojos muy abiertos. Sonríe con una sonrisa que es casi feliz, pero expresa inseguridad. Con cuidado, dobla el papel y lo pone en su bolsillo.)

Rico: Emily es una buena chica. Sí, muy buena chica. *(Su actitud cambia de pronto a una llena de importancia.)* Pero no está tan avanzada como nosotros.

ESCENA 4

(Una mesa de merienda en el patio. Durante el recreo, Emily ayuda a Elena con su tarea. Chicos y chicas están en la parte trasera del escenario, hablando, preparando una cuerda para saltar a la comba, jugando a la pelota, etc. Pero no los oímos, y se deben de mover con cuidado para que la atención se concentre en la conversación.)

Emily: A ver si puedes recordar los nombres ahora. *(Señala su boca.)*

Elena: *Mouth.*

(Emily pretende estar comiendo.)

Elena: *Eat.*

(Emily indica con movimientos que ella come con la boca.)

Elena: *You eat mouth.*

(Emily se ríe, y escribe "with" en una hoja de papel y se la enseña a Elena.)

Elena: *(Riendo.) You eat with your mouth.*

(Emily señala a Elena.)

Elena: *I eat with my mouth.*

(Las dos ríen y aplauden. Elena prepara sus libros para irse. Rico se hace visible. Avanza poco a poco. Parece estar muy enfadado por lo que ve, y quizás celoso. Saca de su bolsillo la hoja de papel que Emily le dio, está a punto de romperla, pero en vez de eso la hace una bola y se la vuelve a meter en el bolsillo. Ahora parece peligroso.)

Emily: Aprendes muy rápido.

Elena: Eso es porque eres una maestra magnífica. Antes estaba preocupada por el examen de inglés, ¡y ahora no puedo esperar a que llegue! ¿Cómo te puedo pagar esto?

Emily: Ya tendrás la oportunidad, pero no creas que estás obligada a nada. No es por eso por lo que te ayudé. Yo creo en ayudar a los demás, sin esperar nada a cambio. Me siento feliz cuando hago una buena acción. Me lo enseñó mi abuela.

Elena: ¿Y tú crees en eso? Bueno, lo que quiero decir es que es muy bonito, pero no todo el mundo piensa así. Mucha gente espera algún tipo de recompensa cuando hacen un favor.

Emily: Sí, pero yo pienso que ayudar a otros sin esperar nada a cambio es bueno en sí mismo. ¡Así que hoy estoy feliz!

Elena: ¡Estupendo! Tengo que contárselo a mi madre. Le encantará. *Until tomorrow*, Emily.

Emily: *Until tomorrow*, Elena. *And good luck with the English test!*

(Elena toma sus libros y se va. Emily se queda allí, copiando un dibujo de un libro. Rico se acerca a ella por detrás, asustándola.)

Rico: *(Chillón.)* ¡Dibújame si puedes! ¡Ja-ja-ja-ja-ja-ja!

Emily: *(Asustada, se vuelve rápidamente.)* ¡Ah!

Rico: Soy yo. ¿Dibujando otra vez?

Emily: Sí. Bueno, copiando esta preciosa casa. Lo que más me gusta hacer en la vida es dibujar.

Rico: ¿Hiciste tú esto? *(Se saca del bolsillo la bola de papel, la alisa.)*

Emily: *(Muy orgullosa.)* ¡Sí!

Rico: *(Le tira el papel, con desprecio.)* Cualquiera puede hacerlo.

(La cara de Emily se entristece. Rico hace una mueca, feliz por haberle hecho daño.)

Rico: *(Con aire importante.)* Deberías de haber visto las acuarelas que la maestra de arte le dio a la señora Zapata para Navidad. ¡Eso es arte! Pero tú no estabas aquí para Navidad.

Emily: *(Pausa.)* No, no estaba aquí.

Rico: *(Acercándose a Emily.)* A ver lo que estás haciendo. *(En tono acusatorio.)* Así que estás copiando directamente del libro.

Emily: Yo—

Rico: Lo que digas no tiene importancia. Puedo ver con claridad lo que pasa. Y ese dibujo que me diste, ¿es tuyo?

(Cuando se menciona la palabra "dibujo" en ese tono, Emily se sobresalta. Cada vez que Rico dice la palabra, ocurre lo mismo: hay una acusación en el tono de Rico que le duele a Emily.)

Emily: Sí, es mío. Lo saqué de mi imaginación.

Rico: Ese dibujo es tuyo, ¿no es así?

(Emily se sobresalta cuando oye la palabra "dibujo". Intenta irse.)

Emily: Sí. Perdón, pero tengo que—

Rico: *(La retiene por el brazo.)* ¡Espera! Todavía no me has enseñado la canción, como prometiste.

Emily: *(Duda.)* Está bien. ¿Sabes . . . , estás estudiando inglés?

Rico: Acabo de comprar un libro con las expresiones más comunes. Buenísimo. Mi mamá me compra todo lo que quiero.

Emily: Bien. Lo leeré sola primero, y entonces—

Rico: No tienes que hacer eso. Vamos a cantar.

Emily: *(Canta de memoria. Rico se saca el papel del bolsillo y lo mira.)*

> *I'm the queen of the seas,*
> *As you'll see.*
> *I drop my kerchief on the ground,*
> *And I pick it up.*
> *Little, little kerchief!*
> *Who could have you*
> *Folded in my pocket,*
> *Like a paper boat!*

(Rico intenta seguirla, con retraso y mal, tropezando con las palabras y cantando sólo la última sílaba. Emily termina la canción.)

Rico: . . . seas . . . see . . . boat.

Emily: Ya sabes cantarla. Practica, y te puedes unir a nosotros en el patio.

(Rico se sorprende de la fuerza de Emily, y de su propia torpeza. Ella toma sus libros y se levanta: incluso sonríe.)

Emily: Es hora de tomar el autobús. ¡Adiós!

Rico: *(Triste.)* Adiós, Emily. *(Pero pronto se convierte en el valentón otra vez.)* ¡Ah! Y esos dibujos . . . no están mal, aunque no sean originales.

(Emily se sobresalta cuando se mencionan los dibujos, lo que complace a Rico. Emily recoge sus cosas y se va. Rico sale del escenario riéndose, con la espalda temblando de placer. De aquí en adelante, los ojos de Rico van a estar muy abiertos y fijos, y una sonrisa burlona complementará la expresión.)

ESCENA 5

(Joselito, Josh, Elena, Mary y las otras chicas que aparecen en las escenas del patio. Están ahora en el pasillo de la escuela. Joselito viene por el pasillo con el teclado de su computadora. Rico lo está esperando, se aproxima a él con pasitos pequeños, le hace señas para que se le acerque más, le susurra algo en el oído con la misma expresión burlona. Joselito imita la sonrisa de Rico, y se va. Llega Josh. Rico hace con él lo mismo que con Joselito, pero Josh no reacciona. Su cara se queda seria. Emily llega, y Josh mira hacia otro lado. Emily parece dolida, y Rico

sonríe desagradablemente. Nadie dice nada. Emily y Josh se van, sin decirse nada. Rico comparte su secreto con Mary, quien parece triste: se va en silencio, como si estuviera avergonzada de sí misma. La maestra llega y Rico la para.)

Rico: Espero que dibujemos hoy.

Maestra: ¡Claro! Estaba yo pensando que hoy tenemos que hacer algo para divertirnos. ¡Habéis trabajado tanto para los exámenes! Sí, hoy vamos a dibujar.

(La maestra va a la clase, donde los estudiantes están ya sentados, seguida de Rico, que sonríe triunfante.)

Maestra: ¡Buenos días, estudiantes! ¿No os parece que hace un día maravilloso? Y vamos a empezar con algo divertido. Sé que habéis trabajado bien duro para esos exámenes de inglés que tuvisteis ayer. *(La maestra se para y mira a Emily. Rico se relame y Joselito sonríe, burlón. Mary y Josh miran al suelo. Emily siente que algo pasa y mira alrededor, sin comprender.)* Emily, gracias por ayudar a Elena a preparar el examen. ¡Me lo ha contado todo! Eso habla muy bien de ti. *(Elena sonríe con gratitud, pero baja los ojos cuando ve que Rico y Joselito se ríen. Se siente confusa.)* Emily, espero que ayudes a Elena otra vez. Lo necesitamos. *(Más risitas de Rico y Joselito. La maestra se para para mirarlos con severidad. Los chicos paran de hacer ruido, pero sus expresiones no cambian. El tono de la maestra es mandón ahora, porque ella tampoco comprende lo que pasa.)* Bueno. Quiero ver a todos con papel y lápiz, y ¡a dibujar!

(El lápiz de Emily cae al suelo. Rico la señala, encantado.)

Maestra: Emily, ¿te gusta dibujar?

Emily: *(Después de un momento.)* Sí.

Maestra: ¡Pues recoge tu lápiz y dibuja!

(Después de dudar por unos momentos, y temblando un poco, Emily recoge su lápiz. Joselito y Rico apenas pueden contener la risa.)

Maestra: ¡Está bien! Vamos a dibujar todos, y . . . ¡a divertirse!

(La maestra mira a Rico y Joselito, que bajan los ojos con miedo. Todos los actores ahora, excepto aquéllos que tienen que hablar o moverse, se quedan inmóviles como estatuas. La idea es la de guiar la atención del público más allá del mundo físico, para que se concentren en los pensamientos y sentimientos de los personajes. Este episodio no se hace en un estilo realista. La maestra deja de moverse completamente, y la atención se concentra en los niños. Cuando hablan, no se dirigen a nadie en particular, aunque pueden elegir a alguien en el público. Si hay luces, se debe enfocar a la persona que habla, mientras que el resto de la clase permanece en penumbra.)

Josh: Yo no digo nada nunca. *Nothing! Ever! Why bother?* Si pregunto qué pasa, me echan a un lado, y cuando digo lo que veo y lo que oigo . . . Pero ya no me pasa eso más, ¡de ninguna manera!

Joselito: La vida es como el teclado de una computadora: aprieta la letra que quieres, eso es todo. ¡Fácil!

(Joselito mira a Emily, se sonríe, y vuelve su atención a la computadora.)

Elena: ¿Estará Rico gastándole una broma pesada a la pobre Emily? Eso parece. No he oído nada todavía, porque soy su amiga y él sabe que no me lo voy a callar. Así que seré la última en enterarse. Pero juro que si es él, esta vez no me voy a callar. ¡Ese pelmazo!

Rico: ¡Ja-ja-ja-ja-ja-ja-ja! ¡Je-je-je-ji-ji-ji! ¡Qué divertida es la escuela! Todo el mundo esperando a que yo le traiga las noticias, a que cuente lo que pasa. ¡Diversión, más diversión, y nada más que diversión!

Emily: *What's going on?* ¿Qué pasa? Algo pasa que me está enfermando. No es el . . . dibujar, porque me gusta mucho. Pasa algo, lo siento aquí en el estómago. Es como cuando se reían de mí en el otro sitio, cuando todavía no hablaba español bien. Es lo mismo. A lo mejor no fue una buena idea ayudar a Elena . La maestra me felicita, pero los otros se ríen. Dicen una cosa, pero piensan otra. Me gustaría hablar con la maestra, pero a lo mejor eso no me ayuda. ¿Qué debo hacer?

Mary: A mí me pasó esto antes, pero ya no estoy donde estaba—ahí abajo. Si digo algo, nadie querrá juntarse conmigo. ¡Pero Emily es tan dulce! Me siento muy mal, porque a nadie le importa nada.

(Sólo Emily y la maestra se mueven ahora. Emily se levanta con determinación , aunque al principio está mareada y sus movimientos no muy seguros. La maestra empieza a caminar de aquí para allá en frente del salón de clase. Emily se le acerca; hablan. No oímos lo que dicen, pero la maestra frunce el ceño mientras que Emily trata de explicar lo que siente. La expresión de la maestra indica frustración, y así termina la conversación. Emily vuelve y se sienta, se queda inmóvil. La maestra mira a Rico, quien se levanta y va a hablarle: la maestra señala a Emily, y mientras hablan la expresión de Rico pasa del miedo, al alivio, y a negar ningún conocimiento de que algo esté pasando. Los otros estudiantes recogen sus dibujos y salen de la habitación, uno a uno, sin mirar a nadie. Rico pasa al lado de Emily y se ríe, pero sin hacer ruido. La maestra no lo ve porque está de espaldas a la clase desde la conversación con Rico. Cuando éste se sienta en su silla, la maestra se da la vuelta y confronta a Emily en un tono acusatorio. Rico está encantado. Si hay luces, un foco de luz roja puede iluminar a Emily mientras la maestra habla con ella.)

Maestra: Bueno, Emily, te estás imaginando cosas, porque Rico dice que no sabe de lo que hablas.

Emily: Claro que lo sabe . . . Sé que está haciendo algo.

Maestra: Algo . . . , como qué.

Emily: Está ridiculizando mis dibujos, y por alguna razón piensa que no estuvo bien el que yo ayudara a Elena.

Maestra: ¿Cómo lo sabes?

Emily: Pues . . . lo sé. Cada vez que dice la palabra dibujo, siento como si estuviera atacando lo que hago. Hasta me ha dicho que mis dibujos no son originales. No me importa lo que él piense, lo que quiero es que pare lo que está haciendo.

Maestra: Emily, ¿no estás viendo cosas que no existen?

Emily: No. Y mis compañeros de clase no me hablan más. ¡Eso es lo que realmente me duele, no lo que Rico piense o deje de pensar!

Maestra: Están demasiado ocupados para hablar.

(La maestra le vuelve la espalda a Emily.)

Rico: ¡Ja-ja-ja! Se cree que va a conseguir algo con explicaciones. ¡No, no y no! Gano yo. ¡Ji-ji-ji-ji-ji!

(Emily oye a Rico y se enfada mucho.)

Emily: ¡No para! ¡No me lo puedo creer!

Maestra: *(Volviéndose hacia Emily.)* Yo no veo nada. Mira, Emily, a lo mejor estás cansada. Eres nueva en esta escuela, y necesitas más tiempo para acostumbrarte a la manera como hacemos las cosas aquí. Además, es hora de tomar el autobús. No llegues tarde.

(Emily y Dick se levantan y dan la cara al público, con la maestra en medio.)

Maestra: *(Dirigiéndose al público.)* Está claro que Emily se imagina cosas que no pasan. ¡Y hay tanto trabajo que hacer en la escuela, sin tener que prestar atención a estas cosas! Es hora de irse a casa. Todo se arreglará.

Emily: *(Dirigiéndose al público también.)* Me pregunto por qué la maestra no ve lo que los demás pueden ver. ¿O es que no se quiere meter? ¿Quién me ayudará?

Rico: *(Al público también.)* Estoy a salvo. Ahora paso por ahí el rumor de que se imagina cosas, y muy pronto nadie querrá saber nada de ella.

(Elena y Josh entran, se paran al frente del escenario mirando al público. Rico, Emily y la maestra vuelven las espaldas al público y no se mueven mientras se desarrolla el diálogo con el público.)

Elena: Me llamo Elena.

Josh: Y yo soy Josh.

Elena: Sabemos como termina este drama, porque somos parte de él.

Josh: De hecho, es por nosotros que esta obra acaba de tomar un camino diferente—y esperamos que sea uno mejor.

Elena: Nos gustaría saber lo que ustedes piensan sobre algunas cosas. Por ejemplo, ¿creen que Rico ganará?

(Elena debe esperar a ver si alguien tiene una opinión, o incluso invitar a participar a la persona que parezca lista para hacerlo. Se les puede decir a los padres y a los maestros, antes de la función, que vengan preparados para responder a los actores si el público joven es tímido al principio.)

Josh: ¿Y qué piensan de Emily? ¿Ha actuado bien al ir a hablar con la maestra, o debería de haber aceptado la situación y quedarse callada?

(Hay que esperar a ver lo que dice el público. Si los actores quieren hacer comentarios sobre las opiniones del público, lo pueden hacer con tal de que no cuenten el final.)

Elena: ¿Se está portando bien la maestra? ¿Es justa con todos los estudiantes?

Josh: ¿Qué piensan que nosotros, los estudiantes, vamos a hacer? O por lo menos, algunos de nosotros.

(Si el público tiene algo que decir, los actores escuchan. Si no, se preparan para presentar la próxima escena.)

Josh y Elena: Bueno, estamos en la escena seis. La última.

(Saludan y salen por la izquierda.)

ESCENA 6

(La maestra, Rico y Emily están en el mismo sitio que estaban, de espaldas al público. Ahora se dan la vuelta, y el resto de los estudiantes—Elena, Mary, Joselito, Josh y los que participaron en las escenas del patio—entran con girnaldas para decorar la clase, una bandeja llena de galletas, una botella de jugo de fruta, etc. Cada uno trae algo para la fiesta.)

Maestra: *(Felizmente sorprendida.)* ¡Qué barbaridad! ¿Qué es todo esto?

Elena: Vamos a hacer una fiesta.

Maestra: ¿Una fiesta? ¿Y a qué se debe?

(El resto de los estudiantes—con la excepción de Josh y Elena, que hablan con la maestra; de Rico, que está desagradablemente sorprendido, y de Emily, que parece muy feliz, preparan la habitación para la fiesta.)

Elena: A nuestra unidad. Queremos tener una fiesta para celebrar eso.

(Los ojos de Rico se abren mucho, llenos de miedo; da unos pasos inseguros hacia atrás, y corre fuera de la habitación. La maestra lo mira irse.)

Maestra: Rico, ¿no te quedas para la fiesta?

(Rico no vuelve. Los otros estudiantes, que han estado sirviendo jugo para que todos tengan un vaso lleno, se juntan.)

Elena: Dudo que vendrá, aunque está invitado.

Maestra: Hay mucho misterio aquí. ¿Qué pasa?

Josh: Yo explico. Ahora quiero hablar, y espero que nunca me callaré en una situación como ésta. Rico es un valentón, muy listillo, un tipo nuevo de valentón.

(Todos asienten con la cabeza. Josh continúa.)

Josh: Rico no se pelea ni con el muchacho más pequeño de la escuela, porque no ganaría. Le da miedo de que la gente sepa quién es en realidad. Pero no le da miedo de abusar a una pobre chica pasando por ahí rumores sobre ella. Todo lo que necesita para ganar es nuestro silencio. Bueno, Elena vino y nos dijo que si permitimos que Rico se salga con la suya, todos perderíamos la amistad de Emily. Y después, de otra persona. Y de otra, y de otra. Y un día, me tocaría a mí.

Maestra: Todo esto me parece muy bien. Pero todavía no sé qué es lo que dijo.

Joselito: Rico me habló en el pasillo, y me dijo que Emily siempre copia sus dibujos de un libro, y que ella estaba muy enojada con Rico porque lo había descubierto y ella quería engañarnos. Así que Rico me dijo que lo que había que hacer era decir dibujo de una manera despectiva, y entonces reír. Eso haría que Emily dejara de mentirnos sobre los dibujos.

Emily: ¡Pero si yo no copio todos mis dibujos!

Joselito: Lo sabemos. Lo siento, Emily.

Mary: A mí me dijo que no me acercara a Emily, porque la había visto ayudando a Elena y tenía la impresión de que ahí había algo extraño. Y que a mí no me gustaría que la gente dijera cosas feas sobre mí si me veían hablando con Emily.

Elena: Bueno, eso nos dice algo sobre la clase de muchacho que es. No te preocupes, Mary.

Mary: No me preocupo. Nunca me lo creí. Pero da miedo pensar que tú serás su próxima víctima si te atreves a decir algo.

Maestra: Así que Emily tenía razón, y algo estaba pasando. Estudiantes, muchas gracias por ayudarme a resolver este misterio. Pero, ¿por qué no se quedó Rico para la fiesta? Podría haber pedido perdón, y todo estaría bien.

Elena: Porque se siente culpable. Pensaba que había ganado, porque nadie dijo nada cuando Emily estaba tratando de decirle a usted que sufría. Hasta que acepte lo que hizo, y le pida perdón a Emily, no podrá darnos la cara.

Emily: Gracias, chicos. Gracias, Elena. ¿Cómo te puedo pagar?

Elena: Fácilmente. Mañana tengo un examen de inglés.

(Todos ríen y continúan con la fiesta. Josh y Elena se dirigen al público de la misma manera que lo hicieron antes, mientras que la fiesta continúa sin ningún ruido. Hablan al público.)

Josh: Bueno, supongo que esta historia tiene una moraleja.

Elena: O dos, o tres, o tantas como puntos de vista haya.

Josh: Tienes razón, Elena. ¿Por qué no decimos cada uno la moraleja que tiene para nostros?

Elena: ¡Por supuesto! Para mí, lo que esta historia me dice es que el preocuparse solamente por lo que me pase a mí no es bastante. Lo que le pase a los demás me va a afectar a mí también.

Josh: Muy bien. Lo que yo quiero decir es que si le has hecho daño a alguien y no pides perdón, no podrás unirte al grupo, no podrás asistir a la fiesta. Así que ten mucho cuidado con lo que haces.

(Josh y Elena saludan y, uno a uno, el resto de los actores se les unen y hacen lo mismo. La maestra se dirige al público.)

Maestra: Si tuviéramos tiempo, me gustaría hacer este drama otra vez—con el público haciendo de actores. Tendríamos un drama diferente, con un final diferente. Pero no tenemos tiempo. ¿Por qué no intentas tú escribir ese drama?

FIN

VOCABULARY–VOCABULARIO

Nouns–Nombres

drawing: *dibujo*
jerk: *pelmazo, memo, pesado*
play: *obra de teatro, drama, comedia*
quiz: *examen, prueba*
victim: *víctima*

Adjectives–Adjetivos

angry: *enfadado, enojado*
nice: *simpático, amable*
guilty: *culpable*
silent: *silencioso*
sorry: *arrepentido, apenado*

Verbs–Verbos

to acknowledge: *admitir, reconocer*
to apologize: *pedir perdón*
to face: *dar la cara*
to forgive: *perdonar*
to hurt: *doler, hacer daño*
to repay: *corresponder a, pagar*

The Coming of Winter

La llegada del invierno

Snowflake

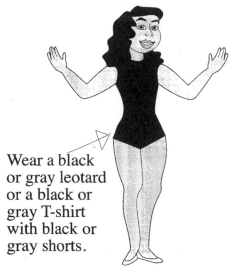

You can also make a snowflake hat out of leftover white posterboard. Cut it 5 inches wide in a strip long enough to go around your head. Next cut star-like shapes, bend around and staple or tape closed.

Wear a black or gray leotard or a black or gray T-shirt with black or gray shorts.

Take a sheet of newsprint or any lightweight paper that measures approximately 22 by 22 inches. Next, fold the paper in half and then in half again. Now you have a smaller square. Next, you fold it to make a triangle. Then you cut out shapes as shown below.

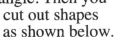

Cut through all the layers and throw away the pieces you cut out. Open it up, and you have your snowflake pattern. Place it on a piece of 22-by-22-inch white posterboard and trace the pattern. Then fill in the areas with black or gray poster paint or a permanent felt tip pen. Wrap yourself in the piece of lightweight cardboard and tape to hold it closed.

Figure 6

The Coming of Winter

Characters

- Old man (Tony)
- Old woman, his wife (Betty)
- The cat
- The mouse
- The first snowflake
- Two pigeons (male, female)
- Children in the audience

> *Note:* An extra character, a narrator, may be added. He or she may read the information in italics if the director and the actors feel this information is needed. Feel free to make any necessary changes. In the text, I refer to the snowflake in the masculine, because the noun is masculine in Spanish, but the part can be played by a girl.

SCENE 1

(The first really cold day of winter. Tony and his wife, Betty, arrive at their apartment's front stairs with one grocery bag each. They put down the bags to rest and to turn up their collars. Their movements say that they feel very cold and very old.)

Old Man: You know, Betty, it's hard being as old as we are.

Old Woman: It sure is, Tony. I think about it every winter.

Old Man: You mean, around this time?

Old Woman: That's right.

Old Man: Then you're smarter than I am. This is the first time I've thought of it.

Old Woman: You silly! We had this very same conversation last year. Here, by the front steps!

Old Man: Is that right, Betty?

Old Woman: You bet!

Old Man: Then, I am sicker than I thought.

Old Woman: Sick? Of what?

Old Man: I don't know. I worry that I don't think as much as you do. But then it turns out that what's happened is I've simply forgotten something. This is not good, Betty. Not good at all!

Old Woman: Just pick up that bag before we freeze out here! Let me see if I can find the key. Where is the key?

Old Man: *(There is a big key hanging from his right wrist. He touches his forehead with this hand, making the key very visible.)* Oh, boy! Now we don't have the key!

Old Woman: What's wrong with you? *You* have the key. Look!

Old Man: That's not true, Betty. I don't have the key. Don't be cruel to a sick man.

Old Woman: *(Grabbing the key, very upset.)* Sick! Look here—what is this?

Old Man: I am so sorry, Betty! I don't know what's wrong with me. Let's go in before we catch a cold. Or I catch a cold. That would be very bad.

Old Woman: *(Turning the key in the lock with great force.)* You only care about yourself!

Cat: *(Pawing at the old man's bag.)* Meoooowwww!

Old Man: *(Patting the cat, but picking up the bag.)* Hi, kitty! I hope you're ready to come in with us. You have had enough of the outdoors, haven't you?

(The man goes in the door first. The cat looks at them, goes in, and then goes out again. The woman closes the door behind them, leaving the cat outside.)

SCENE 2

(The old folks are now in their living room. They put the groceries on the table. A window faces a small balcony at one end of the room. In front of the window, facing the balcony, are two chairs.)

Old Man: *(Sits down.)* I need to rest before I do anything else!

Old Woman: *(She has started to take groceries out of the bag, stops, and then sits down.)* I need to rest, too. *(She sighs.)*

(They look out of the window, and soon they are turning their heads from side to side, fascinated. A mouse wearing a Mexican hat is tap dancing out on the balcony, rushing here and there in a very dainty way.)

Old Woman: Isn't that something! What a cutie!

Old Man: He is cute. Do you suppose he wants to come in? He can keep us entertained during the winter.

Old Woman: *(Pleased at first, but then in a put down manner.)* Yeah! Great idea, with the cat around.

Old Man: I hadn't thought of that!

(The mouse is still doing his dance when the cat shows up at the balcony, eyeing the mouse with delight. The mouse notices the cat, stops dancing, and bows very politely.)

Mouse: ¡Hola, amigo!

Cat: *(Licking his whiskers, mean.)* Amigo-tamigo! I am not your friend, and I hope you remember that.

Mouse: You don't like my dancing?

Cat: What I would like is to have you for supper.

Old Man: *(Opens the window.)* Look here, cat. You have all the food you need if you come in the house. Why do you want to eat this talented mouse?

Cat: *(With a sneer.)* Talented? Don't make me laugh! *(To the mouse.)* Come here, I won't harm youuuuuu!

Mouse: *(Faces the cat, but keeping his distance.)* One moment. I am a modern mouse. You want to eat supper? I want to eat supper, too. Let's talk about it.

Cat: Ha-ha-ha-ha-ha-ha-ha-ha-ha-ha-ha-ha! That's funny. Very funny. What is there to talk about?

Mouse: In the house, there is food. Do you want to go in?

Cat: No.

Mouse: Then I'll go.

Cat: *(Stopping the mouse.)* Wait! Who invited you inside?

Old Woman: We want him in. You are an ungrateful cat. Good-bye!

(The mouse winks at the cat, takes his hat off as if in greeting, then jumps inside the house through the window, which the old woman has opened for him. She closes it promptly after he has entered. The cat is left outside, angry and hurt.)

SCENE 3

(The first snowflake of winter steps onto the balcony. His body is made of six points, all white. He is very graceful and dances in the wind. The cat is crouching to one side, looking cold and upset.)

Snowflake: I am born at last! I am in the world! And I am beautiful! Just as Mother said that I would be: six points, with a white body, like a star. Except that I am small, and cold, and very fast. Look how I move! Wow—wow—wow! Great!

Cat: *(Shivering, hungry.)* Are you hungry?

Snowflake: Hungry? What is that?

Cat: Hungry is . . . to want to eat . . . because if you don't, you die.

Snowflake: *(With an air of superiority.)* I am never hungry.

Cat: Then you cannot die?

Snowflake: Uh . . . yes, I can die. But only if the sun is hot or if the snowplough comes. And I love the cold, because I don't want to die!

Cat: How strange! This cold is going to kill me, but that's what keeps you alive. *(Shaking his head sadly.)* Yes, strange!

Snowflake: *(Looking concerned, approaches the cat.)* I feel bad that you are so unhappy. Is there anything that I can do for you?

Cat: I don't think so. I need heat and food. What can you do?

(They are both sad and thoughtful when two pigeons arrive and sit by the window, making little noises on the glass with their beaks. The old woman enters to see what the noise is all about.)

Old Woman: Tony! There are two nice pigeons here by the window.

Old Man: *(Enters slowly, eating a piece of cake.)* I bet you that they also want food. We have a mouse, an angry cat outside, and now two pigeons. What next?

Female Pigeon: You don't have to worry about us, old man. There is fat under our skin, we have feathers, and we always find some food around.

Male Pigeon: My wife is right. We came to see the first snowflake of winter. He is beautiful.

Snowflake: Thank you!

Old Man: *(Apologetic.)* I'm sorry. I didn't mean to offend you. In fact, we would invite you in if we were not afraid that the cat would eat the house mouse.

Snowflake: Excuse me, sir, but I think that the cat has learned a lesson, and he won't eat the mouse if he has food. I know that there are a lot of people to feed: you, your wife, the two pigeons, the mouse, the cat and . . .

Old Woman: That's enough! We are going to be ruined!

Snowflake: Please, let me finish: I have a great idea! I am a very graceful dancer, and if there are other artists here, we could perform for the children in the neighborhood. We'll ask them to pay for the show with bread and cupcakes so that all the animals can be fed!

Mouse, old man, old woman, and pigeons: Hurrah! What a great idea!

Mouse: I could sing a song to the cat, if he were to become my *amigo*.

(Everyone looks at the cat expectantly. Reluctantly, he goes up to the mouse, shakes hands with him.)

Cat: All right, *amigo*.

Old Man: This is great! There's nothing better to lift the spirits of a sick man than a big family!

Old Woman: Who is sick here? You are sick? How?

(The old woman is becoming angry at her husband, who is afraid.)

Snowflake: The show is about to start! *(Announcing the show outside the balcony.)* All the children in the neighborhood are invited! There will be dancing, singing, and much more! Please, bring cupcakes and bread for the pigeons, the cat, and the mouse! *(Children arrive and sit on the floor around the performers. They carry baskets with bread and cupcakes. The old man and woman sit on their chairs.)*

Snowflake: People, thank you for coming. I will start the show with a dance from my native land, Snowland. I hope that you like it.

(Snowflake dances very gracefully. At the end, everyone applauds. The mouse, with his Mexican hat, stands in the center.)

Mouse: This is a Mexican song. I need two or three singers who say *"miau-miau"* in Spanish.

Cat: I can do that.

(Everyone applauds the cat, who stands a little bit behind the mouse. Anyone who wants to sing can join the chorus.)

Mouse: *(Sings.)*

Yo tengo un gato
(For mouse and chorus)*

Yo tengo un gato,
¡Miau-miau!
con un rabo largo,
¡Miau-miau!
que es muy goloso,
¡Miau-miau!
y está muy gordo.
¡Miau-miau!

---

*The music for this song is printed at the end of the English version of the first play in this collection, *The Farmer Finds His True Friends*, on page 10.

THE END

La llegada del invierno

Personajes

- El viejito (Antonio)
- La viejita, su esposa (Beatriz)
- El gato
- El ratón
- El primer copo de nieve
- Una paloma y un palomo
- Niños del público

> *Nota:* Se puede añadir un personaje más, el de narrador, para leer las instrucciones dadas en paréntesis, si se cree que esto ayudaría. Por favor, no duden en hacer cambios si son necesarios.

ESCENA 1

(El primer día realmente frío del invierno. Antonio y su esposa, Beatriz, llegan a las escaleras que llevan a su apartamento, con una bolsa de comida cada uno. Ponen las bolsas en el suelo para descansar y subirse los cuellos de los abrigos. Sus movimientos nos sugieren que tienen mucho frío y se sienten viejos.)

Viejito: ¿Sabes qué, Beatriz? Es difícil ser tan viejos como lo somos nosotros.

Viejita: Y bien difícil, Antonio. Lo pienso cada invierno.

Viejito: Quieres decir, ¿por este tiempo?

Viejita: Pues claro.

Viejito: Entonces eres más inteligente que yo. Ésta es la primera vez que lo pienso.

Viejita: ¡Qué tonto eres! El año pasado tuvimos la misma conversación. ¡Aquí, en las escaleras!

Viejito: ¿Es verdad, Beatriz?

Viejita: ¡Por supuesto!

Viejito: Entonces, estoy más enfermo de lo que pensaba.

Viejita: ¿Enfermo? ¿De qué?

Viejito: No sé. Me parece que no pienso tanto como tú. Pero luego, lo que realmente pasa es que me olvidé. Eso no es bueno, Betty. ¡Nada bueno!

Viejita: ¡Toma esa bolsa antes de que nos helemos aquí fuera! A ver si puedo encontrar la llave. ¿Dónde estará la llave?

Viejito: (*Una llave enorme le cuelga de la muñeca derecha; se toca la frente con esta mano.*) ¡Ay, vaya! ¡Ahora resulta que no tenemos la llave!

Viejita: ¿Qué te pasa? Tú tienes la llave. ¡Mira!

Viejito: No es verdad, Beatriz. No tengo la llave. No seas cruel con un hombre enfermo.

Viejita: (*Agarrando la llave, muy enfadada.*) Enfermo. ¡Mira! ¿Qué es esto?

Viejito: Lo siento, Beatriz. No sé lo que me pasa. Vamos a entrar antes de que nos resfriemos. O antes de que yo me resfríe. Eso sería malísimo.

Viejita: (*Abriendo la puerta con mucha fuerza.*) ¡Sólo te preocupas de ti mismo!

Gato: (*Arañando la bolsa de Antonio.*) ¡Miau-miau-miauuuuuuuu!

Viejito: (*Acaricia el gato y toma la bolsa.*) ¡Hola, gatito! Espero que estés listo para entrar en la casa con nosotros. Has tenido bastante calle, ¿no?

(*El viejito entra en la casa primero. El gato los mira, entra en la casa, se sale otra vez. La mujer cierra la puerta, dejando al gato fuera.*)

ESCENA 2

(*Ahora están en la sala de estar, y ponen las bolsas con la comida en la mesa. Hay una ventana que da a un pequeño balcón a un lado de la habitación. Frente a la ventana, situadas en dirección al balcón, hay dos sillas, donde la pareja se sienta frecuentemente para mirar a la calle.*)

Viejito: (*Se sienta.*) ¡Necesito descansar antes de hacer nada!

Viejita: (*Ha empezado a sacar la comida de la bolsa, se para, y se sienta.*) Yo necesito descansar también. (*Suspira.*)

(*La pareja mira por la ventana, y de pronto sus cabezas empiezan a moverse de izquierda a derecha y de derecha a izquierda, fascinados. Un ratón con un sombrero mejicano baila un zapateado en el balcón, llendo de aquí para allá de la manera más linda que nadie vió jamás.*)

Viejita: ¿Qué te parece eso? ¡Qué lindo!

Viejito: Es lindo. Me pregunto si le gustaría entrar. Nos mantendría entretenidos durante el invierno.

Viejita: (*Complacida al principio, pero después actúa de forma negativa.*) ¡Qué gran idea! ¡Con el gato por aquí!

Viejito: No había pensado en eso. Cuando tenga hambre, querrá entrar, y entonces . . .

(*El ratón está todavía bailando su zapateado, cuando el gato aparece en el balcón y mira al ratón con alegría. El ratón nota la presencia del gato, para de bailar, y saluda con mucha educación.*)

Ratón: ¡Hola, amigo!

Gato: *(Lamiéndose los bigotes, mezquino.)* ¡Amigo-tamigo! No soy tu amigo, y espero que lo recuerdes.

Ratón: ¿No te gusta cómo bailo?

Gato: Lo que me gustaría es comerte para la cena.

Viejito: *(Abre la ventana.)* Mira, gato, tienes toda la comida que quieras si entras en la casa. ¿Por qué quieres comerte a este talentoso ratón?

Gato: *(Con una mueca desagradable.)* ¿Talentoso? ¡No me hagas reír! *(Al ratón.)* ¡Ven aquí, que no te voy a hacer dañooooooo!

Ratón: *(Le da la cara al gato, pero mantiene su distancia.)* Un momento. Yo soy un ratón moderno: tú quieres cenar, y yo quiero cenar también. Vamos a hablarlo.

Gato: ¡Ja-ja-ja-ja-ja-ja-ja-ja-ja-ja! Es gracioso. Muy gracioso. ¿Qué hay que hablar?

Ratón: En la casa hay comida. ¿Quieres entrar?

Gato: No.

Ratón: Entonces entro yo.

Gato: *(Parando al ratón.)* ¡Un momento! ¿Quién te invitó a entrar?

Viejita: Nosotros lo queremos dentro. Eres un gato desagradecido. ¡Adiós!

(El ratón le guiña un ojo al gato, se quita el sombrero en señal de saludo, entonces salta por la ventana dentro de la casa. La mujer cierra la ventana y deja al gato afuera, enfadado y dolido.)

ESCENA 3

(El primer copo de nieve del invierno entra en el balcón. Su cuerpo, que tiene seis picos, es completamente blanco. Tiene mucha gracia y baila con el viento. El gato está acurrucado a un lado; parece que tiene frío y que está muy enfadado.)

Copo de nieve: ¡Acabo de nacer! ¡Estoy en el mundo! ¡Y soy bellísimo! Exactamente como madre me dijo que sería: con seis picos, con un cuerpo blanco, como una estrella. Excepto que soy pequeño, y frío, y muy rápido. ¡Mira cómo me muevo! ¡Caray! ¡Es fabuloso!

Gato: *(Temblando de frío, hambriento.)* ¿Tienes hambre?

Copo de nieve: ¿Hambre? ¿Qué es eso?

Gato: Tener hambre es . . . querer comer . . . porque, si no, te mueres.

Copo de nieve: *(Con aire de superioridad.)* Nunca tengo hambre.

Gato: Entonces, ¿no puedes morir?

Copo de nieve: ¡Oh, sí! Claro que puedo morir. Pero sólo si el sol calienta o si llega la pala de nieve. Y me encanta el frío, porque no quiero morir.

Gato: ¡Qué extraño! Este frío me va a matar a mí, pero es lo que te mantiene vivo. *(Menea la cabeza con tristeza.)* Sí, muy extraño.

Copo de nieve: *(Preocupado, se acerca al gato.)* No me gusta verte tan infeliz. ¿Hay algo que yo pueda hacer por ti?

Gato: Lo dudo. Necesito calor y comida. ¿Qué puedes hacer tú?

(Los dos están tristes y pensativos cuando aparecen dos palomos, se sientan cerca de la ventana y picotean la ventana con gentileza. La viejita se asoma a ver qué es el ruido.)

Viejita: ¡Antonio! Hay dos lindos palomos aquí en la ventana.

Viejito: *(Sale caminando muy lentamente, comiéndose un trozo de pastel.)* Te apuesto a que también quieren comida. Tenemos un ratón, un gato enfadado afuera, y ahora dos palomos. Y después, ¿qué?

Paloma: No se tiene que preocupar por nosotros, señor. Tenemos grasa bajo las plumas, y siempre encontramos comida por ahí.

Palomo: Mi esposa tiene razón. Vinimos a ver el primer copo de nieve del invierno. ¡Es precioso!

Copo de nieve: ¡Gracias!

Viejito: *(Disculpándose.)* Lo siento. No quise ofenderlos. Los invitaríamos a que entraran si no fuera porque tenemos miedo de que el gato se coma al ratón de la casa.

Copo de nieve: Perdón, señor, pero creo que el gato ha aprendido una lección, y no se comerá el ratón si tiene comida. Sé que hay mucha gente que alimentar: usted, su esposa, los palomos, el ratón, el gato y . . .

Viejita: ¡Eso es bastante! ¡Nos vamos a arruinar!

Copo de nieve: Por favor, déjeme que termine: ¡tengo una idea! Yo bailo muy bien, y si hay otros artistas aquí, podríamos hacer una función para los niños del barrio. Les diremos que paguen su entrada con pan y magdalenas para que todos los animales puedan comer.

Ratón, viejitos, palomos: ¡Viva! ¡Qué gran idea!

Ratón: Yo le cantaría una canción al gato, si se hiciera mi amigo.

(Todos miran al gato para ver su reacción. De mala gana, el gato se acerca al ratón y le da la mano.)

Gato: Está bien, amigo.

Viejito: ¡Fabuloso! ¡No hay nada que anime tanto el espíritu de un hombre enfermo como una familia grande!

Viejita: ¿Quién está enfermo aquí? ¿Tú? ¿De qué?

(La mujer se enfada más y más con su esposo, que tiene miedo.)

Copo de nieve: ¡La función va a empezar! *(Se asoma al balcón y habla en voz alta.)* ¡Todos los niños del vecindario están invitados! ¡Habrá baile, música, y mucho más! ¡Por favor, traed pan y magdalenas para los palomos, el gato y el ratón!

(Los niños llegan y se sientan en el suelo alrededor de los artistas. Los viejitos se sientan en sus sillas.)

Copo de nieve: Muchas gracias por venir, chicos. Voy a comenzar la función con una danza de mi tierra nativa, la Tierra de la Nieve. Espero que os guste.

(El copo de nieve baila con mucha gracia. Todos aplauden cuando termina. El ratón, con su sombrero mejicano, se pone de pie en el centro del escenario.)

Ratón: Ésta es una canción mejicana. Necesito dos o tres cantantes que digan "miau-miau".

Gato: Yo lo haré.

(Aplauso general para el gato, que está de pie detrás del ratón. Todos los que quieran cantar pueden unirse al gato para formar el coro.)

Ratón y coro:

Yo tengo un gato
(Para ratón y coro)

Yo tengo un gato,
¡miau-miau!
con un rabo largo,
¡miau-miau!
que es muy goloso,
¡miau-miau!
y está muy gordo.
¡Miau-miau!

FIN

VOCABULARY–VOCABULARIO

Nouns–Nombres

cupcake: *magdalena*
fat: *grasa*
feather: *pluma*
pigeon: *paloma, palomo*
star: *estrella*
supper: *cena*

Adjectives–Adjetivos

cruel: *cruel*
cute: *lindo*
funny: *gracioso, divertido*
strange: *extraño*
talented: *talentoso*
ungrateful: *desagradecido*

Verbs–Verbos

to be born: *nacer*
to feed: *dar de comer, alimentar*
to harm: *hacer daño*
to rest: *descansar*
to offend: *ofender*
to worry: *preocuparse*

Where Did They Go?
Where Did I Put Them?

¿A dónde se fueron?
¿Dónde las puse yo?

Guilty Conscience

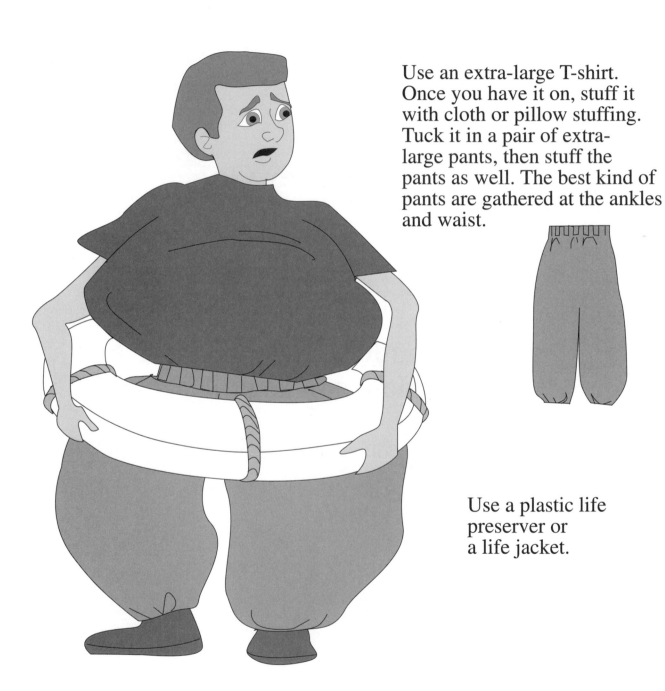

Use an extra-large T-shirt. Once you have it on, stuff it with cloth or pillow stuffing. Tuck it in a pair of extra-large pants, then stuff the pants as well. The best kind of pants are gathered at the ankles and waist.

Use a plastic life preserver or a life jacket.

Figure 7

Where Did They Go?
Where Did I Put Them?

Characters

- Johnny
- Ricky, his cousin
- Mom
- Johnny's conscience (a girl)
- Louis
- The cat
- Ed
- Charles
- Dad

SCENE 1

(Johnny's bedroom on a summer morning. He is in his bed, and his cousin Ricky is in a sleeping bag. The two are sound asleep. The room is a mess, and there are things missing, such as the front wheel of a new bicycle and the "X" of a huge, three dimensional poster, with movable letters, of Mexico. For a few moments, Johnny and Ricky snore loudly. Then, Mom's voice is heard, offstage.)

Mom: Johhhhhhhhnny, do you know what time it is?

(No response from the boys.)

Mom: Well, I'll tell you even if you don't want to know!

(The boys don't move.)

Mom: It is eleven o'clock!

(No response. Mom knocks on the door, from stage right.)

Mom: Knock-knock! *(Opens door and looks in. Her smile turns into shock.)* Johnny!

(Ricky opens one eye, while Johnny turns around and buries his head in the bedclothes.)

Mom: Johnny, wake up! What a mess this place is!

(Ricky responds with a smile which he tries to hide in the sleeping bag. Mom stands by Johnny's bed as he wakes up. When he sees his mother looking so upset, he sits up.)

Johnny: What's this? I mean, what are you doing here? No, that's not what I mean. What time is it?

Mom: Eleven o'clock!

Johnny: Eleven o'clock? What!? Ohhhh, I remember! I had a birthday party yesterday.

(Johnny lies back on the bed, remembering the party with pleasure.)

Ricky: You ate too much cake, he-he!

Johnny: *(Very bossy.)* This is the last time I let you sleep over at my house.

Ricky: All right. But I am your only cousin, and you are going to be alone.

Johnny: *(Sitting on the bed, crossing his arms over his body.)* I have loads of friends.

Ricky: *(Getting out of the sleeping bag, with a superior air.)* Yeah! You don't have friends, you buy them.

(Mom is still there, standing between the two boys, horrified at what she hears. Ricky starts getting dressed and putting his things in order.)

Mom: Johnny, Ricky—stop arguing!

Johnny: *(Really looking at his mother for the first time, showing no emotion.)* Ah, good morning, Mom.

Mom: *(Upset.)* Good morning, Johnny. How can you treat a guest like that?

Johnny: Oh, Mom, it's too early to think.

Mom: Ask Ricky to forgive you.

(Johnny does not like his mother's order. He looks at his cousin sideways. Ricky is not looking at him; he's putting a sweater, his pajama top, and a comb in his knapsack with great determination.)

Mom: Do what I tell you. Please.

(Brief silence. Johnny smiles at Ricky, as if nothing had happened.)

Johnny: Hey, Ricky. Eat breakfast with us.

Ricky: No. I'm leaving.

Johnny: How come? I didn't do anything.

(Mom looks at Johnny with sadness. Ricky picks up his knapsack.)

Ricky: Thank you, Aunt Mary. I . . . I'll walk home.

Mom: Ricky, I need help doing the dishes and putting them away. Would you help me, please?

Ricky: *(After struggling with his feelings for a second, Ricky smiles at his aunt.)* OK, Aunt Mary.

(Mom takes the knapsack from Ricky's hand and leads him out of the room, stage right. Both seem relieved, while Johnny is still sitting on his bed, looking upset.)

Johnny: Rats! What am I going to do now? How can I admit I did something wrong? *If* I did something wrong. I don't think I did!

(Johnny gets out of bed, picks up a towel, and goes to the bathroom, stage left.)

SCENE 2

(Johnny comes back from the bathroom, looking bored and bothered. He picks up objects he finds thrown around—a bicycle with only one wheel, a box of chocolates completely empty, etc. He examines what he finds for a second then throws them aside with contempt. Suddenly, he hears a moan behind him. He turns around with a start, and sees a hideous-looking creature, fat and shapeless. This effect can be created by using balloons or a life preserver.)

Conscience: *(Making awful faces and contorting her body in pain.)* Ahhhh! Ohhhh! Good grief, stop it!

Johnny: Oh, no! Who are you? Get out of here!

Conscience: *(Starts laughing in the middle of her painful noises.)* Get out? I wish I could! Ahhhhh! Ay! Pleeeceaaaaaaaaseeeeeeeeee!

Johnny: Why are you making all those noises? Stop it!

Conscience: I wish I could. Ay! How I hate this!

Johnny: You hate it!? Imagine me, looking at you, listening to you, you horrid thing!

Conscience: You are awful! *(Starts crying.)* You make me this ugly and then call me a horrid thing!

Johnny: I make you ugly? Hah! That's just the way you are! Ugly!

Conscience: *(In a rage.)* No! It's your fault! I wish . . . I wish . . . I wish . . . Oh, what's the point of wishing when I have to live with you?

Johnny: Live with me? Since when? Who are you, anyway?

Conscience: I'm your conscience! Fatter than fat, miserable, and as ugly as they come!

(Johnny is about to laugh when something stops him. He looks at the figure for a long time and very seriously. Then he sits down, looking away.)

Johnny: No. It's not my fault. It . . . it's . . . I . . . I just . . . I can't . . .

Conscience: Well? What are you going to do about it?

Johnny: *(Cold and defensive.)* What am I going to do? What about you?

Conscience: You see, Johnny, what you do makes me what I am. If you were good, I would be beautiful.

Johnny: *(Angry, vindictive.)* Somebody is playing a rotten joke on me, just because yesterday I had a birthday party and received lots of presents. And whoever is playing the joke sent you!

Conscience: *(Contorting with pain and crying desperately.)* There is no way out of this! I wish I could die! Buahhhhhhhhhhhh!

Johnny: Stop it!

(Pause.)

Johnny: All right. How do we end this . . . this . . . collaboration, or whatever it is.

Conscience: You must ask for forgiveness and change your ways.

Johnny: You know I never admit that I'm wrong!

(The door opens, and Mom looks in.)

Mom: Are you all right, Johnny? Were you talking?

Johnny: No, Mom. It . . . it must have been the cat.

(Mom talks while closing the door and returning to the kitchen.)

Mom: The cat? Funny, I haven't seen him since yesterday. I wonder where he's hiding.

(Johnny gives a start.)

Conscience: You are hurting now because you made me feel so guilty.

Johnny: *(Shifty eyed.)* About what.

Conscience: About the cat.

(Johnny gets up quickly and starts walking back and forth across the room.)

Conscience: *(In a calm tone, but merciless.)* You know that you gave the cat to Louis, just because he liked it. And the cat is not yours to give.

Johnny: You make me sick!

Conscience: I could go on with the list.

Johnny: No! I've heard enough. Listen, could we make a deal?

Conscience: No.

Johnny: Why not?

Conscience: I don't make deals. All you have been doing with your life is making deals: to get approval, to pretend that you have more friends than anyone else. Johnny, get real!

Johnny: Yeah! If I get real, what do I have left?

Conscience: *(Smiling for the first time.)* You never know. It may be more than you think.

(Johnny struggles with himself. He sits down, gets up, paces around the room, bites his fingernails, etc. Finally, having made up his mind, he sits next to his conscience, who is patiently waiting.)

Johnny: All right. I guess that when things get bad enough, one has two choices.

Conscience: Which are?

Johnny: Either keep going the same way, or change for the better.

Conscience: Do you know what, Johnny?

Johnny: *(A bit afraid of the answer.)* What?

Conscience: For the first time in a long while, I have a little hope.

(Johnny and his conscience look at each other.)

SCENE 3

(Mom and Ricky are in the kitchen, beating eggs for pancakes. They are singing their favorite song, "Row Your Boat." In the middle of the song, the phone rings. They stop singing, and Mom answers.)

Mom: Hello?

Dad's voice: Hi, dear. I was thinking. Since yesterday was Johnny's birthday and today is Saturday, I'd like to come home early and take you both to the beach.

Mom: I'd love to go to the beach, and I love to have you home early. But tell me—don't you think we're spoiling Johnny? He has not come out of his room yet, and Ricky and I are nearly finished with the dishes and making pancakes.

Dad's voice: Oh, let him have a good time. I'll be home in a jiffy. And I'd love one of those pancakes.

Mom: I think Johnny is always having a good time, and often at people's expense. You are not going to be so pleased when you see his room. But you'll probably let him get away with it, as always.

Dad's voice: Anything wrong today, honey? You sound as if you need to go to the beach. See you.

(Mom hangs up the phone and goes back to what she was doing. Before she and Ricky have time to start singing again, Johnny gets out of his room and heads straight for the phone. He looks very serious and dignified, which startles his mother and cousin. Johnny picks up the phone and dials a number.)

Johnny: Hi, may I talk to Louis? Thank you. *(Mother and cousin exchange a glance of surprise.)* Louis, this is Johnny. Listen, I want the cat back . . . Yes, I know I gave him to you, but I realize that I cannot give away what isn't mine. He belongs to my family. He loves us, and this is his home. I apologize . . . Yes, I know you are disappointed, but I have to do this . . . Thank you, Louis.

(He hangs up and goes back to his own room. While Mom and Ricky look on with amazement, Johnny can be heard talking in his room.)

Johnny's voice: It's incredible! You already look different, and I feel much better.

(There is silence. Mom and Ricky look at each other with wonder, and then continue with the pancakes.)

Johnny's voice: I will never say again, as I used to, "Where did they go?" No . . . you're right, I should say, "Where did I put them?"

(The door bell rings, and Johnny goes out of his room to open it. Mom and Ricky stop cooking to watch what's going on. Louis is at the door with the cat, who rushes into Mom's arms. Louis is very upset.)

Louis: Here's the cat! I'm glad to bring him because he's been a real pain the whole night long, scratching my door like crazy, crying to be let out. My parents couldn't stand it! But still, I think it is cheap of you to ask me to return a gift.

Johnny: I understand how you feel, Louis. Again, I apologize, and I hope you'll continue to be my friend.

Louis: Don't hope for too much. Good-bye!

(Johnny watches Louis leave. He turns around to face his mother, who is hugging the cat, and Ricky, who looks at Johnny with wide eyes, still holding spoon and bowl.)

Mom: My sweet cat! You must have been sooo lonely! Let me give you some kitty cookies.

Cat: Puuurrrrrrrrrr-purrrrr-puuurrrrrrrrr!

Johnny: Sorry, Mom. I'm glad he's all right.

(Ricky is so shocked at Johnny's change, he drops the spoon to the floor. He picks up the spoon. Mom has been busy with the cat food, but once the cat starts eating, she turns to Johnny.)

Mom: *(In a calm, respectful tone.)* Thank you for bringing the cat back, Johnny. He's happy to be home again.

(Johnny smiles, and goes back to his room. Ricky and Mom look at each other and sigh.)

Ricky: I've never heard Johnny say sorry before.

SCENE 4

(Johnny's room. Conscience is sitting by Johnny's desk, reading from a notebook. She looks much better, some of her weight having been taken away from her, and her hair is neatly combed. She is sitting very straight and smiles. Johnny has made the bed and has begun to straighten things up, but the X from the huge poster of MEXICO is missing, as well as the front wheel of the new bicycle.)

Conscience: It's a very good list, Johnny. But one has to start small—and with the most important things. The rest falls into place later. And I'm so glad that the cat is back!

Johnny: *(Sighing with relief.)* So am I! I don't think I have ever felt worse in my life than after I gave the cat away. But, without your help, I would not have been able to make a good decision.

Conscience: I know! How else do you think I got this way? This is old fat, kid! I'm so glad I've lost some of it.

(Johnny looks at his conscience with admiration, while she looks at herself in the mirror. Dad's voice is heard in the kitchen, and soon he's knocking on Johnny's door. Johnny is afraid and looks at his conscience.)

Conscience: Don't worry, only you can see me.

Dad: *(Coming in.)* How are things? *(He interrupts himself when he sees the bicycle without a wheel.)* Hey! Where's the wheel of the new bicycle I gave you yesterday?

(Johnny looks down, but feeling sorry, not avoiding the question.)

Johnny: Listen, Dad, I—

Dad: *(In a rage.)* Don't give me stories! I want the truth.

Johnny: *(Standing up and facing his father, very dignified.)* Dad, I am trying to tell you the truth—if you'll give me a chance. Ed left his bicycle in the driveway, and his father drove in too fast and ran over it, and smashed the front wheel. So I . . .

(Some more weight drops from Conscience, who is very pleased, smiles, and looks at herself in the mirror while Johnny sees her and smiles. Dad, who cannot see Conscience, misunderstands Johnny's look, and is still angrier.)

Dad: Do you realize what that bicycle cost?! What are you smiling at? Don't make fun of your father, on top of everything else!

(Johnny is reaching for Dad's arm when the doorbell rings. This has the effect of calming Dad. Johnny looks outside, leaves the room, and comes back with company—doing all of this very calmly. While Johnny is gone, Dad looks around—he is upset when he sees the bicycle but is pleased that the bed is made and some things are in order. Conscience observes Dad carefully and makes some notes on the sheet of paper she was reading before. Johnny comes back with three of his friends or, rather, his former friends. Two of them are carrying objects—the wheel and the huge X, and look very upset.)

Louis: I told them that you were asking for your things back. They don't want them anyway.

Charles: Here. Now maybe you'll be able to ride the thing.

(The three newcomers laugh with contempt at Johnny after this remark.)

Ed: And I don't need this. It doesn't go with the decorations in my home. But thank you for letting me borrow it.

Johnny: Louis, thank you so much for doing this for me. I'm not sure that you all understand, but I want the things back because they are part of gifts that people gave me. I didn't understand before that it's important to take care of gifts.

Dad: That's right. Thank you for bringing the things back, kids. You wouldn't have had much use for them, anyway. Would you?

(Louis, Charles, and Ed look down, shuffling their feet a little, nodding in agreement.)

Dad: It seems to me that we've all understood what a gift is. It expresses love—or at least friendship and generosity. It has to be taken care of.

(The three boys look at Johnny with respect, speechless. Conscience drops more weight, and looks very beautiful now. Johnny smiles in her direction, but as soon as he notices the others are looking puzzled, his smile fades.)

> **Johnny:** I wonder . . . if I'll have any friends now.

> **Dad:** Goodness, Johnny—do you really mean . . . you think you have to buy friends?

> **Johnny:** Something like that, I guess.

> **Dad:** How did you get that idea?

> **Johnny:** I don't know.

> **Louis:** *(Very impressed and truthfully.)* Johnny, I hope you will want to be my friend in spite of what I did today.

(Johnny holds out his hand to Louis, who takes it in his own. The other two pat Johnny on the shoulder.)

> **Johnny:** I guess . . . we don't have to be perfect to be friends.

> **Dad:** Well, when I came home early, I didn't know I'd have so much to think about—or have such a gang to take to the beach.

> **Ed:** Wow! To the beach!

(Johnny opens a drawer and starts taking towels out, handing one to each of his friends.)

> **Johnny and friends:** Let's go! I can't wait to put my feet in the water!

(Ricky and Mom appear at the door.)

> **Mom:** And what about the pancakes? I've been cooking the whole morning!

> **Dad:** You haven't had breakfast yet?

> **Ricky and Johnny:** No.

> **Dad:** Well, then let's all of us have breakfast! I love pancakes at noon!

(They all laugh. Rick goes to Johnny and gets a towel from him. Dad, Mom, Rick and the three friends leave Johnny's room, very excited with the trip. Johnny puts his things in a little bag. He's smiling. He looks at his conscience, who is radiant and beautiful.)

> **Johnny:** I'll see you soon! And thank you.

> **Conscience:** I'm going with you.

> **Johnny:** You don't trust me?

> **Conscience:** Johnny—I'm always with you.

(They both laugh, and leave to join the others.)

THE END

¿A dónde se fueron?
¿Dónde las puse yo?

Personajes

- Juanito
- Rico, su primo
- Mamá
- La conciencia de Juanito (una chica)
- Luis
- El gato
- Eduardo
- Carlos
- Papá

ESCENA 1

(El dormitorio de Juanito en una mañana de verano. Él está en su cama, y su primo en un saco de dormir. Los dos duermen profundamente. La habitación está muy desordenada y faltan algunos objetos, como la rueda delantera de una bicicleta nueva y la J de un enorme poster tri-dimensional de Méjico con letras movibles. Juanito y Rico roncan ruidosamente por unos minutos. Entonces, se oye la voz de mamá fuera del escenario.)

Mamá: ¡Juaniiiiitoooooooooooo! ¿Sabes la hora que es?

(No hay respuesta.)

Mamá: ¡Bueno, pues te lo voy a decir aunque no quieras saberlo!

(Los muchachos no se mueven.)

Mamá: ¡Son las once de la mañana!

(No hay respuesta. Mamá llama a la puerta, que está a la derecha del escenario.)

Mamá: ¡Tock-tock! *(Abre la puerta y mira dentro. Su sonrisa cambia a una expresión de horror.)* ¡JUANITO!

(Rico abre un ojo mientras que Juanito se da la vuelta y entierra la cabeza en la ropa de la cama.)

Mamá: Juanito, ¡despiértate! ¡Esta habitación está hecha un lío!

(Rico responde con una sonrisa, que trata de esconder tras el saco de dormir. Mamá se para al lado de la cama de Juanito mientras se despierta. Cuando ve que su madre está tan enfadada, Juanito se sienta.)

Juanito: ¿Qué es esto? Digo, ¿qué haces ahí? No, no es eso lo que quiero decir. ¿Qué hora es?

Mamá: Las once.

Juanito: ¿Las once? ¿Qué!? ¡Oh, ya me acuerdo! Tuve una fiesta de cumpleaños ayer.

(Juanito se recuesta en la cama, recordando con placer su fiesta.)

Rico: Comiste demasiado pastel, ¡ja-ja!

Juanito: *(Con actitud mandona.)* Es la última vez que te dejo dormir en mi casa.

Rico: Bueno. Pero recuerda que soy tu único primo, y te vas a quedar solo.

Juanito: *(Se sienta en la cama y se cruza de brazos.)* Tengo montones de amigos.

Rico: *(Se sale del saco de dormir, con aire de superioridad.)* ¡Ya! Tú no tienes amigos: los compras.

(Mamá está todavía en el mismo sitio, horrorizada de lo que oye. Rico se empieza a vestir y a poner sus cosas en orden.)

Mamá: ¡Juanito, Rico, dejad de pelear!

Juanito: *(Mira a su madre realmente por primera vez, y no muestra ninguna emoción.)* Ah, buenos días, mamá.

Mamá: *(Enfadada.)* Buenos días, Juanito. ¿Cómo puedes tratar a un huésped de esa manera?

Juanito: ¡Oh, mamá! Es demasiado temprano para pensar.

Mamá: Pídele perdón a Rico.

(A Juanito no le gusta la orden de su madre. Mira a su primo de reojo. Rico no lo mira: está poniendo un jersey, la camisa del pijama y un peine en su bolsa, con mucha determinación.)

Mamá: Haz lo que te mando, por favor.

(Un silencio breve. Juanito sonríe a Rico, como si no hubiera pasado nada.)

Juanito: Anda, Rico. Desayuna con nosotros.

Rico: No. Me voy.

Juanito: ¿Por qué? No he hecho nada malo.

(Mamá mira a Juanito con tristeza. Rico toma su bolsa.)

Rico: Gracias, tía María. Yo . . . yo me voy a casa caminando.

Mamá: Rico, necesito ayuda lavando los platos y poniéndolos en su sitio. ¿Me ayudas? ¡Por favor!

Rico: *(Lucha con sus sentimientos por unos segundos, y sonríe a su tía.)* Está bien, tía María.

(Mamá toma la bolsa de Rico, y le toma de la mano para llevárselo del dormitorio, por la derecha del escenario. Los dos parecen estar aliviados, mientras que Juanito se queda sentado en la cama, enfadado.)

> **Juanito:** ¡Porras! ¿Qué voy a hacer ahora? ¿Cómo voy a admitir que he hecho algo que no está bien? Si lo hubiera hecho, claro. ¡Pero no!

(Se levanta de la cama, toma una toalla y se va al baño, por la izquierda del escenario.)

ESCENA 2

(Juanito vuelve del baño, aburrido y agobiado. Recoge objetos que encuentra por ahí tirados—una bicicleta que tiene solamente la rueda trasera, una caja de chocolates vacía, etc. Examina por un segundo cada objeto que encuentra, y los tira con desprecio. De repente, oye un quejido detrás de él. Se vuelve, sobresaltado, y ve a una criatura horrible, gorda y deformada. Este efecto se puede conseguir usando un material que se desinfle fácilmente, como globos y chalecos salvavidas.)

> **Conciencia:** *(Haciendo muecas horribles y contorsionando su cuerpo con dolor.)* Ayyyyyyyyy! ¡Ohhhhhh! ¡Para, por favor!
>
> **Juanito:** ¡Oh, no! ¿Quién eres tú? ¡Fuera de aquí!
>
> **Conciencia:** *(Empieza a reírse en medio de sus ruidos de dolor.)* ¿Que me vaya? ¡Ojalá y pudiera! ¡Ayyyyyy! ¡Ay! ¡Por favooooorrrrrrrrrrrrrrrrrr!
>
> **Juanito:** ¿Por qué haces esos sonidos? ¡Para!
>
> **Conciencia:** Ojalá y pudiera. ¡Ay! ¡Lo que odio esto!
>
> **Juanito:** ¿Tú odias esto? ¡Imagíname a mí que te tengo que mirar, cosa horrorosa!
>
> **Conciencia:** ¡Eres odioso! *(Empieza a llorar.)* ¡Me haces así de fea, y encima me dices que soy horrible!
>
> **Juanito:** ¿Que yo te hago fea? ¡Ja! Así es como eres. Fea.
>
> **Conciencia:** *(Con rabia.)* ¡No! ¡Es tu culpa! Me gustaría que . . . me gustaría que . . . me gustaría . . . ¿Pero de qué me vale querer nada si tengo que vivir contigo?
>
> **Juanito:** ¿Vivir conmigo? ¿Desde cuándo? Vamos a ver, ¿quién eres?
>
> **Conciencia:** ¡Soy tu conciencia! Más gorda que nadie, miserable, y de lo más fea.

(Juanito está a punto de echarse a reír, pero algo lo para. Mira a la figura por un rato, con mucha seriedad. Entonces se sienta, y mira para otro lado.)

> **Juanito:** No. No es culpa mía. Es . . . , es . . . , es que . . . no puedo . . .
>
> **Conciencia:** ¿No? ¿Y qué vas a hacer?
>
> **Juanito:** *(Frío y defensivo.)* ¿Que qué voy a hacer yo? Y tú, ¿qué?
>
> **Conciencia:** Verás, Juanito, es que tus acciones me hacen lo que soy. Si fueras bueno, yo tendría buen tipo y sería guapísima.
>
> **Juanito:** *(Enfadado y vengativo.)* Alguien me está jugando una mala pasada, sólo porque ayer tuve una fiesta de cumpleaños y me dieron muchos regalos. ¡Y ese alguien te mandó a ti!

Conciencia: *(Se retuerce de dolor y llora desesperadamente.)* ¡No hay remedio! ¡Quisiera morir! ¡Buáááááá!

Juanito: ¡Calla!

(Silencio.)

Juanito: Bueno. ¿Cómo terminamos esta . . . esta . . . colaboración, o lo que quiera que sea?

Conciencia: Tienes que pedir perdón, y cambiar tu comportamiento.

Juanito: Sabes que nunca admito que estoy equivocado.

(Se abre la puerta, a la derecha del escenario, y madre asoma la cabeza y mira dentro.)

Mamá: ¿Estás bien, Juanito? ¿Estabas hablando?

Juanito: No, mamá. A lo mejor . . . , a lo mejor era el gato.

(Madre habla mientras cierra la puerta para volver a la cocina.)

Mamá: ¿El gato? Es curioso, pero no lo he visto desde ayer. ¿Dónde se estará escondiendo?

(Juanito se sobresalta.)

Conciencia: Sientes dolor ahora porque me hiciste sentir tan culpable.

Juanito: *(Evasivo.)* Sobre qué.

Conciencia: Sobre el gato.

(Juanito se levanta rápidamente y empieza a caminar de un lado para otro.)

Conciencia: *(Tranquila, pero sin piedad.)* Sabes muy bien que le diste el gato a Luis, simplemente porque le gustaba. Y el gato no te pertenece a ti solo.

Juanito: ¡Me pones enfermo!

Conciencia: Te podría decir más cosas.

Juanito: ¡No! He oído bastante. Mira, ¿qué te parece si hacemos un trato?

Conciencia: No.

Juanito: ¿Por qué?

Conciencia: Porque yo no hago tratos. No has hecho otra cosa en toda tu vida más que hacer tratos: para que aprueben de ti, para pretender que tienes más amigos que nadie. Juanito, ¡acepta las cosas como son!

Juanito: ¡Ya! Acepto las cosas como son, y ¿qué me queda?

Conciencia: *(Sonriendo por primera vez.)* Uno nunca sabe. Puede que más de lo que piensas.

(Juanito lucha con sus emociones: se sienta, se levanta, va de aquí para allá, se muerde las uñas, etc. Por fin, habiendo ya tomado una decisión, se sienta al lado de su conciencia, que está pacientemente esperando.)

Juanito: Está bien. Supongo que cuando las cosas se ponen feas, uno tiene que elegir entre dos caminos.

Conciencia: ¿Que son?

Juanito: Sigue como vas, o cambia para mejorar.

Conciencia: ¿Sabes una cosa, Juanito?

Juanito: *(Un poco temeroso de la respuesta.)* ¿Qué?

Conciencia: Que, por primera vez en mucho tiempo, tengo algo de esperanza.

(Juanito y su conciencia se miran.)

ESCENA 3

(Madre y Rico en la cocina, batiendo huevos para hacer panqueques. Cantan su canción favorita, "Row Your Boat", o una en español que les guste a los actores. El teléfono suena cuando van por mitad de la canción. Paran de cantar y madre contesta el teléfono.)

Mamá: ¿Diga?

Voz de padre: Hola, amor. Estaba pensando que, como ayer fue el cumpleaños de Juanito y hoy es sábado, pues que me gustaría volver a casa temprano y llevaros a los dos a la playa.

Mamá: Me encantaría ir a la playa y tenerte en casa temprano. Pero dime, ¿no crees que estamos mimando a Juanito demasiado? Todavía no ha salido de su dormitorio, y Rico y yo casi hemos terminado de lavar los platos y de hacer panqueques.

Voz de padre: ¡Déjalo que se divierta! Estaré en casa en un segundo. Y me encantaría comerme uno de esos panqueques.

Mamá: Creo que Juanito siempre se está divirtiendo, y frecuentemente a costa de otros. No vas a estar muy contento cuando veas su habitación. Pero seguro que dejarás que se salga con la suya, como siempre.

Voz de padre: ¿Te pasa algo hoy, amor? Me parece que necesitas ir a la playa. Hasta la vista.

(Madre cuelga el teléfono y vuelve a donde estaba haciendo los panqueques. Antes de que ella y Rico puedan empezar a cantar otra vez, Juanito sale de su dormitorio y se va derecho al teléfono. Su apariencia es seria y digna, lo que asombra a su madre y primo. Juanito levanta el auricular y marca un número.)

Juanito: Hola. ¿Puedo hablar con Luis? Gracias. *(Madre y primo intercambian miradas de sorpresa.)* Luis, soy Juanito. Mira, me gustaría que me devolvieras el gato . . . Sí, sé que te lo di, pero me he dado cuenta de que no puedo regalar lo que no es mío. Pertenece a la familia. Él nos quiere, y éste es su hogar. Pido disculpas . . . Sí, me doy cuenta que estás desilusionado, pero estoy haciendo lo que tengo que hacer . . . Gracias, Luis.

(Cuelga y vuelve a su dormitorio. Mientras que madre y Rico se miran asombrados, se oye a Juanito hablando en su habitación.)

Voz de Juanito: ¡Es increíble! Ya te ves diferente, y yo me siento mucho mejor.

(Silencio. Madre y Rico se miran otra vez, y continúan con los panqueques.)

Voz de Juanito: Nunca más diré, como antes, "¿A dónde se han ido?" No . . . Tienes razón. Debo de decir, "¿Dónde los puse?"

(El timbre suena y Juanito sale de su habitación para abrir la puerta. Madre y Rico paran de cocinar para mirar lo que pasa. Luis aparece en la puerta con el gato, que corre a los brazos de madre. Luis está muy enfadado.)

Luis: ¡Aquí tienes el gato! Me alegra traerlo porque ha sido una lata toda la noche, sin parar de arañar la puerta para que lo dejáramos salir. Mis padres ya estaban hartos. De todas maneras, me parece de mal gusto que me pidas que te devuelva un regalo.

Juanito: Lo entiendo, Luis. Te pido disculpas otra vez, y espero que continuarás siendo mi amigo.

Luis: No tengas tantas esperanzas. ¡Adiós!

(Juanito mira a Luis irse. Se vuelve a mirar a su madre, que está abrazando al gato, y a Rico, que mira a Juanito con ojos muy abiertos, la cuchara y el cuenco en la mano.)

Mamá: ¡Mi gato dulce! ¡Lo solo que habrás estado! Ven que te dé galletitas.

Gato: ¡Rorro, rorro, rorro!

Juanito: Lo siento, mamá. Me alegra que esté bien.

(A Rico se le cae la cuchara al suelo, de asombrado que está por el cambio de Juanito. Recoge la cuchara. Madre ha estado ocupada dándole de comer al gato, pero cuando el gato empieza a comer se vuelve hacia Juanito.)

Mamá: *(Con voz muy tranquila, respetuosa.)* Gracias por traer al gato, Juanito. Está contento de estar en casa otra vez.

(Juanito sonríe y vuelve a su habitación. Rico y madre se miran otra vez y suspiran.)

Rico: Nunca había oído antes a Juanito decir lo siento.

ESCENA 4

(La habitación de Juanito. Su conciencia está sentada frente al escritorio, leyendo un cuaderno. Está más delgada y atractiva, y lleva el pelo muy bien peinado. Está sentada muy derecha y sonríe. Juanito ha hecho la cama y ha empezado a limpiar, pero la J gigante del poster de Méjico falta, al igual que la rueda delantera de la bicicleta nueva.)

Conciencia: Es muy buena esta lista, Juanito. Pero uno tiene que empezar poco a poco, y por lo más importante. El resto se arregla solo. ¡Y me alegra tanto que el gato haya vuelto!

Juanito: *(Suspirando con alivio.)* ¡Yo también! Nunca me he sentido tan mal en mi vida como cuando regalé el gato. Pero sin tu ayuda, no habría podido tomar una buena decisión.

Conciencia: Lo sé. ¿Cómo crees que me puse así? ¡Ésta es grasa antigua, chico! No sabes lo contenta que estoy de haber perdido alguna.

(Juanito mira a su conciencia con admiración, mientras ella se mira en el espejo. La voz de padre se oye en la cocina, y poco después padre toca en la puerta de Juanito. Juanito tiene miedo y mira a su conciencia.)

Conciencia: No te preocupes, que sólo tú me puedes ver.

Papá: *(Entra.)* ¿Cómo van las co—? *(Se interrumpe cuando ve la bicicleta.)* ¡Eh! ¿Dónde está la rueda de la bicicleta nueva que te di ayer?

(Juanito baja la cabeza con tristeza, no porque esté evitando la pregunta.)

Juanito: Mira, papá. Yo—

Papá: *(Muy enfadado.)* ¡No me cuentes cuentos! Quiero la verdad.

Juanito: *(Levantándose y mirando a su padre con mucha dignidad.)* Papá, estoy intentando decirte la verdad . . . si me das la oportunidad. Eduardo dejó su bicicleta afuera, y su padre iba conduciendo demasiado rápido y le rompió la rueda delantera. Así que yo . . .

(Conciencia pierde más peso, lo que la hace feliz, sonríe, se mira en le espejo más, etc., mientras que Juanito la mira y sonríe. Padre, que no puede verla, malentiende la mirada de Juanito y se enfada todavía más.)

Papá: ¿Te das cuenta de lo que me costó esa bicicleta? ¿Por qué sonríes? ¡No te burles de tu padre, encima de todo!

(Juanito va a tocar el brazo de su padre cuando suena el timbre. Padre se calma. Juanito mira afuera, sale de la habitación y vuelve con compañía—todo hecho con mucha calma. Mientras Juanito está fuera de la habitación, padre lo observa todo: se muestra enfadado cuando ve la bicicleta, pero le agrada ver que la cama está hecha y hay algo de orden. Conciencia, a quien sólo Juanito puede ver, observa a padre con mucha atención y toma notas en el cuaderno que estaba leyendo antes. Juanito ha entrado con tres de sus antiguos amigos. Dos de ellos traen cosas—la rueda y una I enorme , y parecen estar muy enfadados.)

Luis: Les dije que estabas pidiendo tus regalos. De todas maneras, no los quieren.

Carlos: Toma. A lo mejor ahora podrás montarte en esa cosa.

(Los recién llegados se ríen con desprecio de Juanito.)

Eduardo: Yo no necesito esto. No va con las decoraciones de mi casa. Pero gracias por dejármela prestada.

Juanito: Luis, gracias por hacer esto por mí. No sé si lo entendéis, pero quiero estas cosas porque son parte de regalos que la gente me dio. No comprendía antes que es importante cuidar de los regalos.

Papá: Exactamente. Gracias por devolver los regalos, chicos. De todas maneras, no os habrían servido de mucho, ¿no?

(Los tres chicos bajan la vista, se mueven un poco y asienten con la cabeza.)

Papá: Me parece a mí que todos sabemos ahora lo que es un regalo: expresa amor, o por lo menos amistad y generosidad. Hay que cuidarlo.

(Los tres amigos miran a Juanito con admiración, mudos. A la conciencia se le cae más peso; está preciosa ahora. Juanito le sonríe pero, al darse cuenta que los otros no entienden, deja de sonreir.)

Juanito: Me pregunto . . . si tendré amigos ahora.

Papá: ¡Vamos, Juanito! Quieres decir que . . . ¿piensas que tienes que comprar amigos?

Juanito: Más o menos.

Papá: ¿Quién te metió esa idea en la cabeza?

Juanito: No sé.

Luis: Juanito, espero que querrás seguir siendo mi amigo a pesar de lo que hice hoy.

(Juanito extiende la mano a Luis, que la toma en la suya. Los otros dos ponen una mano en el hombro de Juanito.)

Juanito: Supongo . . . que no tenemos que ser perfectos . . . para ser amigos.

Papá: Bueno, cuando vine a casa temprano, no tenía ni idea que tendría tantas cosas en las que pensar, ni tanta gente para llevar a la playa.

Eduardo: ¡Caramba! ¡A la playa!

(Juanito abre un cajón y empieza a sacar toallas, repartiéndolas entre sus amigos.)

Los cuatro amigos: ¡Vámonos! ¡Estoy que me muero por poner los pies en el agua!

(Rico y madre aparecen en la puerta.)

Mamá: ¿Y los panqueques? ¡He estado cocinando toda la mañana!

Papá: ¿No habéis desayunado todavía?

Rico y Juanito: No.

Padre: Bueno, entonces vámonos todos a desayunar. ¡Me encantan los panqueques a las doce del mediodía!

(Risa general. Rico toma una toalla de Juanito. Padre, madre, Rico y los amigos salen del dormitorio de Juanito, muy alborotados con la idea del viaje. Juanito pone sus cosas en una bolsita. Sonríe. Mira a su conciencia, que está radiante y preciosa.)

Juanito: ¡Hasta pronto! Y gracias.

Conciencia: Me voy contigo.

Juanito: ¿No te fías de mí?

Conciencia: Juanito, estoy siempre contigo.

(Se ríen, y salen para reunirse con los otros.)

FIN

VOCABULARY–VOCABULARIO

Nouns–Nombres

cousin: *primo*
knapsack: *mochila*
mess: *lío*
sleeper: *durmiente*
sleeping bag: *saco de dormir*
pancakes: *panqueques*

Adjectives–Adjetivos

cheap: *barato, de mal gusto*
crazy: *loco*
glad: *alegre*
lonely: *solo, aislado*
sorry: *arrepentido, apenado*
wrong: *malo, injusto*

Verbs–Verbos

to admit: *admitir*
to apologize: *pedir perdón*
to belong: *pertenecer*
to hide: *esconder*
to hope: *tener esperanza*
to wonder: *preguntarse, maravillarse*

What Happened in the Garden This Summer?

¿Qué pasó en el jardín este verano?

The Sun

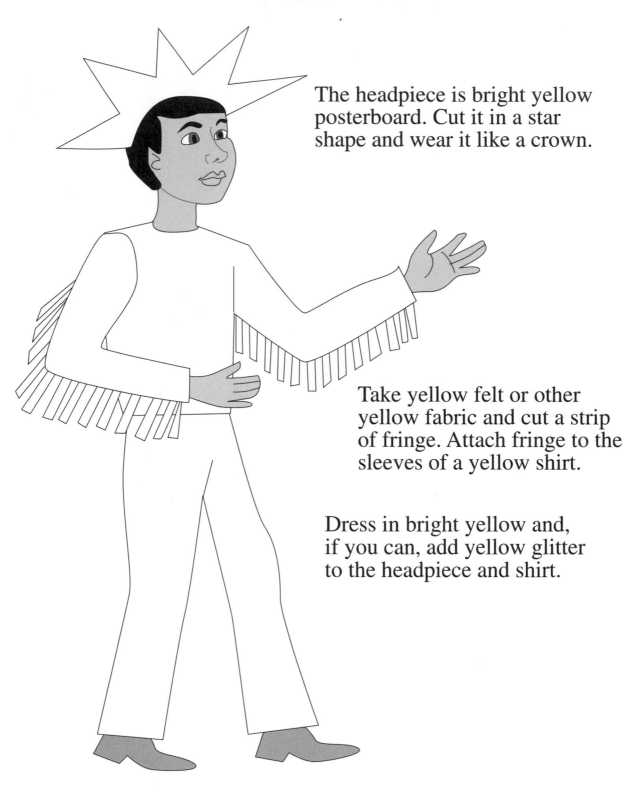

The headpiece is bright yellow posterboard. Cut it in a star shape and wear it like a crown.

Take yellow felt or other yellow fabric and cut a strip of fringe. Attach fringe to the sleeves of a yellow shirt.

Dress in bright yellow and, if you can, add yellow glitter to the headpiece and shirt.

Figure 8

What Happened in the Garden This Summer?

Characters

- Mr. Sun
- Mr. Cloud
- Cloud's Children
- Mother Potato
- Potato's Children
- Father Tomato
- Tomato's Children
- Sunflowers (Mother, Father, Children)
- Ms. Rainbow (Dancer)
- Attendants (Drummer, Fan operator)

> *Note:* The director and cast should determine this play's ending before it is performed. Suggestions are included at the end.

SCENE 1

(The garden. A row of tomatoes, another of potatoes, and a patch of sunflowers. The garden's inhabitants are in an uproar because things have not been going well lately.)

Mother Potato: How wet am I! And I feel so heavy!

Potato's Child 1: You are right, Mother. I am wet too.

Potato's Children 2 and 3: *(Shivering.)* We are wet and cold! Ahhhhh!

Mother Sunflower: You are wet because you are greedy.

Father Sunflower: That's right! You got all the water. Look at my poor children!

Sunflower's Child 1: I am wilting!

Sunflower's Child 2: I wish I could have some water!

Sunflower's Child 3: My colors are fading! Who will love me?

Mother Sunflower: *(To husband, weeping.)* My poor children!

Father Sunflower: *(Hugging his wife.)* Don't worry, wife. Things will get better.

Mother Potato: I hope so! *(Shaking water off.)* I don't want to be wet, and I don't want to be called greedy!

Father Tomato: You should stop fighting! It's a bad example for the children.

Mother Sunflower: A bad example? *(Pointing at the potatoes.)* They have all our water!

Mother Potato: *(Unpleasant.)* Take it!

Father Sunflower: *(Sighs, and his petals wilt some more.)* I wish I could do something for my children!

(All the sunflowers stoop, because they are wilting from lack of water.)

Father Tomato: May I help?

Mother Sunflower: *(Angry, imitating Father Tomato.)* "May I help?" Sure! You have everything! Look at how healthy your children are!

Father Tomato: Of course I'm happy that my children are healthy. But this is not the time to find faults, but solutions.

Sunflower Child 2: Mr. Tomato is right!

Potato Child 1: Yes! Let's hear what he has to say!

Father Tomato: Thank you, kids. You see, from where I am, I can see that something is wrong with the distribution of water. I have just the water that I need. But the potatoes have too much, while the sunflowers have too little.

Mother Sunflower: *(Still unpleasant, making fun of Father Tomato.)* How smart!

Father Sunflower: Quiet, please.

Father Tomato: Thank you, Mr. Sunflower. So, there are two questions to be answered: how did the problem happen, and how do we correct it?

(Mother Sunflower is about to speak, but her husband covers her mouth with his hand. Everyone is silent and thinks.)

Potato Children 2 and 3: What can be done about it, Mr. Tomato?

Father Tomato: There is only one solution! We must ask Mr. Sun, our ruler, what happened.

Father Sunflower: That's right! Let's ask Mr. Sun!

Mother Sunflower: That's easy! I could have thought of that!

(Father Sunflower gives his wife a mean look. They all start getting their things ready, now in a happier mood.)

Father Tomato: It is a nice journey, to go and see Mr. Sun. But only a few of us can go. We cannot leave the garden alone.

(They all nod in agreement, and Father Tomato, Father Sunflower, and Potato Child 1 leave with their knapsacks.)

SCENE 2

(The big hall in Mr. Sun's palace. He's sitting on his throne, while one attendant fans him with a large fan and another plays the drums. Mr. Sun's sprawling position indicates that he is very hot. The drummer plays for a minute, then there is some noise off stage, to the right, and the drummer stops playing and goes out to see what's going on. Mr. Sun immediately sits up, irritated.)

Mr. Sun: Why did the music stop? Who on earth can stand this heat without music?

Fan Attendant: Mr. Sun, in the first place, we are not on Earth.

Mr. Sun: Don't contradict me! Where is the drummer?

Fan Attendant: *(A bit afraid.)* He went to see what the noise was all about.

Mr. Sun: What noise? I don't hear anything!

(The drummer comes in followed by the visitors.)

Mr. Sun: I know that . . . whatever. What's the problem? Make it short.

(The visitors look at each other, puzzled by the cold welcome, and the other two motion Mr. Tomato to speak.)

Father Tomato: We ask Mr. Sun's forgiveness for bothering him on a hot day. The problem is water.

Mr. Sun: *Water!?* Hum! Water? Well, if you want more, I'll send more. If you don't want any, I won't send any. How's that?

(Mr. Sun sprawls on his throne again, closes his eyes and motions the fan attendant to move the fan more vigorously. The visitors, politely, look at the floor.)

Father Tomato: Mr. Sun, it's not that simple.

Mr. Sun: Not simple? Well, explain it to me then.

Father Tomato: The potatoes get too much water and the sunflowers not enough. The tomatoes are just right.

(Mr. Sun puts his index finger on his forehead and thinks deeply for a few seconds.)

Mr. Sun: *(To the drummer.)* Bring in Mr. Cloud at once!

(The drummer bows and exits. Mr. Sun waits impatiently, his fingers drumming on his knees. Mr. Cloud enters, in a panic. The drummer follows.)

Mr. Cloud: Y-y-essss, Mr. Sun?

Mr. Sun: Why did you give the potatoes too much water and the sunflowers too little? That could create a big problem!

Mr. Cloud: D-d-d-did I d-do that, Mr. Sun?

Mr. Sun: You did. And my instructions were correct. They always are.

Mr. Cloud: I-I-I d-d-don't know what happened, Mr. Sun. He-he-here are the instructions you gave us.

(Mr. Cloud, trembling, takes a piece of paper from his pocket and hands it to Mr. Sun.)

Mr. Sun: *(Looks at the paper, turns it over, sideways, etc., trying to read it. Finally, he bursts out laughing.)* I know what happened! I gave you the instructions in Spanish! And you don't read Spanish, do you?

Mr. Cloud: No, sir. My wife does, but she's in bed with a cold.

Mr. Sun: A cold in this weather! Oh, well! I know what we have to do. *(To Mr. Cloud.)* You stand there! *(To Mr. Sunflower.)* That's the sunflowers' side, isn't it? *(Mr. Sunflower nods.)* All right, Mr. Cloud. Rain! And rain hard!

Mr. Cloud: May I call my kids? They are great helpers!

Mr. Sun: Sure! The more the merrier!

(Mr. Sun sits down to rest, fanned by the attendant, while the visitors look on with interest. Mr. Cloud goes to stage left and calls his children.)

Mr. Cloud: Children, bring all the watering cans that you can find! And full to the brim!

(The Cloud's children rush onto the stage with many watering cans.)

Cloud's Children: Here we are, father! What do we do now?

Mr. Cloud: *(Very bossy, not nervous at all.)* Rain here! And very hard! Pour down all the water you brought!

Cloud's Children: *(Scratching their heads and looking at their father, then at Mr. Sun, who nods.)* All right. It will rain hard! Here we go!

(Standing downstage right, the children mime pouring water. They can even go offstage to get more water, if there are enough children. Mr. Sunflower goes up to them and gets his share of the water, which revives him greatly.)

Father Sunflower: Oh, my! This is wonderful! And to know that my children are well again is the greatest gift of all. Water! Water! Water!

Potato Child 1: I am happy for Mr. Sunflower and his family. But—

Mr. Sun: One thing at a time, kid. Come close to me.

(Potato Child 1 does so and retreats quickly because of the heat.)

Mr. Sun: *(Smiling kindly.)* Are you dry now? Yes? Well, now it's your family's turn. *(To fan attendant.)* Stop that fan. I have to be *hot* now.

(He walks downstage left and breathes deeply until he looks very strong. He speaks to the Potato Child.)

Mr. Sun: Is it here where your family lives? *(The child nods.)* Well, watch this! When you get down to Earth, you'll have a story to tell!

(Mr. Sun looks down and exhales a breath so hot that it almost looks like fire, an effect that can be created by blowing on red paper. The others are amazed, with the exception of the drummer and the fan attendant, who take advantage of the situation to squat against the wall and take a short nap.)

Mr. Sun: I just hope that I aimed the heat correctly and haven't burned half the countryside. Well, people, go down to your families, throw a party, and have a ball! I'll be watching from here to make sure that all is well.

Mr. Cloud: Mr. Sun, I am very sorry about what happened. How could I avoid making this mistake again?

Mr. Sun: Very simple. Learn Spanish! It is clear that having only one bilingual person in the family is not enough!

Mr. Cloud: Another job!

Cloud's children: We'll learn with you. That will make it fun!

Mr. Cloud: Well, all right. I'll try.

(The visitors are picking up their knapsacks, ready to go. Mr. Sun is again sprawled on his throne, the drummer and the fan attendant are ready to start their routine. The three visitors bow, and the residents bow as well, with the exception of Mr. Sun, who gets up as soon as the visitors are ready to leave.)

Mr. Sun: I'll be watching!

(The visitors smile and leave. The drummer plays the drums, the fan attendant fans Mr. Sun, and Mr. Cloud and his children pick up the watering cans and take them offstage.)

SCENE 3

(The garden. Everyone is happy because the right conditions have been restored.)

Father Tomato: The trip was nice, but it feels great being home again!

Father Sunflower: *(Dreamy.)* Ahhhhhhhhh! I will remember for the rest of my life the water that gave me strength! Right there, at the source!

Potato Child 1: We are forgetting Mr. Sun's instructions.

Potato Children 2 and 3: Tell us what we have to do to be soooo dry! Hummmm!

Potato Child 1: Mr. Sun thought that we should have a party and be together again.

Mother Potato: I'll go for that. What will we have to eat?

Mother Sunflower: *(In her usual put-down manner.)* How about some deep fried potato chips?

Mother Potato: *(Stepping in front of her children, to protect them.)* Hah! And why not a big dish of nicely roasted sunflower seeds?

Father Sunflower: How insulting! Now, the only thing left to say is that the best thing for the party would be a pizza with lots of tomato sauce!

(Grownups and children start talking at the same time, each facing a member of another family, all angry at each other. They don't realize that Mr. Sun is looking down at them from up-stage left, sternly, and that he is helping Ms. Rainbow step into the garden. When Mr. Sun speaks, the inhabitants of the garden are suddenly quiet and ashamed.)

Mr. Sun: Ahem! Well, well. I see that this garden needs much more than the right amount of water. You must work together at learning to be neighbors.

(The inhabitants of the garden look at each other sideways, shuffle their feet uncomfortably. Ms. Rainbow, a young lady dressed in a flowing dress made in rainbow colors, is dancing among the members of the garden. She invites each one of them to join in her dance, but they are reluctant. The children start participating first, then the grownups join the children. If possible, a simple tune could accompany the movements that Ms. Rainbow and the inhabitants of the garden create. This may be an opportunity for singing a song created at the school, community center, or music class. When it seems that the garden is on its way to cooperating, Mr. Sun smiles, nods, and goes back to his palace. The dance and song may go on for as long as the actors want. Also, if someone comes up with the idea to cook something for the party (unlike the items suggested above, of course) try it—be creative.

THE END

¿Qué pasó en el jardín este verano?

Personajes

- El señor Sol
- El señor Nube
- Los hijos del señor Nube
- Madre Patata
- Las hijas de Patata
- Padre Tomate
- Los hijos de Tomate
- Girasoles (madre, padre, hijos)
- Señorita Arcoiris (bailarina)
- Asistentes (percusionista, operador del abanico)

ESCENA 1

(El jardín: una hilera de tomates, otra de patatas, y una parcela de girasoles. Hay un alboroto en el jardín porque las cosas no han ido bien últimamente.)

Madre Patata: ¡Qué mojada estoy! ¡Y me siento tan gorda!

Hija de Patata 1: Tienes razón, madre. Yo también estoy mojada.

Hijas de Patata 2 y 3: *(Titiritando.)* ¡Estamos mojadas y tenemos frío! ¡Ayyyyyyy!

Madre Girasol: Estáis mojadas por avariciosas.

Padre Girasol: ¡Eso! Vosotras tenéis toda el agua. ¡Mirad a mis pobres niños!

Hijo de Girasol 1: ¡Me estoy marchitando!

Hijo de Girasol 2: ¡Ojalá y tuviera agua!

Hijo de Girasol 3: ¡Me estoy descoloriendo! ¿Quién me va a querer a mí?

Madre Girasol: *(A su esposo, llorando.)* ¡Mis pobres hijos!

Padre Girasol: *(Abrazando a su esposa.)* No te preocupes, esposa. Las cosas mejorarán.

Madre Patata: ¡Espero que sí! *(Sacudiendo el agua.)* ¡No quiero estar mojada, y no me gusta que me llamen avariciosa!

Padre Tomate: Debéis de dejar de pelear, familia. Es mal ejemplo para los niños.

Madre Girasol: ¿Mal ejemplo? *(Señalando a las patatas.)* ¡Tienen toda nuestra agua!

Madre Patata: *(Muy desagradable.)* ¡Llévatela!

Padre Girasol: *(Suspira, y los pétalos se le caen un poco más.)* ¡Ojalá pudiera hacer algo por mis hijos!

(Todos los girasoles se marchitan más por falta de agua.)

Padre Tomate: ¿Puedo ayudar?

Madre Girasol: *(Enfadada, imitando a Padre Tomate.)* "¿Puedo ayudar?" ¡Claro! ¡Como lo tienes todo! ¡Mira lo saludables que están tus hijos!

Padre Tomate: Sí, me alegro de que mis hijos estén sanos. Aunque éste no es el momento de buscar faltas, sino soluciones.

Hijo de Girasol 2: ¡El señor Tomate tiene razón!

Hija de Patata 1: ¡Sí! ¡Oigamos lo que tiene que decir!

Padre Tomate: Gracias, chicos. Mirad, desde donde yo estoy puedo ver que algo no funciona bien con la distribución de agua. Yo tengo justamente el agua que necesito. Pero las patatas tienen demasiada, mientras que los girasoles no tienen bastante.

Madre Girasol: *(Todavía muy desagradable, burlándose de Padre Tomate.)* ¡Qué listo!

Padre Girasol: ¡Silencio, por favor!

Padre Tomate: Gracias, señor Girasol. Bueno, hay dos preguntas que necesitan respuesta: por qué ocurrió el problema, y cómo corregirlo.

(Madre Girasol está a punto de hablar cuando su esposo le cubre la boca con la mano. Todo el mundo está en silencio, pensando.)

Hijas de Patata 2 y 3: ¿Qué podemos hacer, señor Tomate?

Padre Tomate: ¡Hay solamente una solución! Tenemos que preguntarle al señor Sol, nuestro jefe, qué pasó.

Padre Girasol: ¡Exactamente! ¡Preguntemos al señor Sol!

Madre Girasol: ¡Eso es fácil! Yo misma podría haber pensado en eso.

(Padre Girasol mira a su esposa con desaprobación. Todos empiezan a arreglar sus cosas para el viaje, sintiéndose más contentos.)

Padre Tomate: El ir a ver al señor Sol es un viaje muy interesante. Pero sólo podemos ir unos cuantos. No podemos dejar el jardín solo.

(Todos están de acuerdo, y Padre Tomate, Padre Girasol y la Hija de Patata 1 toman sus mochilas y se van.)

ESCENA 2

(El gran salón en el palacio del señor Sol. Está sentado en su trono, mientras que un asistente lo abanica con un enorme abanico y otro toca el tambor. La postura del señor Sol, todo espatarrado, nos indica que tiene mucho calor. El percusionista toca por un minuto, y entonces

oye ruido fuera del escenario, a la derecha, y sale a ver lo que pasa. El señor Sol se levanta inmediatamente, irritado.)

Señor Sol: ¿Por qué paró la música? ¿Quién en esta tierra puede aguantar el calor que hace sin música?

Operador de Abanico: Señor Sol, en primer lugar, no estamos en la Tierra.

Señor Sol: ¡No me contradigas! ¿Dónde está el percusionista?

Operador de Abanico: *(Algo temeroso.)* Fue a ver qué era el ruido ese.

Señor Sol: ¿Qué ruido? ¡No oigo nada!

(El percusionista entra seguido de los visitantes.)

Señor Sol: Ya sé que . . . lo que sea. ¿Qué pasa? Y breve.

(Los visitantes se miran entre sí, algo sorprendidos por la fría bienvenida, y los otros le indican al señor Tomate que hable.)

Padre Tomate: Pedimos disculpas al señor Sol por molestarlo en un día tan caluroso. El agua es el problema.

Señor Sol: ¡Agua! ¡Ummmmmm! ¿Agua? Bueno, si queréis más, mandaré más. Si no queréis ninguna, pues no mando ninguna. Qué tal eso.

(El señor Sol se espatarra en su trono otra vez, cierra los ojos y le hace una señal al operador del abanico para que lo mueva con más fuerza. Los visitantes, con mucha educación, fijan los ojos en el suelo.)

Padre Tomate: Señor Sol, no es tan sencillo.

Señor Sol: ¿Que no es tan sencillo? Bueno, explica.

Padre Tomate: Las patatas recibieron demasiada agua, y los girasoles no tienen bastante. Los tomates están bien.

(El señor Sol se toca la frente con el dedo índice y piensa profundamente por unos segundos.)

Señor Sol: *(Al percusionista.)* ¡Que venga el señor Nube ahora mismo!

(El percusionista saluda y sale. El señor Sol espera impacientemente, moviendo los dedos como si estuviera tocando música sobre las rodillas. El señor Nube entra, aterrorizado. Le sigue el músico.)

Señor Nube: S-s-s-síí, señor Sol.

Señor Sol: ¿Por qué le diste demasiada agua a las patatas, y no la suficiente a los girasoles? ¿Eh? Eso podría crear un gran problema.

Señor Nube: ¿Hi-hi-hi-ce e-e-eso, señor Sol?

Señor Sol: Sí. Y te di las instrucciones correctas, como siempre.

Señor Nube: Y-y-y-yo no sé lo que pasó, señor Sol. A-a-a-a-quí están las instrucciones que nos dio.

(El señor Nube, temblando, le da al señor Sol una hoja de papel que lleva en el bolsillo.)

Señor Sol: *(Mira al papel de esta manera y de la otra, le da la vuelta, etc., intentando leerlo. Al fin se echa a reír.)* ¡Ya sé lo que pasó! ¡Te di las instrucciones en inglés! Y tú no sabes inglés, ¿no es así?

Señor Nube: Sí, señor. Mi esposa sabe, pero está en la cama con un resfriado.

Señor Sol: ¡Un resfriado en este tiempo! ¡Vaya por Dios! Ya sé lo que tenemos que hacer. *(Al señor Nube.)* Usted, ¡póngase aquí! *(Al señor Girasol.)* Ése es el lado de los girasoles, ¿no? *(El señor Girasol asiente con la cabeza.)* Muy bien, señor Nube. ¡Que llueva! ¡Y que llueva fuerte!

Señor Nube: ¿Llamo a mis hijos? Son grandes ayudantes.

Señor Sol: ¡Por supuesto! Cuantos más, mejor.

(El señor Sol se sienta a descansar, abanicado por el asistente, mientras que los visitantes miran la escena con interés. El señor Nube va a la izquierda del escenario y llama a sus hijos.)

Señor Nube: ¡Chicos, traed todas las regaderas que encontréis, y llenas hasta el filo!

(Los hijos del señor Nube entran corriendo, con muchas regaderas.)

Hijos del señor Nube: ¡Aquí estamos, padre! ¿Qué hacemos ahora?

Señor Nube: *(Sin nerviosismo, muy mandón.)* ¡Que llueva aquí! ¡Y fuerte! ¡Echad toda el agua que habéis traído!

Hijos del señor Nube: *(Arrascándose las cabezas y mirando a su padre, y luego al señor Sol, que asiente con la cabeza.)* Está bien. ¡Lloverá fuerte! ¡Ahí vamos!

(De pie en el frente del escenario, a la derecha, los niños representan con gestos el acto de regar. Si hay bastantes niños, pueden salir del escenario a por más agua. El señor Girasol se les acerca y recoge su porción de agua, que lo revive mucho.)

Padre Girasol: ¡Ah! ¡Es fabuloso! Y el saber que mis hijos están bien de nuevo es el mejor de los regalos. ¡Agua! ¡Agua! ¡Agua!

Hija de Patata 1: Me alegro por el señor Girasol y su familia, pero—

Señor Sol: Cada cosa a su tiempo, chica. Acércate a mí.

(La chica se acerca al señor Sol, y retrocede rápidamente a causa del calor.)

Señor Sol: *(Sonriendo amablemente.)* ¿Estás seca ahora? ¿Sí? Bueno, ahora le toca a tu familia. *(Al operador del abanico.)* Para de abanicarme. Tengo que estar CALIENTE ahora.

(Camina al frente del escenario, a la izquierda, e inhala aire hasta que parece muy fuerte. Le habla a la chica.)

Señor Sol: ¿Es aquí donde vive tu familia? *(La chica asiente.)* ¡Pues mira esto! Cuando vulevas a la Tierra, tendrás algo que contar.

(El señor Sol mira hacia abajo y echa una bocanada de aire tan caliente que casi parece fuego: este efecto se puede conseguir soplando en papel rojo. Los otros están asombrados, con la excepción de los asistentes, que se aprovechan de la situación para sentarse contra la pared y tomar una siestecita.)

Señor Sol: Espero que apunté bien y no quemé la mitad del campo. Bueno, amigos, regresen al lado de sus familias, hagan una fiesta, ¡y disfruten! Estaré observando desde aquí para estar seguro que todo marcha bien.

Señor Nube: Señor Sol, siento mucho lo que ha pasado. ¿Cómo puedo evitar que pase otra vez?

Señor Sol: Es muy fácil. ¡Aprende inglés! Está claro que una sola persona bilingüe en la familia no es bastante.

Señor Nube: ¡Otro trabajo!

Hijos de Nube: Aprenderemos contigo. ¡Así será muy divertido!

Señor Nube: Bueno, está bien. Lo intentaré.

(Los visitantes empiezan a recoger sus mochilas, listos para marcharse. El señor Sol está otra vez espatarrado en su trono, y sus asistentes están listos para continuar su rutina. Los tres visitantes saludan, los residentes saludan también, con la excepción del señor Sol, que se pone de pie tan pronto como los visitantes están listos para irse.)

Señor Sol: ¡Estaré observando!

(Los visitantes sonríen y se van. El percusionista toca el tambor, el otro asistente abanica al señor Sol, y el señor Nube y sus niños recogen las regaderas y las sacan del escenario.)

ESCENA 3

(El jardín. Todo el mundo está feliz desde que las cosas se arreglaron.)

Padre Tomate: ¡El viaje fue lindo, pero es fabuloso estar en casa otra vez!

Padre Girasol: *(Soñador.)* ¡Ahhhhhhhhh! Toda mi vida recordaré aquella agua que me dió fuerza. ¡Allí, en la misma fuente!

Hija de Patata 1: Nos estamos olvidando de las instrucciones del señor Sol.

Hijas de Patata 2 y 3: ¡Dinos lo que tenemos que hacer para estar siempre así de secas! ¡Ummmm!

Hija de Patata 1: El señor Sol dice que debemos de hacer una fiesta para estar unidos otra vez.

Madre Patata: Me gusta la idea. ¿Qué podemos comer?

Madre Girasol: *(Con su actitud desagradable de siempre.)* ¿Qué te parece unas patatas bien fritas?

Madre Patata: *(Poniéndose en frente de sus hijas, para protegerlas.)* ¡Vaya! ¿Y por qué no un plato grande de pipas bien tostaditas?

Padre Girasol: ¡Qué insulto! Lo único que queda por decir ahora es que lo mejor que podemos comer en la fiesta es pizza con un montón de salsa de tomate.

(Los mayores y los niños empiezan a hablar todos a la misma vez, cada uno dándole la cara a un miembro de otra familia, enfadados los unos con los otros. No se dan cuenta que el señor Sol los está mirando, situado a la izquierda de fondo atrás del escenario, muy serio, y que está

ayudando a que la señorita Arcoiris entre en el jardín. Cuando el señor Sol habla, los habitantes del jardín se quedan callados de repente, muy avergonzados.)

> **Señor Sol:** ¡Ajem! Vaya, vaya. Veo que este jardín necesita mucho más que una cierta cantidad de agua. Necesitan cooperar para aprender a ser vecinos.

(Los habitantes del jardín se miran de reojo y arrastran los pies, incómodos. La señorita Arcoiris, una joven vestida en un traje con los colores del arcoiris que fluye con el viento, danza entre los habitantes del jardín. Los invita a que bailen con ella, pero se retraen. Los primeros en empezar a participar son los niños, y luego se les unen los mayores. Si se puede, una melodía sencilla podría acompañar los movimientos creados por la señorita Arcoiris y los habitantes del jardín. Ésta sería una buena oportunidad para cantar una canción creada en la escuela, el centro de la comunidad o la clase de música. Cuando parece que el jardín está aprendiendo a cooperar, el señor Sol sonríe, mueve la cabeza en señal de aprobación, y se vuelve a su palacio. La danza y la canción pueden durar todo el tiempo que los actores quieran. También, si de esta danza sale una idea para cocinar algo para la fiesta que no se parezca en nada a lo que provocó la pelea, sería bueno intentarlo. Usen su imaginación.)

FIN

VOCABULARY–VOCABULARIO

Nouns–Nombres

attendant: *asistente, sirviente, acompañante*
distribution: *distribución*
fault: *defecto, falta, culpa*
ruler: *gobernante; regla*
sunflower: *girasol*

Adjectives–Adjetivos

fun: *diversión, alegría*
greedy: *codicioso, avaro*
hard: *duro, sólido, firme*
healthy: *sano, saludable*
wet: *mojado*

Verbs–Verbos

agree: *estar de acuerdo*
aim: *apuntar, dirigir*
contradict: *contradecir*
fade: *marchitarse, descolorarse*
forgive: *perdonar, disculpar*
drum: *tamborilear*

Ay, Carmelo!

¡Ay, Carmelo!

Cold or Hot?

Use a big man's overcoat.
Wear earmuffs and mittens
and hold a thermometer
that shows a temperature of 110°.

Make the thermometer out of
white posterboard. Cut it to
be 14 inches long. Draw the
lines on with a ruler and make
the long, dark line red. Print
the numbers 110° on it as
shown.

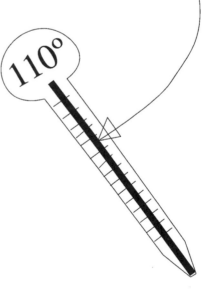

Figure 9

Ay, Carmelo!

A Play in One Scene

Characters

- The Storyteller
- Carmelo
- Carmelo's Mother
- Elisabeth
- Elisabeth's Cousin
- Anthony 1
- Anthony 2

(The town square of a small seaport village on a Caribbean island. It is a hot summer afternoon, and the town seems to be deserted, except for one person: Carmelo. Wrapped in a thick, long woolen coat, Carmelo shivers from cold in the middle of the square.)

Carmelo: Br . . . brrrr . . . brrrrrrr . . .

(A strong and youthful figure appears in the square, dressed in cool summer clothes and a straw hat. He looks at Carmelo without surprise, says nothing to him, and then goes downstage and addresses the audience.)

Storyteller: Hi! I could start by saying "Once upon a time . . ." the way that fairytales start. But I'm not going to do that. I am the Storyteller of this town, and my job is to tell what happens here, now. *(Looks back at Carmelo, who is still shivering with cold and doesn't seem to notice the Storyteller.)* This is Carmelo, a native. He has a mother, a . . . but wait! What you want to know is why he's dressed like this on a hot day, right? That's where I come in.

(A boy, dressed in white clothes and a red kerchief around his neck enters from stage left, a fishing pole hanging from his shoulders. He doesn't look at Carmelo. He is in the middle of the stage when he notices the Storyteller, and he stops.)

Anthony 1: Good afternoon, Storyteller.

Storyteller: Good afternoon. Are you going fishing?

Anthony 1: That's where I'm going. I guess you have to know. *(He points at the audience.)* But tell me, are you going to tell them about how it was that we got a chorus?

Storyteller: Hmmm! I don't think so . . . not now, anyway.

Anthony 1: Well, I thought I would mention it. Have a good afternoon.

(Anthony exits stage right. The Storyteller looks at the audience again.)

Storyteller: That was Anthony . . . Anthony . . . *(He seems a bit confused, but regains his self-assurance soon.)* Yes, Anthony . . . He was in a hurry to catch some fish for supper, I'm sure. But I am here to tell you about Carmelo and why he's dressed like this on a hot summer day.

(Just then, Anthony crosses the stage, from right to left, dressed as he was before, carrying now a watering can and a hoe. He doesn't look at Carmelo, but stops when he sees the storyteller.)

Anthony 2: Good afternoon, Storyteller.

Storyteller: Good afternoon, Anthony. You are returning from your fishing early. Not many fish around, eh?

Anthony 2: I don't know what you're talking about. I am going to water my flowers. I don't see how they can do well in this heat if I don't give them some water.

Storyteller: *(Very puzzled, but polite.)* S-sure. Well, good luck, An-Anthony!

Anthony 2: Say, are you going to tell them how was it that we got a chorus in town? *(As before, he points at the audience.)*

Storyteller: *(Very confused now.)* N-no. I mean, maybe. Later, yes. Good-bye.

Anthony 2: Well, I just thought that I would mention it. Good-bye.

Carmelo: Br . . . brrrrrrrrr . . . brrrrrrrr . . .

Storyteller: *(Addressing the audience again, less sure of how to do things now.)* Ah, yes! Car-Carmelo is s-s-till here. In his wool coat . . . that you can see f-f-from where you are, and-and-and a ther-thermometer in his hand, which says that . . .

(The Storyteller takes a few steps backward to where Carmelo is standing and takes a quick look at a thermometer that Carmelo holds in his hand.)

Storyteller: The thermometer says it's 110 degrees where he's standing. I don't doubt that. It's hot!

(A woman, dressed in a white shirt and flower-print skirt, enters from the right and approaches Carmelo with a cup in her hand.)

Mother: Here, Carmelo. Drink this. It will make you feel better.

Carmelo: No, Mother. I can't drink this. It's too cold outside for a cool drink. Br . . . brrrrrr . . . .brrrrrrrrrrrr . . .

Mother: Ay, Carmelo!

(She takes the cup with her, starts to leave, taking sips from the cup. But she turns to the Storyteller as soon as she sees him.)

Mother: Good afternoon, Storyteller.

Storyteller: Good afternoon. So, he doesn't want the lemonade.

Mother: He'll drink some later. Say, are you going to tell them how it was that—

Storyteller: *(Cold, stopping her.)* Maybe later. I am busy now. Good afternoon, Mother.

Mother: Well, I thought I would mention it. Good afternoon.

(She looks at her son, waves at him, and leaves stage right.)

Storyteller: As I was saying, this is Carmelo . . . in his wool coat . . . on a hot summer afternoon . . . in the middle of the town square. The thermometer says that it's 110 degrees, and Carmelo's mother—

(From stage left, a girl and a boy, dressed as if they were part of a traditional dance troupe, come on stage from the left rehearsing some dance steps. They don't say anything to Carmelo, but they stop to talk with the Storyteller.)

Elisabeth: This is my cousin, Storyteller.

Storyteller: *(Annoyed by the new interruption, but tries to avoid being impolite.)* Hi, cousin . . . Forgive me, but I am trying to inform this wonderful audience what—

Elisabeth: *(Very enthusiastic.)* Oh! So, you are finally going to tell them how it was that we—

Storyteller: *(Losing his patience and yelling at Elisabeth.)* No! I am not going to tell them! Good afternoon, Elisabeth. And please, take your cousin with you.

Elisabeth: No problem, we are late to the—

(And without finishing her sentence, Elisabeth takes her cousin by the hand and both leave, stage right. Just then, from stage right, Anthony comes in, with a bucket full of fish. The Storyteller opens his eyes very wide and looks at the audience, then at Anthony, speechless.)

Anthony 1: So, I'm back. And happy! Say, have you done your job of telling them how it was that—

Storyteller: No, I didn't! How could I! I was interrupted every two seconds by someone who wanted me to tell . . . But I don't have time for that. And tell me, how is it that you have a bucket full of fish when you have gone to water your flowers?

Anthony 1: Flowers? Not I! That must have been my brother.

Storyteller: That's right! You have a brother! I forgot, in the middle of all this!

Carmelo: Br . . . brrrrrrr . . . . .. brrrrrrrrrrrrrrrrrr . . . .

Anthony 1: *(Taking Carmelo into account for the first time, and looking at his watch.)* Excuse me, but I mustn't be late for—

(And without finishing his sentence, he takes another look at Carmelo and rushes off with his bucket.)

Storyteller: *(Looking at the audience with a sigh of relief.)* I hope that that's the last interruption of the afternoon, and, although it's getting late, I would like to tell you about Car—

(The Storyteller stops suddenly, because he realizes that Carmelo has stopped shivering, has looked at his watch and left the stage at right.)

> **Storyteller:** Well, I guess not. If he has left, that's an old story, and since I am the town storyteller I'm supposed to be telling you what happens in the town here and now!

(A happy crowd, playing musical instruments, singing and laughing, is heard outside. The Storyteller, surprised, looks around to see what's going on. Anthony 2 enters with a beautiful flower arrangement, Anthony 1 with a tray full of broiled fish. They stand, each at one side of the stage, holding their treasures, in a festive mood. Carmelo, in cool white clothes and a red kerchief around his neck, walks to center stage. The other members of the cast—his mother, Elisabeth, Elisabeth's cousin, and any other actor or actress available—come behind Carmelo and stand in a semicircle, which he faces, his back turned to the audience, raising his arms like a conductor. He is conducting a chorus of singers. They may sing any song the actors choose, or they may make up a tune for the following words.)

> **Chorus:**
>
> > Ay, Aaaaayyyyy,
> > A-a-a-a-ayyyyyyyyy!
> > Ay! Carmeeeelo!

(The conducting ended, Carmelo takes a bow, Anthony 2 gives him the flowers, and Anthony 1 passes the fish around to the hungry performers. Everyone is happy, except the Storyteller, who is spellbound.)

> **Storyteller:** *(Quite upset.)* I am the storyteller of this town! How is it that I didn't know about this?

> **Mother:** *(Busy, eating her fish.)* We all have been trying to tell you, haven't we?

(Everyone nods in agreement while eating their fish.)

> **Storyteller:** *(Still upset.)* Well, I was busy figuring out why Carmelo dressed in a long woolen coat on a hot summer afternoon! That's an important story to tell!

> **Anthony 1:** A great story!

> **Anthony 2:** And what do you know about it?

> **Storyteller:** Well, I . . . I . . . I . . . Who can tell me? I am the town storyteller and—

> **Carmelo:** I will tell you. I have always liked music, always. The problem is that I don't know how to play an instrument, and I can't sing!

> **Mother:** But! He can put it all together! That's what he was doing in the middle of the square with his winter coat on! At first, I didn't understand it either. But I talked it over with his teacher, and then with Carmelo himself. All geniuses have strange habits when they are visited by inspiration. And, what we need to learn to do is . . .

> **Carmelo:** O.K., chorus! Let's sing!

(They all put the rest of their fish on the tray, and sing, conducted by Carmelo.)

Chorus:

> Respect a genius,
> Be quiet when he works;
> And when you see him
> Do something quite
> Out of the ordinary,
> Think of the play called
> *Ay, Carmelo!*
> Ah, and the story equally
> Applies to girls!

Storyteller: Ahem! Well, people, I have learned this lesson from you: if you are the town's Storyteller, don't turn away those who have important information, and, above all, go to the person in question and *listen!*

THE END

¡Ay, Carmelo!

Obra en una escena

Personajes

- El Cronista
- Carmelo
- Madre de Carmelo
- Isabel
- Primo/a de Isabel
- Antonio Uno
- Antonio Dos

(La plaza de un pequeño pueblo costero en una isla caribeña. Es por la tarde de un día muy caluroso, y el pueblo parece desierto, con la excepción de una persona: Carmelo. Envuelto en un abrigo largo de lana, Carmelo está titiritando de frío en la mitad de la plaza.)

Carmelo: Ti-tiri-ti-ti-titititititi . . .

(Una figura fuerte y juvenil aparece en la plaza, vestido con ropas veraniegas y un sombrero de paja. Mira a Carmelo sin mostrar sorpresa, no le dirige la palabra, y luego se va al frente del escenario y le habla al público.)

Cronista: ¡Hola! Podría empezar con las palabras érase una vez, como pasa en los cuentos de hadas. Pero no voy a hacer eso. Soy el Cronista de este pueblo, y mi trabajo es el de contar lo que pasa aquí, ahora, en este momento. *(Mira a Carmelo, que tirita de frío y no parece notar la presencia del Cronista.)* Es Carmelo, nativo de este pueblo. Tiene una madre, un . . . ¡Un momento! Ustedes quieren saber por qué va vestido así en un día tan caluroso como éste, ¿no? Bueno, pues aquí es donde yo entro en acción.

(Un chico, vestido de blanco y con un pañuelo rojo al cuello, entra por la izquierda, llevando una caña de pescar al hombro. No mira a Carmelo, pero se para en la mitad del escenario cuando ve al Cronista.)

Antonio 1: Buenas tardes, Cronista.

Cronista: Buenas tardes. ¿Vas de pesca?

Antonio 1: Eso es exactamente lo que voy a hacer. Supongo que usted tiene que enterarse. Y dígame, ¿les va usted a contar cómo fue que conseguimos tener un coro? *(Señala al público.)*

Cronista: ¡Ummmmmm! Creo que no, o por lo menos esta tarde no.

Antonio 1: Bueno, pensé que sería bueno mencionarlo. Buenas tardes.

(Antonio sale por la derecha. El Cronista mira al público otra vez.)

Cronista: Es Antonio . . . , Antonio . . . *(Parece estar confundido por alguna razón, pero recupera su confianza pronto.)* Sí, Antonio . . . Estoy seguro que tenía prisa por llegar pronto a pescar algo para la cena. Pero yo estoy aquí para hablarles de Carmelo, y porqué está vestido así en un día caluroso de verano.

(Entra en ese momento Antonio, vestido como antes, y cruza el escenario de derecha a izquierda, llevando consigo una regadera y un azadón. No mira a Carmelo, pero se para cuando ve al Cronista.)

Antonio 2: Buenas tardes, Cronista.

Cronista: Buenas tardes, Antonio. Vuelves de la pesca temprano. No hay muchos peces, ¿eh?

Antonio 2: No tengo ni idea de lo que está hablando. Voy a regar mis plantas. No pueden aguantar este calor si no les doy un poco de agua.

Cronista: *(Confundido, pero con mucha educación.)* Por-por-por supuesto. Bueno, que todo te salga bien, An-Antonio.

Antonio 2: Dígame, ¿les va a contar cómo fue que conseguimos tener un coro? *(Y señala al público.)*

Cronista: *(Bastante confundido.)* N-no. Quiero decir, quizás. Sí, sí, luego. Adiós.

Antonio 2: Bueno, pensé que sería bueno mencionarlo. Buenas tardes.

Carmelo: Ti-ti tiriri-ti-tiri-ti-titi . . .

Cronista: *(Dirigiéndose al público, no muy seguro de cómo hacer las cosas ahora.)* ¡Ah, sí! Carmelo es-está aquí todavía. Con su abrigo de lana . . . eso lo pueden ustedes ver desde sus asientos, y y y un termómetro en la mano, que dice que . . .

(El Cronista toma unos pasos hacia atrás, se para al lado de Carmelo y mira rápidamente al termómetro que éste tiene en la mano.)

Cronista: El termómetro dice que hace una temperatura de ciento diez grados donde él está. Y no lo dudo. ¡Hace calor!

(Una mujer entra por la derecha, vestida con una blusa blanca y una falda de flores, y se acerca a Carmelo con una taza en la mano.)

Madre: Toma, Carmelo. ¡Bébete esto! Te sentará bien.

Carmelo: No, Madre. No me lo puedo beber. Hace demasiado frío para tomar una bebida fresca. Titi-ri, titititititi-ri, tiriti, tiriti . . .

Madre: ¡Ay, Carmelo!

(Se lleva la taza y se dispone a salir, tomando sorbitos de la taza. Pero se vuelve al Cronista en cuanto lo ve.)

Madre: Buenas tardes, Cronista.

Cronista: Buenas tardes. Así que no quiere la limonada.

Madre: Ya la querrá más tarde. Y dígame, ¿les va a contar cómo fue que—?

Cronista: *(Frío, interrumpiéndola.)* Quizás más tarde. Estoy ocupado ahora. Buenas tardes, Madre.

Madre: Bueno, pensé que sería bueno mencionarlo. Buenas tardes.

(Mira a su hijo, lo saluda con la mano, y sale por la derecha.)

Cronista: Como iba diciendo, éste es Carmelo . . . con su abrigo de lana . . . en una tarde calurosa de verano . . . en el medio de la plaza del pueblo. El termómetro dice que hace una temperatura de ciento diez grados, y la madre de Carmelo . . .

(Por la izquierda entran una chica y un chico, vestidos con los trajes típicos de un grupo de bailarines folklóricos. Van ensayando unos pasitos de baile. No le dicen nada a Carmelo, pero se paran para hablar con el Cronista.)

Isabel: Éste es mi primo, señor Cronista.

Cronista: *(Enfadado por la nueva interrupción, aunque intenta no ser desagradable.)* Hola, primo . . . Perdonadme, pero estoy intentando informar a este fabuloso público so—

Isabel: *(Con mucho entusiasmo.)* ¡Oh! Así que por fin les va a contar cómo fue que—

Cronista: *(Perdiendo la paciencia completamente.)* ¡No! ¡No se lo voy a contar! Buenas tardes, Isabel. Y, por favor, llévate a tu primo contigo.

Isabel: No se preocupe. Vamos a llegar tarde a—

(Y sin terminar lo que iba a decir, Isabel toma a su primo de la mano y salen por la derecha. Entra entonces Antonio por la derecha también, con el cubo lleno de pescado. El Cronista abre mucho los ojos, mira al público, luego a Antonio, sin poder hablar.)

Antonio 1: Estoy de vuelta. ¡Y muy feliz! Dígame, ¿les ha contado cómo fue que—?

Cronista: ¡Por supuesto que no! ¿Cómo lo iba a hacer, si no han parado de interrumpirme cada dos segundos pidiéndome que les contara . . . ? Pero no tengo tiempo para eso. A ver, ¿cómo es que apareces aquí con un cubo lleno de pescado cuando acabas de ir a regar tus flores?

Antonio 1: ¿Flores? Yo no. Sería mi hermano.

Cronista: ¡Es verdad! ¡Tienes un hermano! Se me olvidó, con tanta cosa.

Carmelo: Titiri-titititi-ri-titiri . . .

Antonio 1: *(Notando a Carmelo por primera vez, y mirando su reloj.)* Perdón, pero voy a llegar tarde a—

(Y sin terminar la frase, mira otra vez a Carmelo y sale corriendo con su cubo.)

Cronista: *(Con alivio, se dirige al público.)* Espero que ésta sea la última interrupción de la tarde y, aunque se hace tarde, me gustaría contarles la historia de Car—

(El Cronista se para de repente, pues se da cuenta que Carmelo ha parado de titiritar, ha mirado a su reloj y se ha ido del escenario por la derecha.)

Cronista: ¡Vaya! Pues a lo mejor no. Si se ha ido, es una historia antigua y como soy el cronista del pueblo, mi trabajo es el de contar lo que pasa aquí, ahora mismo.

(Un grupo de gente, felizmente cantando y tocando instrumentos musicales, se oye fuera del escenario. El Cronista, sorprendido, se vuelve a ver lo que pasa. Antonio 2 entra con un bello ramo de flores, quizás trenzado en forma de corona, y Antonio 1 lleva una bandeja de pescado asado. Cada uno toma su posición a un lado diferente del escenario, felices con sus tesoros. Carmelo entra, vestido de blanco y con un pañuelo rojo al cuello, y se para en el centro del escenario. Los otros personajes, y cualquier otro actor que quiera participar en esta escena, entran por detrás de Carmelo y forman un semicírculo; Carmelo se vuelve, dándole la espalda al público, y levanta los brazos como lo hace un conductor: está dirigiendo un coro de cantantes. Los cantantes pueden ponerle música al texto que sigue, o pueden cantar una canción que les guste.)

Coro:

¡Ay, aaaayyyyyyyyyyyy!
¡A-a-a-a-a-ayyyyyyyyyyy!
¡Ay! ¡Caa-ar-arrrr-meeelo!

(Se termina la canción, Carmelo saluda, Antonio 2 le da las flores y Antonio 1 pasa la bandeja de pescado para que los cantantes coman. Todos están felices, excepto el Cronista, que está asombrado.)

Cronista: *(Bastante enfadado.)* ¡Yo soy el Cronista de este pueblo! ¿Cómo es que yo no sabía nada de esto?

Madre: *(Ocupada, comiéndose el pescado.)* Todos hemos intentado decírselo, ¿no es verdad?

(Todos asienten con la cabeza mientras se comen su pescado.)

Cronista: *(Enfadado todavía.)* ¡Vaya! Estaba bien ocupado, intentando saber porqué Carmelo lleva un abrigo largo de lana las tardes calurosas de verano. ¡Es una historia importante que hay que contar!

Antonio 1: ¡Una gran historia!

Antonio 2: ¿Y qué sabe usted del asunto?

Cronista: Pues yo . . . yo . . . yo . . . ¿Quién me va a decir algo? ¡Yo soy el Cronista, y—!

Carmelo: Yo lo informaré. Verá, a mí siempre me ha gustado la música. El único problema es que yo no sé tocar ningún instrumento musical, y canto muy mal.

Madre: ¡Pero puede armonizarlo todo! Eso es lo que hace en la plaza con su abrigo de invierno. Al principio yo no lo entendía. Pero lo hablé con su maestra, y luego con Carmelo. Todos los genios tienen costumbres extrañas cuando los visita la inspiración. Y lo que tenemos que aprender a hacer es . . .

Carmelo: ¡Coro, vamos a cantar!

(Los cantantes ponen el resto de sus pescados en la bandeja y cantan, dirigidos por Carmelo.)

Coro:

> Respeta a un genio,
> y no hagas ruido cuando trabaja.
> Cuando lo veas hacer algo
> fuera de lo ordinario,
> piensa en el drama
> que se llama
> "¡Ay, Carmelo!"
> Y este cuento
> es también bueno
> cuando de chicas se trata.

Cronista: ¡Ajem! Bueno, amigos, me habéis enseñado una lección: si uno es el Cronista de un pueblo, es una buena idea no rechazar a los que quieren darte información, y, sobre todo, ¡acércate a la persona en cuestión y *escúchalo*!

FIN

VOCABULARY–VOCABULARIO

Nouns–Nombres

cousin: *primo, prima*
inspiration: *inspiración*
seaport: *puerto de mar*
storyteller: *cuentista, narrador, cronista*
village: *pueblecito*

Adjectives–Adjetivos

cool: *fresco*
festive: *festivo, alegre*
impolite: *descortés, mal educado*
woolen: *de lana*
youthful: *juvenil, de aspecto joven*

Verbs–Verbos

to conduct: *conducir, dirigir*
to figure out: *entender, imaginar*
to listen: *escuchar*
to play an instrument: *tocar un instrumento musical*
to shiver: *titiritar, temblar*
to turn away: *rechazar, despedir, volver la cara*

Don Quijote in America

Don Quijote en América

Don Quijote

(Directions for the helmet are below.)

Use a broomstick for the pole.

A garbage can cover is perfect for the shield. Hold the side that has the handle.

Take an old baseball hat and cut off the brim.

Wear tights or tight-fitting pants. Wear a T-shirt or jersey with it.

Next, take a sheet of 8 1/2" x 11" paper. Cut the sheet as shown below.

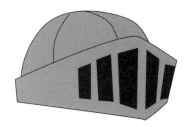

Paint blocks as shown in the directions. Using tape, attach the front piece to the baseball hat. You could also sew it to the hat.

Fold line

Cut line

Cut line

Figure 10

Don Quijote in America

A play with music for a multigenerational group

Characters

- Don Quijote de la Mancha
- Sancho Panza
- Alicia (about twelve years old)
- Jared, her brother (about fifteen)
- Dana, their sister (about eight)
- Father and/or Mother
- Efraín, a homeless man
- Boy 1 (Christopher)
- Girl 1 (Marisa)
- Girl 2 (Erica)
- Boy 2 (Papote)
- Boy 3 (Israel)
- Boy 4 (Ramón)
- Two Bag Ladies
- Animals for Central Park
- Two businessmen
- Musicians: keyboard, alto saxophone, or another instrument for Efraín

Note. This play was written for a community-based group, Teatro Latino de New London. Everyone who wished to participate had a part. That's how scene 2, with the singers and the Central Park animals, was born because we had a sizable group of children aged 5 to 7 and a number of good musicians eager to share their gifts with the community. But this scene can be cut if these conditions do not exist within the group that would like to produce this play. Other adaptations may be necessary, such as presenting the Sancho song as a recitativo or a speech if the group does not have a Broadway-style actor/singer taking the part of Sancho. For copies of the music, write to the composer or the author at 265 Gardner Avenue, New London, Connecticut 06320. Also, we had only one thirteen-year-old girl to play the part of a parent, so we combined the roles of father and mother. The original script, however, including parts for two parents, is given here.

SCENE 1

(The living room of an expensive New York apartment. There are decorative items that suggest it is the home of a Hispanic family. Before the actors appear on the stage, there is an offstage solo played on the saxophone (or whatever instrument the actor playing Efraín is able to play) and that will be repeated at the start of scene 3. Three young people sit in the living room: Alicia at the computer, Jared on a sofa, and Dana on the floor. They are trying to amuse themselves with video games and gadgets. They are bored, except Dana, who is absorbed in her crossword puzzle. Alicia is looking at a new game.)

Jared: *(Pushing his gadget away.)* I've had it! These games get more boring by the second. Who's the nerd who thinks them up? I bet you he's rich by now. Shoot!

Alicia: Whatever you want, you get. We have nice parents.

Jared: You're so smart, you make me sick!

Dana: Why do you two have to fight all the time? I can't find where the pieces belong when you get going like that.

Jared: We're not fighting. We're expressing our reality.

Alicia: Our reality? Don't get me into this!

Jared: I am getting you into this! Do you like your games?

Alicia: That's different.

Dana: I'm getting out of here!

(She picks up her puzzle and leaves.)

Jared: *(Cooly aggressive.)* I don't like my games. You don't like yours. That's our reality!

Alicia: You wanted junk games, with action, war! I wanted cultural things.

Jared: Well, you got them.

Alicia: I know it! You don't have to rub it in. It's just that . . .

Jared: Yes, I'm listening.

Alicia: I don't know why, but—I just can't relate to this stuff.

Jared: Maybe the same jerk designed all our games—yours and mine.

Alicia: Jared, leave me alone. I don't want to sit here complaining.

Jared: Complaining? Who's complaining? I'm not.

Alicia: All right.

(Silence.)

Alicia: Jared, could you do me a favor?

Jared: If it doesn't take money, work, or intelligence, yes.

Alicia: I'd like to be alone.

Jared: Alone?

Alicia: Yes. I want to think.

(Jared is surprised and a bit contemptuous. He gets up slowly.)

Jared: Think?! All right! Think big, sister. Big! Don't settle for less.

(He leaves, and his sister lets out a big sigh.)

Alicia: How can he stand himself?

(Alicia looks at the computer screen, which is on, and then at the window. The sky is purple, as it often is in the early evening in winter. A crescent moon is seen through the window. Silence.)

Alicia: Why is it that we are not happy? Why are we so lonely in the middle of so much . . .

(The door that leads into the living room from the far end of the kitchen opens, and Alicia's father [or mother] comes in. He or she is dressed in a business suit, carries a suitcase, and is affable but in a hurry.)

Father: Where is everyone? Where are the kids?

(He kisses Alicia.)

Alicia: Hi, Father! They are in their rooms.

(Father picks up one of the rejected computer games and looks at it.)

Alicia: Don't worry. Jared is very hard to please.

Father: Do you mean that he doesn't like this? But he almost drove me crazy until I got it for him!

Alicia: There is something going on . . . *(She touches her head.)* I don't know, I can't explain.

Father: *(Smiles and puts the package down. Sits next to Alicia.)* Must be his age. He's fifteen years old! I was like Jared when I was his age, too.

Alicia: Did you have games like these?

Father: Oh, no! Things were . . . quite different. For one thing, grandma didn't have much money to spend on us at first, when grandpa was financially responsible for so many family members. He was also going through medical school to become a surgeon. And then, there were no computers. But I remember at one time suddenly feeling too grown up to get the same presents as the other kids. I was a grown man [woman]!

Alicia: *(Looking at her father with love.)* It is so nice talking to you!

Father: We'll talk more some other time. I have to go now.

Alicia: But it's almost dark!

Father: I have an important meetinr. Mother [Father] will be home soon. Bye!

Alicia: *(A bit disappointed.)* I know your meeting will go well. *(More cheerfully.)* And thank you for the nice CD on Spanish Monuments.

Father: Do you like it?

Alicia: Of course! I'll tell you more about it some other time. Bye!

(Father gives Alicia a little kiss and leaves. Alicia, after a moment, picks up the disk, inserts it into the computer. She sighs, and fiddles with the keys and mouse.)

Alicia: Another cathedral! Nice, very nice. And here is the building date, the name of the architect, and I can play with this and that, and with architectural styles and names of cities and whatnot. Big deal! But I can't say this to Father. He'll be disappointed . . . Wait a minute, Alicia! Is that all you are concerned about? About disappointing Father? Grow up, Alicia! Grow up! Jared is more mature than you if that's your whole point—not to disappoint Father.

(Alicia has been moving keys and suddenly she stops and looks at the screen.)

Alicia: What's this? It's familiar, but I don't know why. A monument, but I'm glad it's not another cathedral! Two guys, dressed in weird costumes, carved in stone, standing in the middle of the street. What on earth can that teach us kids? Info: it says Madrid, Plaza de España, Don Quijote and Sancho Panza. Yeah! And I'm Alicia González, New York City, United States of America, pleased to meet you.

(She pauses. Looks at the screen again, very thoughtful.)

Alicia: If I could only figure out how to explain it, maybe my father would understand why the information they feed us, saying it's important, really feels to us like a whole bunch of nonsense. But they try, at least my father really tries . . . And Miss Harper tries, too. What if I were to think up something really neat that I could give to them as gifts? Nothing that can be bought with money—a real gift. What if I could tell my father tomorrow, "Look, this Don Quijote and I have this and this and this in common, and it's great that you are passing on to us your culture, because it is ours, too." I wish I could say that, but I don't see how. Let's see . . . where did my creativity go today? Don Quijote, if you and my great-great-great-grand uncle went to the same elementary school, speak up.

(Silence. Alicia waits and thinks.)

Alicia: No connection there. *(Sighs.)* Don Quijote, if you or Sancho had a cousin called Alicia González, send me a signal that we have something in common. *(Silence.)* Naggghhh, nothing there either. This cultural heritage thing is proving to be pretty loose. Let me see . . . . Don Quijote or Sancho—if either of you had a grandfather who was a surgeon, please come and sit next to me.

(A sudden noise scares Alicia. Don Quijote and Sancho have landed next to her, with all their equipment, and lie on the floor, bewildered. Alicia stands up, unable to speak. She looks at the screen, and then at the two men trying to straighten up from their fall on the floor.)

Don Quijote: ¿Qué es esto, Sancho? Another adventure?

Sancho: ¡Vaya! And I thought that we had earned eternal fame and rest when the tales of our deeds and misfortunes throughout Spain were published! Why do we need another adventure? Enough is enough—and even too much sometimes! ¡Ay, otra aventura!

Don Quijote: One never knows, Sancho, what el destino has in store for us. We are the sirvientes of those who need us. I think that this young señorita is in peligro.

(Alicia, moving slowly and showing that she's very afraid, stretches her body to reach a dictionary which is on a shelf.)

Alicia: Good thing that the dictionary is here. I hope I can get them to speak slower and maybe we'll understand each other a bit. *(Looking up, as if speaking to heaven.)* Mother and Father, where are you now that I need you?

Don Quijote: What did I tell you, Sancho? Not only is she in peligro, but she is bewitched as well. Get ready, porque—

(The phone rings, and Alicia rushes to pick it up, relieved. The two men retreat to a corner, afraid.)

Alicia: Hello? . . . Hi, Mom! I am so happy to hear from you . . . . All right? Yes, of course everything is all right . . . Oh, no, nothing happens here, I was just watching one of the CDs that you got me for Christmas, the one about monuments. Of course I like it . . . Yes. I'm sure. . . . You are going to be late? Father is not here. . , , Yes, we will warm up the Chinese food you left, maybe cook a pizza in the microwave. . . . Thank you, Mom. . . . I love you too.

(Alicia, a bit disappointed, hangs up the phone, and looks at the two men who are huddling in the corner, Don Quijote with his lance drawn. They look at each other, unsure of what to do. Don Quijote puts the lance down.)

Don Quijote: Señorita, please tell me what gigante has made you a prisoner, and in what bewitched castillo we are, so that we can break the spell quickly.

Alicia: *(Dictionary in hand, looking up words.)* Tú, Don Quijote. Yo, Alicia González. Pleased to meet you. ¡Hola!

Don Quijote: *(Turning to Sancho, satisfied.)* ¿Oyes, Sancho? The spell is half broken already. We understand more of what she's saying.

Sancho: *(Yawns loudly.)* I don't like this—¡no me gusta esto! But, since I am at the servicio of your highness . . .

Don Quijote: Mira, Sancho, I don't force you to follow me. If you want to return to el pueblo, just say so.

Sancho: *(He cries and takes out of his sleeve a giant handkerchief to dry his tears.)* ¿A qué pueblo? I wish it were that easy! When we were immortalized together, they condemned us to this and to much more, together, forever! I just want to know how we are going to escape this place and return to sleep to our estatuas, where we were so happy, ¡tan felices!

Alicia: *(Delighted that she is understanding.)* ¡Estatuas! ¡Mira! Tú, y tú.

(Alicia guides the two gentlemen, who are afraid of the computer, and places them in front of the screen.)

Don Quijote: ¡Qué maravilla de castillo, Sancho, aunque esté encantado! The gigante knew that we would come, and he put our portraits here, so that the señorita would recognize her saviors!

Sancho: *(Between pleased and distrustful. He looks at his portrait, then away.)* It is true that it is you and I! ¡Y elegantes! But I don't like this situation at all. It is very different from what we saw before we became famous statues.

Don Quijote: Los tiempos cambian, Sancho, pero no la vida del espíritu. Let's inspect the castle. Let's see where this window . . .

(Don Quijote approaches the window, is about to open it, and Alicia shouts for the first time. The two visitors freeze, not knowing what to do.)

Alicia: No! ¡La alarma!

(Jared shows up by the kitchen door, looks shocked.)

Jared: ¡Alicia! Are you all right? ¿Qué es esto? Why were you talking in Spanish in the first place? Our parents are not here, are they? Who are these people?

Don Quijote: I told you, Sancho. Half bewitched, half unbewitched. ¡Y aquí estamos nosotros, listos!

Alicia: *(To Jared.)* I don't know how it happened, but you must help with the Spanish. I was using the monument CD and wanted proof that I was culturally connected to something in it. And I got the proof!

Jared: *(Sighs, speaks after a while.)* We are not dreaming, so we have to deal with it. I only wish it had been my idea—it's kind of cool.

(Dana appears at the door and screams. Sancho is alarmed, but Don Quijote is expectant.)

Alicia: Dana, come here. These are friends: Don Quijote y Sancho Panza. Dana.

(Dana hides behind Alicia but looks at the visitors with curiosity. Alicia now speaks more Spanish, although with difficulty.)

Don Quijote: Another señorita under a spell! ¡Da-na!

Alicia: Yo soy Alicia, y él es Jared.

Don Quijote: Don Quijote y mi squire, Sancho. A su servicio. It is very important that we inspect the castle.

(Dana, afraid, hides behind Alicia. Alicia and Jared exchange looks, and they make a quick decision.)

Jared: *(Speaking with comic seriousness.)* Sí, of course! This way.

(Jared opens doors, while Don Quijote inspects everything carefully, his lance ready. Sancho stays behind, somewhat bored and never losing sight of his image on the computer screen, which he clearly likes. Several modern objects upset Don Quijote: water dripping from a faucet, which he opens and closes a few times with much show of emotion; a refrigerator, and any other modern gadget available. Don Quijote scratches his head, because he does not understand anything.)

Don Quijote: *(To Jared, in a confidential tone.)* Todo, everything must be examined, hijo, to discover the secret of el gigante!

Jared: *(Feigning seriousness.)* Sí, I understand.

Don Quijote: ¿Y el gigante? Where is the giant?

Alicia: *(Speaking in Spanish with difficulty.)* ¿Qué gi-gan-te?

Don Quijote: The giant who made you prisoners, and half bewitched, in this strange palace. I admit that he has imagination and great magical powers, because I've never seen anything like this!

(Don Quijote goes to the faucet again, opens it and reacts with so much fear that Jared has to run to turn it off, while Don Quijote is lost in deep thought. If there are no faucets, the action should concentrate around the refrigerator and freezer. After the objects have been examined, Jared and Alicia look at each other, unsure of what to do next.)

Alicia: *(Using mime to compensate for her imperfect Spanish.)* I am hambre. ¿Comida?

Sancho: *(Turning his attention away from the computer.)* It seemed to me that supper should be here at this time! Because I feel as much hunger as three men together! I could eat three whole cows right this minute!

(Alicia goes to the fridge, opens the freezer and takes out a pizza. Don Quijote is fascinated by the steam coming out of the freezer, and touches the ice. He takes the pizza away from Alicia's hand, and puts his inside the freezer. He takes it out immediately, shouting, at the same time that he attacks the open freezer, and then throws the pizza on the floor.)

Don Quijote: ¡Ayyyyyyyyyyy! ¡Ayuda, Sancho! I am being burnt by this frozen hell! Open that door down there! It has to be the entrance we are looking for! I'll get inside this dark window, even if it leaves me blind!

(Don Quijote, crazed, puts his head inside the freezer. At that moment, the refrigerator's motor starts, which freaks out the two visitors.)

Sancho: ¡Rápido, señor! Quick! I hear nearby the rumbling of the giant, and we still do not know where our dinner is coming from!

(Alicia takes the pizza cake and Jared, leading Sancho to one side before he opens the refrigerator door, tries with much difficulty to get Don Quijote's head out of the freezer. Don Quijote's head finally comes out and Jared closes the door.)

Jared: Ésa . . . That's not the giant's door, but where we keep our food.

(Don Quijote, exhausted, sits down on a chair. Sancho, who has heard the word food, comes forward in a friendly manner.)

Sancho: It seemed to me to be a very small door for such a powerful lord. Let's eat now, since my master is half dead from his efforts, and let's wait a little while to do the job for which we were called. It is early evening now, and full darkness is much better to undo matters of witchcraft.

Don Quijote: Ven aquí, Sancho . . . Come here. If I die in this adventure, please see to it that I get buried in a holy place, because I swear that I have seen hell, and it doesn't burn as I thought. It freezes, it freezes even one's heart.

Sancho: *(Impatient.)* Lo prometo. I promise it.

Jared: *(Recovered from such an unexpected scene, he places his arm around Alicia's.)* Alicia, you have heard that our guests are hungry. Put the pizza inside the microwave

(Alicia opens the door of the microwave, which alerts Don Quijote. He stands up, takes the pizza from Alicia, gets afraid when he realizes that it is so cold, and drops it on the floor. He picks up his lance and attacks the pizza.)

Don Quijote: Whatever it is that you are, evil and hellish thing; may you be giant's heart or body of unfortunate mortal—your destiny is to die at my hands, so that we may contemplate how frozen injustice dies, how liberty's sun illuminates!

(Don Quijote strikes the frozen dough, and tries very hard to kill something that sticks to his lance. Jared, looking at the damage being done to the floor, stops the gentleman and throws the pizza into the trash.)

Jared: ¡Bien hecho! Well done, and the thing is finished. Bad things always end up in the trash. And now, let's eat whatever we can find. *(Turning to Sancho.)* Did you say that you wanted cows for supper?

Sancho: Sí. That's what I said. Although I would be happy with sausages, bread, and sardines.

(Alicia and Jared look at each other, smiling.)

Jared: Bring the box that father keeps in the pantry for grandpa and uncle Catalino. *(To Sancho.)* En mi opinión . . . in my opinion, sardines are always better for one's stomach at this time of the night.

(Jared motions to Dana for her to help him move the table in front of Don Quijote, who is sitting on his chair, eyes half closed, exhausted. The lance is still in his hand. Sancho takes a chair and sits next to Don Quijote, quite pleased by the fact that they are going to eat. Suddenly, he notices that Dana, who has helped her brother move the table closer to the guests, is standing openmouthed, looking at him. Sancho motions for her to sit next to him on a chair, but she doesn't move, a bit afraid.)

Sancho: Da-na . . . ¿A comer?

Dana: *(Warming up a little, she sits next to Sancho.)* I don't speak Spanish, but Jared does. And Alicia, a little bit. Maybe more, I don't know. And I want to know what happened to your animals.

(Jared is helping Alicia bring a few dishes and a board on which to put a big round loaf of bread, a huge string of sausages, and sardines—either in a can or in a heap. He sees Dana talking to Sancho and approaches them to translate.)

Jared: A Dana le gustan los rompecabezas—she likes crosswords puzzles and . . .

Sancho: En ese caso, I am sure that she'll find employment with my master. Although first she must be completely free of the spell she's under, because my master doesn't like people talking to him in Arabic or in any other language that reminds him of magic spells.

Jared: Dana quiere saber . . . she wants to know what you people did with your animals. She likes to put things in order, and there in the . . .

(Jared points at the computer, where the picture of the two men is still on the screen. Sancho, who had forgotten the statues, gets up, approaches the screen, and starts weeping.)

Sancho: ¡Mi pobre rucio! My poor donkey! Here I am, warm and about to eat my supper, while you are there alone, quite alone, and very hungry—I am sure of that.

Jared: The donkey is not hungry. Can't you see that it's a statue? Come on, eat. It's getting late.

Sancho: If my donkey is a statue, ¿por qué estoy yo aquí? I didn't ask to be drawn into another adventure!

(Sancho, saddened, returns to his place at the table. Dana is also sad, and places her hand on the man's shoulders to make him feel better.)

Dana: *(Giving him some bread.)* Eat. It's good.

Alicia: *(Sitting between Don Quijote and Sancho. She speaks Spanish well, but hesitantly.)* Lo siento. I am sorry. It was I who called you and created this mess. I hope that you like your dinner! ¡Espero que les guste la cena!

(Alicia shares the food with the two men. Sancho has almost forgotten his sadness and starts eating with appetite. Don Quijote, who has been lost in his thoughts and is a little sleepy, wakes up and joins in the conversation. He eats very little, daintily.)

Don Quijote: No me molesta . . . I am not bothered that you woke us up, and this dinner is very good. And now that we can rest, please tell us your story, beautiful damsel. Tell us how it happened that you were made a prisoner, and any other matters of importance.

(Alicia and Jared look at each other. Dana is delighted with Sancho, who eats, having forgotten about his donkey.)

Jared: If you want, we can go outside for a walk after dinner.

Don Quijote: ¡Pasear por los alrededores del castillo, en triunfo! To take a walk around the castle, in triumph!

Sancho: *(As if talking to himself.)* I hope that we won't find more aventuras.

Alicia: ¿Perdón? Excuse me?

Sancho: Oh, no, nada, estaba cantando. I was just singing. To eat and to sing, to sing and to eat is what I like best.

Jared: The surroundings of this . . . castillo are very different from the ones that you have seen in your other adventures.

Don Quijote: ¡Bueno, bueno! Come on! You shouldn't be too sure. I've seen a lot, and more than that.

Alicia: Jared is right. Are you ready to see something completely new?

(Sancho drops his food.)

Sancho: ¡Para qué! Why? Why so much novelty?

Alicia: *(Ignoring Sancho, who is quite irritated.)* Otherwise, you won't be able to understand why I called you, why I woke you up from your dream . . . I cannot explain with words, and now I feel guilty.

Jared: Don't feel guilty, Alicia! To start a conversation, a dialogue with others means to wake them up from their dream to bring them into ours, into our enchanted castle. That's why I was so bored with the videos about war and all that stuff . . . because I was not sharing my dreams with anyone. You have taught me that.

(Alicia and Jared embrace. Don Quijote is in a conciliatory mood.)

Don Quijote: Iremos, Alicia, iremos. We'll go, Alicia. As soon as Sancho finishes his food, because I have finished eating. It is good to share dreams, very good. That's why I went out into the world, although at times I doubt whether I did things well.

Sancho: ¡Por eso es por lo que me fastidia que nos despierten! That's why I don't like people to wake us up, just in case you plan again more trips along the roads of Spain.

Jared: No se preocupe . . . don't worry, because we are not in Spain.

Don Qujiote y Sancho: ¡Que no estamos en España!? We are not in Spain? Where then?

Alicia: En América. And I feel so guilty!

(Silence. The two visitors digest the news, each in a different way: Don Quijote is delighted, while Sancho feels more mistrust.)

Don Qujiote: ¡América! At the other end of the ocean! Is that why this castle is so different from the other castles? Or is this really a castle? I wonder whether it is under a spell! Were you really in danger? I understand now . . . *(Somewhat irritated, addressing Alicia.)* Why did you call me?

Alicia: ¡Lo siento! I am sorry! I should not—

Jared: Un momento. Just one moment! This gentleman wants to know why you called him, and there is a reason. Let's take that walk!

Don Quijote: Sí, vamos. Let's go. I never refuse to hear whoever needs to explain a request for my services.

(They all get up from the table. Don Quijote is about to pick up his lance, which Jared tries to prevent. But Don Quijote insists, and Jared goes along. Sancho also gets up, very sorrowful. Before going out, he stops by the computer screen.)

Sancho: Adiós, my donkey. If this is the last time we see each other, I want you to know that my last thought will be of how warm I was riding on your back.

(He wipes a tear with a huge handkerchief, and exits after the others, dejected.)

SCENE 2

(Central Park. There are two benches, one at each side of the stage, leaving a space in the middle. The first bag lady enters stage right, sits down slowly on the bench. She picks up a newspaper someone has left there and opens it.)

Bag Lady 1: Huh? What's this? *Wall Street Journal.* Great! Gimme a chance to check on my investments. Well, anyhow—make a blanket for tonight.

(She continues looking at it, while Erica enters stage left with a schoolbag or a skateboard. She sits down on the other bench, bored. A second bag lady enters stage right and sits down next to the first bag lady.)

Bag Lady 2: Anything new?

(Bag Lady 1, with contempt, turns her back on the newcomer, and starts rummaging in her bag, looking for something. This is what the two bag ladies will do when not singing: they open and fold old newspapers, arrange pencils, pick up useable objects from the ground, etc. Efraín enters stage left with a musical instrument, hopefully a saxophone, in its case, which he puts on the ground. Efraín nods at the two bag ladies, sits next to Erica, who pats him on the hand as a form of greeting. Efrain's expression and movements suggest that he is at peace. The two bag ladies start singing the song "So many animals!" The animals get ready to come on stage and take their places, in character. It is important to remind the young actors to make the sounds and movements that the animals they portray would make, for example, bark, look for food in a trash can, sleep, and so forth. All animals come on stage from stage left, in this order: two cats, two mice, a dog, two pigeons.)

Bag Lady 1:

Have you ever thought of the kinds
Of wild animals that live in New York?

Bag Lady 2:

Of course!
The cats and the mice,
The dogs and the pigeons
Live here.
Of course!

(The animals enter at this moment, and the singing stops until the animals do their mime and take their places.)

Bag Lady 1:

Besides, did you know that there is
A pair of hawks in their nest
On a roof in Park Avenue?

(The hawks enter, moving in a circle around Efraín and Erica, and scare the pigeons before leaving stage right.)

Bag ladies, Erica, and Efraín:

What are these doing,
And so many more!—
Around here?

They are looking for food,
And a place to rest,
And, each one in his own way,
For love.
Ahhhhhh!
But let's not forget that these animals
Are intelligent
And carefully avoid

(Two businessmen enter stage left, in such a hurry that they almost step on the two cats, and leave stage right.)

The two-legged giants
Who go by in a hurry,
Looking for food,
And a place to rest,
And, each in his own way,
For love, love, love.

(The two bag ladies wave good-bye to Efraín and exit. Efraín starts getting his instrument ready to play. As if they were in another part of Central Park, Alicia and Dana, followed by Don Quijote and Jared, and by Sancho, who barely avoids bumping into things as he observes his surroundings with awe, cross the front of the stage, from left to right. At this moment, the two businessmen appear again, start to cross the stage from right to left, and stop in the middle, looking at the five friends in amazement. The five friends go off, stage right.)

Businessman 1: Hey, look at that—*The Man of La Mancha!*

Businessman 2: I didn't know the play was on Broadway again! But why would they want to go out into the streets with their costumes? Actors don't do that!

Businessman 1: You're right. Some loony dressed up for a kick. Hey, it's not Halloween!

(Laughing, the two men go off, stage left.)

SCENE 3

(Efraín has been getting ready to play his instrument. The children who habitually come to visit Efraín arrive, making lots of noise. They sit on the bench, which is on stage left, and on the floor. The children are very happy to be together, as if they were a family. When they have taken their places, Efraín starts playing. The children are in complete silence, delighted. When the music ends, they applaud with much enthusiasm.)

Christopher: ¡Chévere, Efraín, chévere! That's great!

Marisa: When are you going to teach us to play, Efraín?

Efraín: The day in which the moon dresses herself in silk and comes down from the sky to bring us tiny pineapple cakes on a tray of gold and emeralds, that same day I'll teach you kids my first saxophone lesson.

Erica: Efraín, you'll drive us crazy before you teach us anything! Last week you told us that you would teach us to play on the day in which all the cars parked around turned into white, blue, and pink butterflies!

Efraín: *(Laughing quietly.)* Did I say that? Está bonito; if I really said that, it is very nice!

Papote: What happens is that you don't want to teach us anything.

Erica: Tiene razón. He's right! And what would happen if the cars turn into green butterflies? What would you say then?

Efraín: Buena pregunta, sí. Good questions! In that case, I would think about it.

Israel: And what if, instead of turning into butterflies, they become clowns? You do not want to teach us anything! You want everything for yourself, for yourself, for yourself!

(Efraín runs toward Israel, who hides behind a bench or a tree. Efraín grabs him by an ear. They pretend to be fighting, while the other kids laugh.)

Erica: ¡Te atrapó! He caught you! That happened because you insulted the great Efraín.

Israel: *(Pretending to be repentant.)* I won't do it anymore, I swear!

Efraín: In that case, I'll leave you alone. If you repent forever, of course.

Israel: I swear it! I won't do it ever again, never, never!

(The other children laugh.)

Ramón: *(Pretending to consult a watch on his bare wrist, very seriously.)* He'll do it again in five minutes.

(More laughter.)

Efraín: Kids, since you have been so good today, I'll teach you something very special. I'm going to play the musical phrase that puts us in direct communication with heaven, with eternity. There is only one, and only the great Efraín knows it.

(Efraín plays a long musical phrase on his saxophone. The children, very serious, look at the sky. The five friends enter the stage at this moment, and stop, delighted.)

Don Quijote: *(Approaching Efraín and the children.)* Oh, God! What a calm and worthy congregation you place before my tired eyes! Tell me, who are you? Are you on a pilgrimage to any church or shrine? Or are you those in need of help, and in search of whom I travel to the four corners of the earth?

Sancho: *(To Don Quijote's right, touches his arm, in the hope that he'll stop talking.)* Look, my lord, we have eaten already and do not need to do any more work today. It's bad for my digestion. It seems to me that these good people are here enjoying the weather and do not need anything from anyone.

(The children who surround Efraín giggle, wink at each other, amused by the visitors' appearance. Alicia and her brothers remain near the bench and glance at each other, but say nothing.)

Don Quijote: *(Gives Sancho a look full of sorrow.)* ¡Ay, Sancho! ¡Sancho, Sancho! Your lack of generosity saddens me. Have we come this far to be unworthy of our good reputation? *(Sancho lowers his head, feeling burdened and ashamed. The children, who have been listening, take advantage of the silence to continue joking and laughing.)*

Israel: *(Stands up, behaving like a wise guy.)* ¿Cena? Did anyone mention dinner? I would give a night like this one—many nights like this one!—for a good supper.

Efraín: I was hoping to hear that from you, ungrateful! The great Efraín shows you the road to eternity with his saxophone tonight, and the best thing that you have to say is that you would exchange this night for a good supper. Bah!

Erica: Wouldn't you, Efraín?

(Everyone laughs: Efraín, Alicia, Jared, and the children, but not Don Quijote and Sancho. Dana, very close to Alicia, looks at everything with fear. Jared and Dana sit down on a bench.)

Alicia: *(Between Efraín and Don Quijote, center stage.)* These are my friends, Efraín. You have already met Jared and Dana.

Efraín: Heyyyyyy! Alicia, how you doing? Nice friends you got there.

Alicia: *(Pretending to be upset.)* I decide to speak Spanish on my own for once, and then you respond in English.

Efraín: *(Pretending to be very serious.)* That's because I am suspicious of generosity in a Yankee. You want something in return.

(The children, Alicia, and Jared laugh.)

Alicia: How do you know that?

Efraín: Because life has taught me that a truly generous spirit is a thing of the past. Today, hoy en día, you are nice to the person who can give you something or who may do you harm. That's why I want nada de nada.

Alicia: *(Thinks for a second.)* I agree with you this time, Efraín.

Efraín: *(Truly surprised.)* You do?

Alicia: Yes. *(Looking at Don Quijote.)* I came to show you a truly generous spirit from the past.

Efraín: *(Looking at the two visitors, amused.)* Are they actors?

Sancho: *(Smiling at his own wisdom.)* Mi no inglés.

(Don Quijote looks at Sancho and falls backward. In the original script, which is bilingual, it is here that Sancho begins speaking English, and Don Quijote thinks that Sancho is abandoning him. Don Quijote is very sad, while the others look on, not knowing what to do.)

Don Quijote: ¡Tú también me abandonas, Sancho! You also abandon me, Sancho! ¡Tú también te dejas encantar! You also allow yourself to be bewitched!

Sancho: ¡Nadie está encantado aquí, vuestra merced! No one is bewitched here! Stop talking nonsense. They have already told us that we are in America. And, as we say in my hometown, when in Rome, do as the Romans do.

Efraín: *(Touched by Don Quijote's sadness, he helps the man stand up.)* Es el gigante, the giant, who devours everything. Nothing and nobody remains untouched for long.

(Sancho, noticing that Efraín seems to agree with his master, shakes his head and sits down on a bench. He tries, with movements of his hands, to get Efraín to stop talking, but without success.)

Don Quijote: *(Getting excited as he stands up.)* ¡Así que hay un gigante! So, there is a giant!

Efraín: Y grande, huge! *(Opens his arms very wide.)* Do you see this man? *(He points at himself.)* This man has been devoured by the giant.

Christopher: *(Looking very sad.)* Efraín, don't talk that way. It makes us sad.

Erica: *(Almost shouting.)* Don't speak that way anymore, Efraín! ¡Nooooo!

(The other children cover their ears with their hands, to express agreement with their friends.)

Don Quijote: *(Ignoring the children, approaching Efraín in great excitement.)* ¡Lo derrotamos! We'll defeat him! Together, this time, we'll defeat him, forever! *(He kneels, looking up to heaven, as if praying.)* Thank you, Lord, for bringing me to the place where the spirit which continues the work that I started lives; the spirit which continues fighting against injustice, helping those who cannot defend themselves.

Efraín: ¡Ajajá! I used to think that way when I was young. And look where it has landed me!

Papote: Efraín, you still think that way; at least, that's what you said the other day!

Efraín: *(In a good mood, pointing at Papote.)* Do you believe everything that the great Efraín says, eh? Well, careful, or you'll end up like him, sleeping in Central Park.

Alicia: I'm also sad when you speak that way, Efraín. But I know that you speak the truth, and that's why I like listening to you.

Efraín: Mira, mira, ¡cuánto español de un tirón! Listen to her, speaking lots and lots of Spanish! Kids, a round of applause for Alicia!

(The children applaud, laugh, wink, push each other playfully . . . Sancho and Jared also laugh. Don Quijote is surprised by the wisdom revealed in Alicia's words.)

Don Quijote: ¡Por eso me gusta escucharte! Alicia, how is it that I didn't realize it before? That's why you called me. You are the other spirit that—

(Sancho stands up, very determined to stop his master.)

Sancho: Todo eso del espíritu está muy bien—that business about the spirit is fine, my lord, and we have heard it before. But it seems to me that these kids need more happiness, and I would like to sing them a song.

Efraín: ¡Adelante! Go ahead! Stand here, which is where the flower blossoms and the star shines!

(Efraín offers Sancho his place centerstage, which the other occupies with much happiness.)

Sancho: La canción, the song is called "My belly comes first."

(Don Quijote is horrified, kneels with his lance in his hand, while the children laugh and applaud Sancho.)

> Oh, I'm loyal to my master,
> However strange his ways.
> I keep my place beside him
> Through all his dangerous days.
> Ah, but when he raves of justice
> In some exalted phrase,
> Then I know that my belly comes first.
> Oh, I comb old Rocinante,
> Make sure he's warm at night,
> And whisper to him calmly
> To help him conquer fright.
> Ah, but when our Don Quijote
> Pulls out his sword to fight,
> Then I know that my belly comes first,
> Last and always!
> I know that my belly comes first!
> Mi amo me prometió que sería
> De una ínsula gobernador.
> ¡Sí, yo, Sancho, gobernador!
> Pero nunca soñé
> Que yo vendría de viaje
> A Nueva York.
> Pero nunca soñé
> Que yo vendría de viaje
> A Nueva York.
> So, I dare to sing en inglés,
> Perhaps not very well.
> I've learned to listen closely,
> Though I can scarcely spell.
> Oh, but all I see around me
> Rings out like some great bell
> What I know—yes, my belly comes first!
> ¡Sí, primero! ¡Yo sé que mi panza
> Comes first!

(They all enjoy the song, except Don Quijote and Efraín. There is lots of applause, laughter, noise. Sancho takes a bow.)

Israel: *(Stands up and imitates Sancho, in an irreverent way.)* "My belly comes first!" I already said that. Everything has been said already, and Efraín became very angry. The grownups sometimes don't know what they want. That's why one can go nuts if one pays attention to them!

(Israel sits down. Sancho looks at him in silence until the boy lowers his eyes, smiles, and sits down on the other bench.)

Marisa: *(To Sancho.)* We can also sing.

Efraín: *(Slowly, to the girl.)* Sí, cantas bien. Yes, you sing very well, Marisa. *(To Israel, in a very serious tone.)* And you, Israel, you are right. We grownups sometimes do not know what we want. Or whatever it is that we want is impossible, a dream. Only a dream. Sólo un sueño.

(Don Quijote, his lance drawn and crazed, stands in front of Efraín, who is back again on center stage.)

Don Quijote: ¡No hay tal cosa, vive Dios, que lleve el nombre de sueño con propiedad! There is no such thing that properly bears the name of dream! Because if a man wants to have freedom as his doctrine, let him have it! If he craves the open road and the starry sky as his only refuge and roof, let him have it! And if bread alone is not enough to sustain him, allow his mouth to drink sun, to eat laughter, to sing justice, allow him to name things by their own name, and not by what others want them to be called. If a man throws away the yoke of selfishness and fear which has been sown all through the earth, let that man live, bless him! Because it is not a dream to wish to live life fully, nor stupidity to dare to fight the giants for it.

(There is a great silence. Efraín nods, somewhat sad, while Alicia looks at her hands, then at Don Quijote and back at her hands, not knowing what to do or say. The others' silence infuriates Don Quijote, who starts charging at the space around him; the others retreat to protect themselves.)

Don Quijote: *(To Efraín.)* Where is the giant who devoured you? *(To everyone.)* Where are all the giants, so that I may finish them all for once, so that peace and justice may rule throughout the earth?

(Don Quijote continues moving his lance for a few moments more, then stops, exhausted.)

Efraín: Do not tire yourself out. The giant exists, but he cannot be seen. He is everywhere, and nowhere. He cannot be defeated that way. Many have tried it.

(Don Quijote lowers his lance, defeated. The children laugh now louder than ever, pushing each other, etc. Sancho sighs, changing his position on the bench, ill at ease.)

Don Quijote: *(Looking around, disillusioned.)* Silence. And, if not silence, ridicule.

(The children stop what they were doing, fall silent. Everyone looks at Don Quijote. Efraín defends the children, who really understand Don Quijote.)

Efraín: Silence, yes, but not ridicule. The kids laugh when they don't know what to say, but they are not mocking you.

(The kids nod in silence. Some of them look at Efraín, others have their eyes lowered.)

Don Quijote: And who will teach them to say what needs to be said, to find one's way, and not to abandon it when everything seems lost?

Alicia: That's why I called you, señor Don Quijote.

Don Quijote: ¡Ay, Alicia! I feel old, very old. *(He points at the children whom he believed were making fun of him.)* Besides, I remember that one day, many years ago, I confessed to having failed.

Alicia: How can you speak of having failed if, when I called you, you came? You wanted to save me from danger, and you managed to do it. *(She opens her arms very wide, the same way Efraín opened them before.)* I felt so alone in this city, which is so full of people, that I was about to be . . . *(Smiles, winks an aye at Efraín.)* devoured by the giant!

Efraín: Not if the great Efraín can prevent it.

(Alicia and Efraín shake hands with great force, until they hurt. The kids laugh, relieved. The solemn moment has passed. They start joking again.)

Erica: Alicia, Alicia! I am going to ask a question I always wanted to ask: why do you come to visit us when we are poor and you are rich?

Papote: Don't ask that!

Marisa: ¿Pero no la has oído? Haven't you heard what she said? She comes because she's not lonely with us. For the same reason that you and I come here.

Papote: One doesn't ask those questions, Erica.

Alicia: Of course it can be asked. Marisa is right. I come here because I am not lonely with you and Efraín.

Don Quijote: ¡Ahhhhhhhh! Ahora entiendo. I understand now. You called me to know whether it is possible to become old and not to lose one's heart. To see whether it is possible to go out into the world with a beautiful dream and not have to see it smashed when it meets reality.

(Alicia nods. Jared takes her hand. Dana has fallen asleep, her head on Jared's shoulder.)

Efraín: *(Having a good time.)* So, after all, there is a dream.

Don Quijote: *(Smiling.)* Yes, there is a dream. And I have just understood what needs to be done to keep it forever: to really want to speak with someone, to speak truly, it doesn't matter with whom. Alicia has taught me that. Thank you for waking me up, Alicia. I won't go back to sleep anymore.

Sancho: *(Alarmed.)* ¡Ay de mí! Poor me! There is no end to adventures now.

Don Quijote: Don't worry, Sancho, because we return to our statues not to sleep, but to wait to hear the voice of a child who, somewhere, needs to understand, needs to feel without being afraid, a child who needs to be with someone.

Sancho: Bueno, after all, that doesn't seem to be a bad fate—especially if we can sit on our animals once in a while to rest.

Efraín: Buena casa, sus caballos. Yes, a good home. I also need a home, to be warm for many, many years, and where I can invite all my friends to a good supper once in a while.

(The children stand up and embrace Efraín, all speaking at the same time. While the children embrace Efraín, the two bag ladies appear, from stage left, and join the scene.)

Christopher: Will I be the one to be invited to your house first?

Erica: Efraín, invite me!

Marisa: ¡No! ¡A mí, a mí! No, invite me!

Erica: I'll make you a bunch of paper flowers to decorate it!

Ramón: And I'll bring you the arroz con gandules my mother makes. You'll see!

Papote: ¡Va a ser la mejor casa, tu casa! You house is going to be the best of all homes!

Efraín: *(Laughing.)* For all, or for none!

All the children: For all, for all!

(The visitors look at them, smile, and stand up, walking away from Efraín and the children. Jared rouses Dana, who wakes up slowly. She starts walking away, holding her brother's hand. Alicia and Don Quijote walk first.)

Don Quijote: It's time to go. The work for which you called me, Alicia, is fi-ni-to: we have conquered the giant! You have to go home, and Sancho and I will return to our statues.

Sancho: *(Skeptical, although he also feels happy.)* That's if we know how.

Don Quijote: Don't doubt any more, Sancho. The past is the past.

(Efraín and the children realize that the others are getting ready to leave.)

Efraín: Until soon, my friends. While you walk home, the children will sing you a song, so that you find your way back.

Don Quijote: *(Very slowly, smiling.)* Until soon, amigos!

Sancho: *(Trying very hard to find the correct words in English.)* We . . . have to leave you now. But . . . we . . . shall be with you . . . always. Siempre. Siempre.

(The children and the bag ladies sing "El mejor adiós" ("The Best Good-bye") all standing around Efraín. The five friends raise their hands, wave good-bye, and leave.)

Singers:

When you come to see me,
When you come here,
I put aside what I'm doing
In order to run toward you.

Amiguito, do not go away,
Amiguito, stay!
Otherwise, there will be no one
To be happy with me.
Otherwise, there will be no one
To keep me company.
There are thousands of games
That I love to play.
There are clouds in the sky
That I love to watch.
But I know that a great friend
Is not easy to find.
Amiguito, when you arrive
I give you a beautiful welcome,
And when you leave
I'll give you the best good-bye
So that you'll return another day.
The best of good-byes
I keep within my heart
For you.

SCENE 4

(A little bit later, back in the apartment, Dana, Jared, and Alicia sit in front of the computer, their eyes glued to the screen, and they look very sad.)

Dana: I can't believe they're gone!

Jared: It was kind of neat to meet them in person. I wonder how . . . But never mind.

Alicia: Jared, I would like to speak en español, siempre.

Jared: *(Points at the computer screen.)* To talk con ellos?

Alicia: ¡Claro! *(Alicia and Jared smile.)* At least we know now that we can identify with something from our parent's heritage, don't we?

Dana: I don't always understand everything you say. Will you teach me Spanish?

(Mother enters, looking tired. She takes off her jacket.)

Madre: Hi, kids. Did you have supper?

Dana: Mama, will you teach me Spanish? We—Alicia and Jared and—

Madre: And who?

Dana: And those two guys who are in the CD that you gave Alicia for Christmas . . .

(Alicia and Jared look at each other, smile a bit, waiting to see what Dana will say and what they will have to explain. Mother looks at the computer, smiles, nods, and goes to the kitchen as Dana follows.)

Dana: They also speak Spanish, and I would like to know what they say.

Mother: Of course, honey. I'll ask Father to speak more Spanish at home. He speaks better Spanish than I do. Will you help me with the laundry, Dana?

Dana: Yes, Mama. And while we are doing the laundry, will you tell me all you know about those guys and whether you can get me a puzzle—

(Mother and Dana go inside the house. Alicia and Jared look after them and breathe with relief.)

Alicia: Wow! I thought she was going to tell the whole thing.

Jared: She will. The question is whether we will have to explain. And, why not? At least Father will love it.

Alicia: But how do we explain such a thing?

Jared: They were here! They were. I know it. We know it.

Alicia: *(Smiles, nods.)* Father will understand.

(They keep looking at the computer screen with Don Quijote and Sancho on it.)

THE END

Don Quijote en América

Una obra de teatro bilingüe, con música

Personajes

- Don Quijote de la Mancha
- Sancho Panza
- Alicia, de 12 años de edad
- Jared, su hermano, de 15
- Dana, la hermana menor, de 8
- Padre y/o Madre
- Efraín, vagabundo
- Niño 1 (Christopher)
- Niña 1 (Marisa)
- Niña 2 (Erica)
- Niño 2 (Papote)
- Niño 3 (Israel)
- Niño 4 (Ramón)
- Dos mujeres vagabundas
- Animales
- Instrumentos musicales: keyboard; saxofón alto u otro instrumento para Efraín

> Nota: Esta obra se escribió para un grupo de teatro de la comunidad, Teatro Latino de New London. A todos los interesados en trabajar fuerte y en mostrar sus destrezas se les ofreció la oportunidad de hacerlo, y así es como nació la escena 2, en que un grupo de niños hicieron de animales. Si no se tienen niños ni músicos entrenados, hay modificaciones que se le puede hacer a la obra para que sea asequible a cualquier grupo que trabaje con seriedad pero no tenga los artistas con los que nosotros trabajamos. Por ejemplo, la escena 2 se puede cortar completamente; la canción de Sancho se puede recitar, y Madre y Padre pueden ser representados por la misma persona, haciendo los cambios necesarios al texto. Doy las instrucciones en español y en inglés para mantener la atmósfera bilingüe de la obra, y ayudar a mantener a los actores pensando en los dos idiomas.

ESCENA 1

(The living room of an expensive New York apartment. There are decorative items that suggest it is the home of a Hispanic family. Before the actors appear on the stage, there is an offstage solo played on the saxophone (or whatever instrument the actor playing Efraín is able to play) and that will be repeated at the start of scene 3. Three young people sit in the living room: Alicia at the computer, Jared on a sofa, and Dana on the floor. They are trying to amuse themselves with

video games and gadgets. They are bored, except Dana, who is absorbed in her crossword puzzle. Alicia is looking at a new game.)

Jared: I've had it! These games get more boring by the second. Who's the nerd who thinks them up? I bet you he's rich by now. Shoot!

Alicia: Whatever you want, you get. We have nice parents.

Jared: You're so smart, you make me sick!

Dana: Why do you two have to fight all the time? I can't find where the pieces belong when you get going like that.

Jared: We're not fighting. We're expressing our reality.

Alicia: Our reality! Don't get me into this!

Jared: I am getting you into this! Do you like your games?

Alicia: That's different.

Dana: I'm getting out of here!

(Picks up her puzzle and leaves.)

Jared: *(Cooly aggressive.)* I don't like my games. You don't like yours. That's our reality!

Alicia: You wanted junk games, with action, war! I wanted cultural things.

Jared: Well, you got them.

Alicia: I know it! You don't have to rub it in. It's just that . . .

Jared: Yes, I'm listening.

Alicia: I don't know why, but— I just can't relate to this stuff.

Jared. Maybe the same jerk designed all our games: yours and mine.

Alicia: Jared, leave me alone. I don't want to sit here complaining.

Jared: Complaining? Who's complaining? I'm not.

Alicia: All right.

(Silence.)

Alicia: Jared, could you do me a favor?

Jared: If it doesn't take money, work or intelligence, yes.

Alicia: I'd like to be alone.

Jared: Alone?

Alicia: Yes. I want to think.

(Jared is surprised and a bit contemptuous. He gets up slowly.)

Jared: Think?! All right! Think big, sister. Big! Don't settle for less.

(He leaves, and his sister lets out a big sigh.)

Alicia: How can he stand himself?

(Alicia looks at the computer screen, which is on, and then at the window. The sky is purple, as it often is in the early evening in winter. A crescent moon is seen through the window. Silence.)

Alicia: Why is it that we are not happy? Why are we so lonely in the middle of so much . . .

(The door that leads into the living room from the far end of the kitchen opens, and Alicia's father (or mother) comes in. He or she is dressed in a business suit, carries a suitcase, and is affable but in a hurry.)

Father: Where is everyone? ¿Dónde están los niños?

(He kisses Alicia.)

Alicia: Hi, Father! They are in their rooms.

(Father picks up one of the rejected computer games and looks at it.)

Alicia: Don't worry. Jared is very hard to please.

Father: Do you mean that he doesn't like this? But he almost drove me crazy until I got it for him!

Alicia: There is something going on . . . *(She touches her head.)* I don't know, I can't explain.

Father: *(Smiles and puts the package down. Sits next to Alicia.)* Must be his age. ¡Tiene quince años! I was like Jared when I was his age, too.

Alicia: Did you have games like these?

Father: Oh, no! Things were . . . quite different. For one thing, grandma didn't have much money to spend on us at first, when grandpa was financially responsible for so many family members. He was also going through medical school to become a surgeon. And then, there were no computers. But I remember at one time suddenly feeling too grown up to get the same presents as the other kids. ¡Yo era todo un hombre [una mujer]!

Alicia: *(Looking at her father with love.)* It is so nice talking to you!

Father: We'll talk more some other time. I have to go now.

Alicia: But it's almost dark!

Father: I have an important meeting. Mother will be home soon. ¡Hasta luego!

Alicia: *(A bit disappointed.)* I know your meeting will go well. *(More cheerfully.)* And thank you for the nice CD on Spanish Monuments.

Father: ¿Te gusta?

Alicia: ¡Mucho! I'll tell you more about it some other time. ¡Adiós!

(Father gives Alicia a little kiss and leaves. Alicia, after a moment, picks up the disk and inserts it into the computer. She sighs and fiddles with the keys and mouse.)

Alicia: Another cathedral! Nice, very nice. And here is the building date, the name of the architect, and I can play with this and that, and with architectural styles and names of cities and whatnot. Big deal! But I can't say this to my father. He'll be disappointed . . . Wait a minute, Alicia! Is that all you are concerned about? About disappointing Father? Grow up, Alicia! Grow up! Jared is more mature than you if that's your whole point—not to disappoint Father.

(Alicia has been moving keys and suddenly she stops and looks at the screen.)

> **Alicia:** What's this? It's familiar, but I don't know why. A monument, but I'm glad it's not another cathedral! Two guys, dressed in weird costumes, carved in stone, standing in the middle of the street. What on earth can that teach us kids? Info: it says Madrid, Plaza de España, Don Quijote y Sancho Panza. Yeah! And I'm Alicia González, New York City, United States of America, pleased to meet you.

(She pauses. Looks at the screen again, looks very thoughtful.)

> **Alicia:** If I could only figure out how to explain it, maybe my father would understand why the information they feed us, saying it's so important, really feels to us like a whole bunch of nonsense. But they try, at least my father really tries . . . And Miss Harper tries too. What if I were to think up something really neat that I could give to them as gifts? Nothing that can be bought with money—a real gift. What if I could tell my father tomorrow, "Look, this Don Quijote and I have this and this and this in common, and it's great that you are passing on to us your culture, because it is ours, too." I wish I could say that, but I don't see how. Let's see . . . where did my creativity go today? Don Quijote, if you and my great-great-great-grand uncle went to the same elementary school, speak up.

(Silence.)

> **Alicia:** No connection there. *(Sighs.)* Don Quijote, if you or Sancho had a cousin called Alicia González, send me a signal that we have something in common. *(Silence.)* Naggghhh, nothing there either. This cultural heritage is proving to be pretty loose. Let me see . . . . Don Quijote or Sancho—if either of you had a grandfather who was a surgeon, please come and sit next to me.

(A sudden noise scares Alicia. Don Quijote and Sancho have landed next to her, with all their equipment, and lie on the floor, bewildered. Alicia stands up, unable to speak. She looks at the screen, and then at the two men trying to straighten up from their fall on the floor.)

> **Don Quijote:** ¿Qué es esto, Sancho? ¿Otra aventura?

> **Sancho:** ¡Vaya! ¡Y yo que pensaba que me había ganado la fama y el descanso eternos cuando se publicaron nuestras dichas y desdichas por España! ¿Para qué necesitamos otra aventura? Bastante es bastante, y hasta demasiado a veces. Pues sí señor, ¡otra aventura!

> **Don Quijote:** Uno nunca sabe, Sancho, lo que el destino nos tiene guardado. Somos servidores de los que nos necesitan. Para mí, que esta doncella está en peligro.

(Alicia, moving slowly and showing that she's very afraid, stretches her body to reach a dictionary which is on a shelf.)

Alicia: Good thing that the dictionary is here. I hope that I can get them to speak slower and maybe we'll understand each other a bit. *(Looking up, as if speaking to heaven.)* Mother and Father, where are you now that I need you?

Don Quijote: ¿Qué te dije, Sancho? No está solamente en peligro, sino encantada. Prepárate, que—

(The phone rings, and Alicia rushes to pick it up, relieved. The two men retreat to a corner, afraid.)

Alicia: Hello? . . . Hi, Mother! I am so happy to hear from you. . . . All right? Yes, of course everything is all right. . . Oh, no, nothing happens here, I was just watching one of the CDs that you got me for Christmas, the one about monuments. Of course I like it . . . Yes I'm sure. . . . You are going to be late? Father is not here. . . . Yes, we will warm up the Chinese food you left, maybe cook a pizza in the microwave. . . . Thank you, Mother. . . . I love you too.

(Alicia, a bit disappointed, hangs up the phone, and looks at the two men who are huddling in the corner, Don Quijote with his lance drawn. They look at each other, unsure of what to do. Don Quijote puts the lance down.)

Don Quijote: Doncella, decidnos de qué gigante sois prisionera, y en qué castillo encantado estamos, que deshagamos cuanto antes el encanto.

Alicia: *(Dictionary in hand, looking up words.)* Tú, don Quijote. Yo, Alicia González. Pleased to meet you. ¡Hola!

Don Quijote: *(Volviéndose a Sancho, satisfecho.)* ¿Oyes, Sancho? El encanto está medio deshecho ya. Vamos entendiendo algo.

Sancho: *(Bostezando.)* A mí no me gusta esto, pero como estoy al servicio de su merced . . .

Don Quijote: Mira, Sancho, que yo no te fuerzo a que me sigas. Si quieres volver al pueblo, no tienes más que decirlo.

Sancho: *(Llorando, saca un pañuelo enorme para secarse las lágrimas.)* ¿A qué pueblo? ¡Ojalá fuera tan fácil! Cuando nos inmortalizaron juntos, nos condenaron a esto y Dios sabe a qué más, juntos para siempre. A ver cómo salimos de este sitio y nos volvemos a dormir en nuestras estatuas, que tan bien estábamos.

Alicia: *(Delighted that she is understanding.)* ¡Estatuas! ¡Mira! Tú, y tú.

(Alicia takes the two men, who are afraid of the computer, and places them in front of the screen.)

Don Quijote: ¡Qué maravilla de castillo, Sancho, aunque esté encantado! El gigante sabía que vendríamos, y ¡puso nuestras figuras aquí para que la doncella reconociera a sus salvadores!

Sancho: *(Vanidoso, pero receloso. Mira a su imagen, luego desvía la mirada.)* Es verdad que somos nosotros, y elegantes. Pero no me gusta esto un pelo, no me gusta nada. Es muy diferente a lo que vimos antes de que nos hicieran estatuas famosas.

Don Quijote: Los tiempos cambian, Sancho, pero no la vida del espíritu. ¡A inspeccionar el castillo! A ver a dónde da esta ventana.

(Don Quijote se aproxima a la ventana, va a abrirla, y Alicia grita por primera vez. Todos se quedan helados, sin saber qué hacer.)

Alicia: ¡No! ¡La alarma!

(Jared aparece en la puerta, se queda de piedra.)

Jared: ¡Alicia! ¿Estás bien? ¿Qué es esto? Why were you talking in Spanish in the first place? Our parents are not here, are they? Who are these people?

Don Quijote: Ya te lo dije, Sancho. Medio encantados, medio desencantados. ¡Y aquí estamos nosotros, listos!

Alicia: *(To Jared.)* I don't know how it happened, but you must help with the Spanish. I was using the monument CD, and wanted proof that I was culturally connected to something in it. And I got the proof!

Jared: *(Sighs, speaks after a while.)* We are not dreaming, so we have to deal with it. I only wish it had been my idea—it's kind of cool.

(Dana appears at the door, and screams. Sancho is alarmed, but Don Quijote is expectant.)

Alicia: Dana, come here. These are friends: Don Quijote y Sancho Panza. Dana.

(Dana hides behind Alicia but looks at the visitors with curiosity. Alicia empieza a hablar español, pero con dificultad al principio.)

Don Quijote: ¡Otra dama encantada! ¡Da-na!

Alicia: Yo soy Alicia, y él es Jared.

Don Quijote: Don Quijote y mi escudero, Sancho. A su servicio. Es muy importante que inspeccionemos el castillo.

(Dana, temerosa, se esconde detrás de Alicia completamente. Alicia y Jared intercambian miradas, y toman una decisión rápida: le mostrarán la casa.)

Jared: *(Con cómica seriedad.)* Sí, cómo no. Por aquí.

(Jared empieza a abrir puertas, mientras que Don Quijote lo inspecciona todo, con la lanza lista. Sancho se queda algo atrás, un tanto aburrido y nunca perdiendo de vista su imagen en la computadora, que obviamente le gusta. Varias escenas de la vida moderna le asustan a Don Quijote: un grifo abierto, que cierra y abre una y otra vez, con timidez; un frigorífico, y otros objetos modernos si se pueden conseguir. Don Quijote se rasca la cabeza, pues no entiende nada de lo que ve.)

Don Quijote: *(A Jared, confidencial.)* Todo ha de ser examinado, hijo, para descubrir el secreto del gigante.

Jared: *(Fingiendo seriedad.)* Sí, comprendo.

Don Quijote: ¿Y el gigante?

Alicia: ¿Qué gi-gan-te?

Don Quijote: El gigante que los tiene prisioneros, y medio encantados, en este curioso palacio. Admito que tiene imaginación y grandes poderes mágicos, pues jamás vi cosa similar.

(Don Quijote va otra vez al grifo, lo abre completamente, se asusta, y Jared tiene que ir corriendo a cerrarlo mientras Don Quijote piensa profundamente. Si no hay grifos, la acción se puede concentrar alrededor del frigorífico. Jared y Alicia se miran, inseguros de cómo continuar.)

Alicia: *(Usando la mímica para compensar por su español imperfecto.)* Tengo hambre. ¿Comida?

Sancho: *(Volviendo de donde está la computadora.)* Ya decía yo que la hora de la cena estaba cerca. Porque siento hambre por tres al menos. Me comería tres vacas ahora mismo.

(Alicia va al frigorífico, abre el congelador, y saca una pizza. Don Quijote se queda fascinado al ver y sentir el vapor del hielo y se adelanta, para la mano de Alicia, y mete la suya dentro del congelador. La saca inmediatamente, gritando, a la vez que empieza a acometer al congelador abierto con la lanza.)

Don Quijote: ¡Ahhhhh! ¡Ayúdame, Sancho, que me quema este infierno helado! ¡Abre esa puerta que está debajo también, que de seguro es la entrada que buscamos! ¡Yo me meto por esta ventana oscura, aunque me deje ciego!

(Don Quijote, enloquecido, mete la cabeza dentro del congelador. En ese momento, se oye el ruido de la máquina, que espanta a los dos visitantes.)

Sancho: ¡Dése prisa, vuestra merced, que se oye cerca el rugido del gigante, y todavía no hemos visto de dónde nos va a llegar la cena!

(Alicia se queda con la pizza en la mano, y Jared, apartando a Sancho, que va a abrir la puerta del frigorífico, se echa sobre Don Quijote, intentando con mucha dificultad sacarle la cabeza del congelador. Tira de él, y al final, con don Quijote medio muerto, lo logra, y cierra la puerta del congelador.)

Jared: Ésa no es la puerta del gigante, sino donde se guarda la comida.

(Don Quijote está exhausto, se sienta en una silla. Sancho, al oir la palabra "comida", se acerca solícito.)

Sancho: Ya me parecía a mí una puerta muy pequeña para señor tan poderoso. Podemos comer ahora, puesto que mi amo está medio muerto del esfuerzo, y dejamos el trabajo para el que nos llamaron para más tarde, cuando esté más anochecido, que de todas maneras la noche es mejor hora para derribar encantos.

Don Quijote: Ven aquí, Sancho. Si muero en esta aventura, que me entierren en lugar santo, que te juro que he visto el infierno: y no quema como yo creía. Hiela, hiela hasta el mismísimo corazón.

Sancho: *(Impaciente.)* Lo prometo.

Jared: *(Reponiéndose algo de la escena tan imprevista, y poniendo el brazo alrededor de los hombros de su hermana.)* Alicia, ya oyes que nuestros invitados tienen hambre. Mete la pizza en el microwave.

(Alicia abre la puerta, lo que despierta a Don Quijote de su sueño; se levanta, toma la pizza congelada de las manos de Alicia, se asusta de la temperatura, y la deja caer en el suelo. Toma su lanza y la dirige a la pizza.)

Don Quijote: Seas lo que seas, cosa maldita e infernal—corazón de gigante o cuerpo de mortal desafortunado—, tu destino es morir a mis manos, que veamos cómo se apaga la helada injusticia, cómo se ilumina el sol de la libertad.

(Mete la lanza en la masa helada, y pone mucho empeño en matar algo que se queda pegado a la lanza. Jared, mirando el daño que se le hace al suelo, para al caballero, y tira la pizza en la basura.)

Jared: ¡Bien hecho, y ya está terminado! Lo malo siempre encuentra su fin en la basura. Y ahora, ¡a cenar lo que se pueda! *(Se vuelve a Sancho.)* ¿Dijo usted que quería vacas?

Sancho: Eso dije, aunque me contentaría con chorizo, pan y sardinas.

(Alicia y Jared se miran, sonriendo.)

Jared: Bring the box that father keeps in the pantry for grandpa and uncle Catalino. *(To Sancho.)* En mi opinión, las sardinas sientan mejor al estómago a esta hora de la noche.

(Jared motions to Dana for her to help him move the table in front of Don Quijote, who is sitting on his chair, eyes half closed, exhausted. The lance is still in his hand. Sancho takes a chair and sits next to Don Quijote, quite pleased by the fact that they are going to eat. Suddenly, he notices that Dana, who has helped her brother move the table closer to the guests, is standing openmouthed, looking at him. Sancho motions for her to sit next to him on a chair, but she doesn't move, a bit afraid.)

Sancho: Da-na . . . ¿A comer?

Dana: *(Warming up a little, she sits next to Sancho.)* I don't speak Spanish, but Jared does. And Alicia, a little bit. Maybe more, I don't know. And I want to know what happened to your horses.

(Jared is helping Alicia bring a few dishes and a board on which to put a big round loaf of bread, a huge string of chorizo, and sardines—either in a can or in a heap. He sees Dana talking to Sancho and approaches them in order to translate.)

Jared: A Dana le gustan los rompecabezas, y—

Sancho: En ese caso, de seguro que encuentra servicio con mi amo. Aunque se debe de desencantar por completo, que a él no le gusta que le hablen en algarabía o en lengua de encantos.

Jared: Dana quiere saber lo que hicieron con los caballos. Le gusta poner las cosas en orden, sin que falte nada, y en la . . . .

(Jared señala la computadora, con la imagen de los dos todavía en la pantalla. Sancho, que se había olvidado de las estatuas, se levanta, se acerca a la pantalla, y empieza a llorar.)

Sancho: ¡Mi pobre rucio! Yo aquí, bien caliente y pensando en mi cena, mientras tú estás allí solo, bien solo, y me temo que hambriento.

Jared: El caballo no tiene hambre. ¡No ve que es una estatua! Hala, a cenar, que se hace tarde.

Sancho: Si mi rucio es estatua, ¿por qué estoy yo aquí? ¡No fui yo quien pedí que me metieran en otra aventura!

(Sancho, entristecido, se vuelve a su sitio en la mesa. Dana está triste también y pone su manecilla encima de la del hombre, para consolarlo.)

Dana: *(Giving him some bread.)* Eat. It's good.

Alicia: *(Sitting between Don Quijote and Sancho. She speaks Spanish well, but hesitantly.)* Lo siento. Yo soy quien los llamó y creó este lío. Espero que les guste la cena.

(Alicia pasa comida a los dos hombres. Sancho medio se olvida de su tristeza, y empieza a comer con ganas. Es Don Quijote ahora, que ha estado sumido en sus pensamientos y algo adormilado, quien se despierta y se une a la conversación. Come un poco, muy delicadamente.)

Don Quijote: No me molesta que se nos despertara, y la cena está muy bien. Y ahora que podemos descansar, contadnos vuestra historia, bella doncella. Cómo es que fuísteis hecha prisionera, y otros detalles de importancia.

(Alicia y Jared se miran. Dana está encantada con Sancho, que ahora come, olvidado de su rucio.)

Jared: Si le parece bien, después de la cena nos damos un paseo por los alrededores.

Don Quijote: ¡Pasear por los alrededores del castillo, en triunfo!

Sancho: *(Como para sí.)* Espero que no encontremos más aventuras.

Alicia: ¿Perdón?

Sancho: Oh, no, nada, estaba cantando. Comer y cantar, cantar y comer—lo que más me gusta hacer.

Jared: Las afueras de este . . . castillo son muy diferentes de las que usted ha visto en sus otros viajes.

Don Quijote: ¡Bueno, bueno, no es para tanto! Yo he visto mucho, y más.

Alicia: Jared tiene razón. ¿Está usted listo para ver algo completamente nuevo?

(A Sancho se le cae el pan y chorizo de las manos.)

Sancho: ¡Para qué! ¿Para qué tanta novedad?

Alicia: *(Ignorando a Sancho, quien está bastante irritado.)* Si no, no podrán comprender para qué los llamé, para qué los desperté de su sueño . . . No lo puedo explicar con palabras, y ahora me siento culpable.

Jared: No te sientas culpable, Alicia. El dialogar con otros es despertarlos de su sueño para traerlos al nuestro, a nuestro castillo encantado. Es por eso que me aburría tanto con los videos de guerras y esas cosas . . . , porque no intercambiaba mi sueño con nadie. Tú me has enseñado eso.

(Alicia y Jared se abrazan. Don Quijote está conciliatorio.)

> **Don Quijote:** Iremos, Alicia, iremos. En cuanto termine Sancho su cena, que yo ya he terminado. Es bueno compartir sueños. A eso fue a lo que salí yo al mundo, aunque cuando estoy despierto me acomete la duda de si lo hice bien.

> **Sancho:** Por eso es por lo que me fastidia que nos despierten, por si acaso se le ocurre a vuestra merced el irse otra vez por esos caminos de España.

> **Jared:** No se preocupe, que no estamos en España.

> **Don Qujiote y Sancho:** ¡Que no estamos en España!? Pues, ¿dónde?

> **Alicia:** En América. ¡Y me siento tan culpable!

(Silencio. Los dos visitantes digieren la noticia de manera diferente: Don Quijote se queda maravillado, mientras que Sancho siente todavía más desconfianza.)

> **Don Qujiote:** ¡América! ¡Al otro lado del océano! ¿Es por eso que este castillo es tan diferente de los otros castillos? ¿Será acaso un castillo? ¿Estará encantado? ¿Estábais en peligro de verdad? Ahora comprendo . . . *(Algo irritado.)* ¿Para qué me llamásteis?

> **Alicia:** ¡Lo siento! No debí—

> **Jared:** Un momento: el caballero quiere saber para qué lo llamaste, y hay una razón. Vamos a dar ese paseo.

> **Don Quijote:** Sí, vamos. Nunca le niego la oportunidad de que se explique al que ha necesitado mis servicios.

(Todos se levantan. Don Quijote va a tomar su lanza, Jared intenta disuadirlo, pero Don Quijote insiste y Jared tiene que acceder. Sancho también se levanta, con bastante pena. Antes de salir detrás de los otros, se para ante la pantalla de computadora.)

> **Sancho:** Adiós, mi rucio. Si es la última vez que nos vemos, quiero que sepas que en lo caliente que estaba cuando te montaba será lo último que pienso.

(Se seca una lágrima con el inmenso pañuelo, y sale detrás de los otros, cabizbajo.)

ESCENA 2

(Central Park. Hay dos bancos, uno a cada lado del escenario, dejando un espacio libre en el centro. La primera mujer vagabunda entra por la derecha, se sienta lentamente en el banco. Toma un periódico que alguien ha dejado abandonado, lo mira atentamente.)

> **Vagabunda 1:** Huh? What's this? *Wall Street Journal.* Great! Gimme a chance to check on my investments. Well, anyhow—make a blanket for tonight.

(Se pone a mirar el periódico, y Erica entra por la izquierda con un patín o su bolsa de la escuela. Se sienta en el banco de la izquierda, aburrida. Entra la otra vagabunda por la derecha, se sienta al lado de la primera.)

> **Vagabunda 2:** ¿Algo nuevo?

(Vagabunda 1, con una mueca de desprecio, le da la espalda a la recién llegada, que se pone a buscar algo en la bolsa vieja que lleva. Las dos vagabundas, cuando no están cantando, sacan

y meten en sus bolsas papeles viejos, trozos de lápices y cigarrillos a medio fumar, etc. Entra Efraín por la izquierda con su instrumento musical. Si toca el saxofón—alto—, lo debe de llevar en su funda, que pone en el suelo. Efraín saluda con la cabeza a las vagabundas, se sienta al lado de Erica, a la que toca la mano en señal de saludo. Los movimientos y expresión de Efraín sugieren paz. Las vagabundas empiezan a cantar la canción "¡Cuántos animales!", y los animales se preparan para salir y distribuirse por el escenario. Es importante recordarles a los animales, especialmente si los actores son niños, que mientras estén en el escenario deben de comportarse en todo momento como lo haría el animal que ellos representan: pueden maullar, ladrar, buscar comida en la basura, acurrucarse contra las piernas de las vagabundas, dormir, etc. El orden de aparición de los animales, que salen de la izquierda, es: gatos, dos ratones, perro, palomas.)

Vagabunda 1:

¿Has pensado en las clases de animales salvajes
que viven en Nueva York?

Vagabunda 2:

¡Por supuesto!
Los gatos y los ratones,
los perros y las palomas
viven aquí.
¡Por supuesto!

(Los animales entran en este momento, y los cantantes dejan de cantar hasta que los animales mencionados entran y se ponen en sus sitios, haciendo los movimientos indicados.)

Vagabunda 1:

Además, ¿sabías que existía
un par de halcones en su nido
en un tejado en Park Aveníu?

(Entran los halcones, que se mueven en círculo alrededor de Efraín y Erica, y asustan a las palomas antes de desaparecer por la derecha.)

Vagabundas, Erica, Efraín:

¿Qué hacen esos,
¡y tantos más!,
por aquí?
Buscan comida,
y un lugar para descansar,
y, cada uno a su manera,
amor.
¡Ahhhh!
Y no nos olvidemos que estos animales
son inteligentes, y cuidadosamente evitan

(Entran los dos hombres de negocios por la izquierda, cruzan el escenario con tanta prisa que casi chocan contra los gatos, y desaparecen por la derecha.)

a los gigantes de dos patas
que pasan con prisa
en busca de comida,
y un lugar para descansar,
y, cada uno a su manera,
amor, amor, amor.

(Las dos vagabundas dicen adiós a Efraín con un gesto de la mano y salen. Los animales también se van. Efraín empieza a preparar su instrumento para tocar. Como si estuvieran en otra parte de Central Park, Alicia y Dana, seguidas de Don Quijote y Jared, y luego de Sancho, que apenas evita el tropezar con las cosas de absorto que está en las muchas novedades que hay a su alrededor, cruzan el frente del escenario, de izquierda a derecha. En este momento aparecen otra vez los dos hombres de negocios, que van a cruzar el escenario de derecha a izquierda, y se paran en la mitad a mirar con asombro al grupo de amigos que lentamente desaparece por la derecha.)

Hombre de negocios 1: Hey, look at that—*The Man of La Mancha!*

Hombre de negocios 2: I didn't know that the play was on Broadway again! But why would they want to go out into the streets with their costumes? Actors don't do that!

Hombre de negocios 1: You're right. Some loony dressed up for a kick. Hey, it's not Halloween!

(Riendo, los dos hombres desaparecen por la izquierda.)

ESCENA 3

(Mientras tanto, Efraín y Erica han estado preparando el instrumento musical, compartiendo alguna historia, etc. Los niños que habitualmente vienen al parque a reunirse con Efraín llegan con mucho ruido. Se sientan en el banco de la izquierda si hay sitio, y en el suelo. Los niños se comportan como si estuvieran más acostumbrados a estar en la calle que en casa, y muestran mucha alegría de estar juntos—como si el grupo de amigos fuera la familia. Cuando cada uno está en su sitio, Efraín empieza a tocar. Los niños, en absoluto silencio, escuchan, encantados. Cuando termina, aplauden con mucho entusiasmo.)

Christopher: ¡Chévere, Efraín, chévere!

Marisa: ¿Cuándo nos vas a enseñar a tocar, Efraín?

Efraín: Cuando la luna se vista de seda y se baje del cielo a traernos pastelitos de piña en una bandeja de oro y esmeraldas, ese mismo día empezaré mi primera clase de saxofón para ustedes.

Erica: Efraín, nos vas a volver locos antes de que nos enseñes nada. La semana pasada nos dijiste que sería el día en que los carros que hay en las calles se convirtieran en mariposas blancas, azules y rosa.

Efraín: *(Riendo un poco.)* ¿Eso dije? Está bonito, si dije eso, bien bueno.

Papote: Lo que pasa es que no nos quieres enseñar nada.

Erica: Tiene razón. ¿Y si los carros se convierten en mariposas verdes? ¿Qué dirías entonces?

Efraín: Buena pregunta, sí. Buena pregunta . . . En ese caso, me lo pensaría.

Israel: ¿Y si en vez de en mariposas se convierten en payasos? Tú no nos quieres enseñar nada. Lo quieres todo para ti, para ti, para ti.

(Efraín corre hacia Israel, quien pretende esconderse detrás de un árbol. Efraín logra traerlo, cogido de una oreja. Pretenden luchar, mientras los otros niños ríen.)

Erica: ¡Te atrapó! Eso te pasa por insultar al gran Efraín.

Israel: *(Pretendiendo estar arrepentido.)* No lo haré más, lo juro.

Efraín: En ese caso, te suelto. Si te arrepientes para siempre, claro.

Israel: Lo juro, lo juro. Nunca, nunca más.

(Los otros niños se ríen.)

Ramón: *(Pretendiendo consultar un reloj que no tiene, muy serio.)* En cinco minutos lo repetirá.

(Más risas.)

Efraín: Niños, como han sido tan buenos hoy, les voy a enseñar algo muy especial. Voy a tocar la frase musical que nos pone en comunicación directa con el cielo, con la eternidad. Solamente hay una, y sólo el gran Efraín sabe la que es.

(Efraín toca una frase musical, larga. Los niños, muy serios, contienen el aliento mientras miran hacia el cielo. Entran los cinco amigos y se quedan encantados, como lo están los niños.)

Don Quijote: *(Acercándose a Efraín y los niños, que están a la izquierda-centro del escenario.)* Dios, qué congregación tan sosegada y valerosa presentas a mis ojos cansados. Mas, ¿quiénes sois? ¿Vais en romería a alguna ermita? ¿O sois los menesterosos en pro de los que voy por las cuatro partes del mundo?

Sancho: *(A la derecha de Don Quijote. Le toca el brazo, para que no siga hablando.)* Mire, vuestra merced, que ya hemos cenado y no necesitamos más trabajos hoy. Malo para la digestión. Me parece que esta buena gente está aquí gozando de la noche, y no necesita nada de nadie.

(Los niños que rodean a Efraín se dan codazos y se ríen entre dientes de los dos visitantes. Alicia y sus hermanos se quedan cerca del banco, y se miran rápidamente pero no dicen nada.)

Don Quijote: *(Mira a Sancho, lentamente, con pena.)* ¡Ay, Sancho! Tu falta de caridad me entristece. ¿Hemos venido tan lejos para desmerecer de nuestro buen nombre?

(Sancho baja la cabeza, entre abrumado y avergonzado. Todos los niños han estado mirando a los recién llegados con curiosidad, y aprovechan el silencio para seguir con sus bromas. Empiezan a reir.)

Israel: *(Levantándose.)* ¿Cena? ¿Mencionó alguien la cena? Yo daría una noche como ésta, y muchas más, por una buena cena.

Efraín: Esperaba yo oir eso de ti, ¡ingrato! El gran Efraín te muestra el camino de la eternidad con su saxofón esta noche, y lo mejor que se te ocurre decir es que la cambiarías por una buena cena. ¡Bah!

Erica: ¿Y tú no, Efraín?

(Todos se ríen: Efraín, Alicia y Jared, pero no Don Quijote y Sancho. Dana, muy cerca de Alicia, lo mira todo con un poco de miedo. Jared y Dana se sientan en el banco.)

Alicia: *(Se pone entre Efraín y Don Quijote, en el centro del escenario.)* Éstos son mis amigos, Efraín. A Jared y a Dana los conoces.

Efraín: Heyyyyyy! Alicia, how you doing? Nice friends you got there.

Alicia: *(Pretending to be upset.)* I decide to speak Spanish on my own for once, and then you respond in English.

Efraín: *(Pretending to be very serious.)* That's because I am suspicious of generosity in a Yankee. You want something in return.

(The children, Alicia, and Jared laugh.)

Alicia: How do you know that?

Efraín: Because life has taught me that a truly generous spirit is a thing of the past. Today, hoy en día, you are nice to the person who can give you something or who may do you harm. That's why I want nada de nada.

Alicia: *(Thinks for a second.)* I agree with you this time, Efraín.

Efraín: *(Truly surprised.)* You do?

Alicia: Yes. *(Looking at Don Quijote.)* I came to show you a truly generous spirit from the past.

Efraín: *(Looking at the two visitors, amused.)* Are they actors?

Sancho: *(Sonriéndose de su propia sabiduría.)* Mi no inglés.

(Don Quijote mira a Sancho y se cae de espaldas, asustado ante la falta de pureza lingüística de Sancho. Los otros lo miran sin saber qué hacer. Desde el suelo, Don Quijote le habla a Sancho, entristecido.)

Don Quijote: ¡Tú también me abandonas, Sancho! ¡Tú también te dejas encantar!

Sancho: Nadie está encantado aquí, vuestra merced. Déjese de tonterías. Ya nos han dicho que estamos en América. Y como decimos en mi pueblo, cuando estés en Roma, haz como los romanos.

Efraín: *(Ayudando a Don Quijote a levantarse, muy afectado por la tristeza del hombre.)* Es el gigante, que lo devora todo. Nada ni nadie permanece puro por mucho tiempo.

(Sancho, viendo que Efraín parece estar de acuerdo con su amo, mueve la cabeza, suspira, y se sienta en el banco—o, antes de sentarse, puede intentar disuadir a Efraín, por medio de movimientos de la cabeza y las manos, de que siga hablando del tema a don Quijote. Pero Efraín no hace caso de Sancho.)

Don Quijote: *(Emocionándose mientras se levanta.)* ¡Así que hay un gigante!

Efraín: Y grande, ¡enorme! *(Extiende los brazos alrededor.)* ¿Ve a este hombre aquí? *(Se señala a sí mismo.)* Este hombre ha sido devorado por el gigante.

Christopher: *(Triste.)* No hables así, Efraín, que nos ponemos tristes.

Erica: *(Casi gritando.)* ¡No hables más así, Efraín! ¡Nooooo!

(Los otros niños se ponen las manos sobre los oídos, como confirmando lo que dicen sus compañeros.)

Don Quijote: *(Ignorando a los niños, acercándose a Efraín con mucha ansiedad.)* ¡Lo derrotamos! Juntos, esta vez lo derrotamos, para siempre. *(Hinca una rodilla en el suelo, mira al cielo, como si estuviera orando.)* Gracias, Señor, por traerme al lugar donde vive el espíritu que continúa el trabajo que yo empecé—el de enderezar entuertos y luchar contra los que injustamente tratan a los que no pueden defenderse.

Efraín: ¡Ajajá! Yo también pensaba así, cuando era joven. ¡Y mire a dónde me llevó!

Papote: Efraín, tú todavía piensas así; al menos, eso dijiste el otro día.

Efraín: *(Con humor, apuntando el dedo al que habló.)* ¿Te crees todo lo que dice el gran Efraín, eh? Pues cuidado, que acabarás como él, durmiendo en Central Park.

Alicia: A mí también me pone triste cuando hablas así, Efraín. Pero sé que dices la verdad, y por eso me gusta escucharte.

Efraín: Mira, mira, ¡cuánto español de un tirón! Niños, un aplauso para Alicia.

(Los niños aplauden, ríen, se dan codazos, guiñan los ojos, etc, y Sancho y Jared también ríen. Don Quijote está sorprendido por la sabiduría de las palabras de Alicia.)

Don Quijote: "¡Por eso me gusta escucharte!" Alicia, ¿cómo no me había dado cuenta antes? Por eso es por lo que me llamaste. Tú eres el otro espíritu que-

(Sancho se pone de pie, con mucha determinación.)

Sancho: Todo eso del espíritu está muy bien, vuestra merced, y ya lo hemos oído antes. Pero me parece a mí que estos niños necesitan más alegría, y me gustaría cantarles algo.

Efraín: ¡Adelante! Póngase aquí, que es donde florece la flor y donde brilla la estrella.

(Efraín le da a Sancho su puesto en el centro del escenario, que Sancho toma satisfecho.)

Sancho: La canción se llama "My belly comes first".

(Don Quijote se horroriza, se hinca de rodillas con su lanza en la mano, mientras los niños ríen y aplauden. Sancho canta.)

Oh, I'm loyal to my master,
however strange his ways.
I keep my place beside him
through all his dangerous days.
Ah, but when he raves of justice
in some exalted phrase,
then I know that my belly comes first.
Oh, I comb old Rocinante,
make sure he's warm at night,
and whisper to him calmly
to help him conquer fright.
Ah, but when our Don Quijote
pulls out his sword to fight,
then I know that my belly comes first,
last and always!
I know that my belly comes first!
Mi amo me prometió que sería
de una ínsula gobernador.
¡Sí, yo, Sancho, gobernador!
Pero nunca soñé
que yo vendría de viaje
a Nueva York.
Pero nunca soñé
que yo vendría de viaje
a Nueva York.
So, I dare to sing en inglés,
perhaps not very well.
I've learned to listen closely,
though I can scarcely spell.
Oh, but all I see around me
rings out like some great bell
what I know—yes, my belly comes first!
¡Sí, primero! ¡Yo sé que mi panza
comes first!

(Todos escuchan muy divertidos, hasta el final—menos Don Quijote y Efraín. APLAUSOS generales, risas, ruido. Sancho recibe el aplauso con una reverencia.)

Israel: *(De pie, imitando a Sancho, irreverente.)* "My belly comes first!" Eso ya lo dije yo antes—¡todo se ha dicho ya antes!—, y Efraín se puso bien enfogonao. Los mayores a veces no saben lo que quieren. Por eso es que uno se puede volver loco si les hace mucho caso.

(Israel se sienta. Sancho lo mira en silencio hasta que el niño baja los ojos, se sonríe, y se sienta también en el banco.)

Marisa: *(A Sancho.)* Nosotros también sabemos cantar.

Efraín: *(A la niña.)* Sí, cantas muy, pero que muy bien, Marisa. *(A Israel, muy despacio y serio.)* Y tú, Israel, tienes razón. Los mayores a veces no sabemos lo que queremos. O lo que queremos es imposible, un sueño. Sólo un sueño.

(Don Quijote, con la lanza por delante y enloquecido se planta frente a Efraín, que ha vuelto a tomar el centro del escenario.)

Don Quijote: ¡No hay tal cosa, vive Dios, que lleve el nombre de sueño con propiedad! Que si un hombre ansía la libertad por doctrina, el camino abierto y la noche estrellada por único cobijo y techo, ¡que lo tenga! Y si el pan no es bastante para su alimento, que su boca beba sol, coma risa, cante justicia, llame a las cosas por lo que son y no por lo que los otros quieren que sean. Que si un hombre arroja de su cuello el yugo del egoísmo y del miedo que hay sembrado por toda la tierra, ¡viva ese hombre, que viva! Que no es sueño querer vivir la vida entera, ni necedad atreverse a luchar contra los gigantes por ella.

(Silencio general. Efraín asiente con la cabeza, algo triste, mientras Alicia se mira las manos y a Don Quijote, sin saber qué hacer ni decir. El silencio hace que Don Quijote se enloquezca más, y empieza a dar palos en el aire con la lanza a todo su alrededor, lo que hace que los otros se echen al suelo o se agachen para protegerse.)

Don Quijote: *(A Efraín.)* ¿Dónde está el gigante que lo devoró a usted? *(A todos en general.)* ¿Dónde están todos los gigantes, que acabe con ellos de una vez por todas, que reine la paz y la justicia por toda la tierra?

(Don Quijote sigue con la lanza unos momentos más. Se para, cansado y mareado, y Alicia le extiende la mano para que no se caiga.)

Efraín: No se canse, que el gigante existe, pero no se puede ver: está en todos sitios, y en ninguno. Así, como usted lo hace, no se le puede derrotar. Muchos lo han intentado.

(Don Quijote baja la lanza, como derrotado. Entonces los niños se ríen como locos, se dan empujones. Sancho suspira, se mueve inquieto en su asiento.)

Don Quijote: *(Mirando a su alrededor, desilusionado.)* Silencio. Y si no es silencio, burlas.

(Los niños se quedan muy callados. Todos miran a Don Quijote. Efraín toma la defensa de los niños, que realmente no comprenden a Don Quijote bien.)

Efraín: Silencio sí, pero no burlas. Los niños se ríen cuando no saben lo que decir, pero no se burlan.

(Los niños asienten en silencio. Unos miran a los que hablan, otros bajan la cabeza.)

Don Quijote: ¿Y quién les enseñará a decir lo que hay que decir, a encontrar el camino, a no abandonarlo cuando todo parece inútil?

Alicia: Para eso lo llamé, señor don Quijote.

Don Quijote: ¡Ay, Alicia! Yo ya estoy viejo, muy viejo. *(Señala a los niños que se han reído de él.)* Además, me parece recordar que un día, hace muchos muchos años, confesé el haber fracasado.

Alicia: ¡¿Cómo puede hablar de fracaso si, cuando lo llamé, vino? Usted quiso sacarme de un peligro, y me sacó. *(Hace un movimiento con los brazos extendidos, similar al que hizo Efraín.)* Me sentía tan sola en esta ciudad llena de gente, que estaba a punto der ser . . . *(Se sonríe, guiña el ojo a Efraín.)* ¡devorada por el gigante!

Efraín: No si el gran Efraín puede evitarlo.

(Alicia y Efraín se aprietan la mano, hasta que a los dos les duele el apretón. Los niños se ríen, aliviados, porque el momento solemne ha terminado. Empiezan a hacerse bromas.)

Erica: ¡Alicia, Alicia! Ahora voy a hacer la pregunta que siempre quise preguntar: ¿por qué vienes a visitarnos, si nosotros somos pobres y tú eres rica?

Papote: ¡Eso no se pregunta!

Marisa: ¿Pero no la has oído? Viene a vernos porque está sola. Por lo mismo que tú y yo venimos.

Papote: Pero eso no se pregunta, Erica.

Alicia: Sí que se pregunta. Marisa tiene razón, vengo aquí porque con ustedes y Efraín no me siento sola.

Don Quijote: ¡Ahhhhhhhh! Ahora entiendo. Me llamaste para ver si es posible hacerse viejo y no perder el corazón. Para ver si puede uno salir al mundo con un bello sueño, y que no se hiele cuando choque con la realidad.

(Alicia asiente con un movimiento de cabeza. Jared le coge la mano. Dana se ha dormido en el banco, la cabeza en el hombro de Jared.)

Efraín: *(Divertido.)* Así, que hay un sueño.

Don Quijote: *(Sonriendo.)* Sí, hay un sueño. Y yo acabo de comprender lo que hay que hacer para guardarlo para siempre: el querer realmente hablar con alguien, hablar de verdad, no importa con quién. Alicia me lo ha enseñado. Alicia, gracias por despertarme. Ya no me dormiré más.

Sancho: *(Alarmado.)* ¡Ay de mí! No se acaba la aventura ahora.

Don Quijote: No te preocupes, Sancho, que volvemos a nuestras estatuas, pero no a dormir, sino a esperar escuchar la voz de un niño que, en algún lugar, necesite entender, sentir sin tener miedo, estar acompañado.

Sancho: Bueno, después de todo, no me parece un mal destino—especialmente si nos podemos sentar en nuestros animales de vez en cuando y descansar.

Efraín: Buena casa, sus animales. Yo también necesito una casa en que estar caliente por muchos, muchos años, donde invitar a todos mis amigos a una buena cena de vez en cuando.

(Los niños se levantan y abrazan a Efraín, todos abrazándolo y hablando a la misma vez. Mientras los niños abrazan a Efraín, las vagabundas, que ayudarán a cantar la última canción, entran por la izquierda y sin distraer mucho se integran a la escena.)

Christopher: ¿Me vas a invitar a mí el primero a ver tu casa?

Erica: ¡No, Efraín, invítame a mí!

Marisa: ¡No! ¡A mí, a mí!

Erica: Te voy a hacer un ramo de flores de papel para que la adornes.

Ramón: Y yo te voy a llevar arroz con gandules de los que hace mi mamá . . . Ya verás.

Papote: ¡Va a ser la mejor casa, tu casa! ¡La mejor de todasssssssss las casas!

Efraín: *(Riendo, muy feliz.)* ¡A todos, o a ninguno!

Todos los niños: ¡A todos, a todos!

(Los visitantes los miran sonriendo, y se levantan, empezando a separarse de Efraín y los niños. Jared levanta a Dana, que se despierta lentamente. Se va cogida de la mano de su hermano. Alicia y Don Quijote van primero, seguidos de Sancho, que está contento de volver.)

Don Quijote: Ya es hora de que nos vayamos. El trabajo para el que me llamaste, Alicia, está terminado: hemos conquistado al gigante. Os tenéis que ir a vuestra casa, y Sancho y yo tenemos que volver a nuestras estatuas.

Sancho: *(Escéptico, aunque sin dejar de estar contento.)* Si sabemos cómo.

Don Quijote: No dudes más, Sancho. El pasado es el pasado.

(Efraín y los niños se dan cuenta que los otros se van.)

Efraín: ¡Hasta pronto, amigos! Mientras caminan a casa, los niños los acompañarán con una canción. Para que encuentren el camino y no se pierdan.

Don Quijote: *(Lentamente, sonriendo.)* ¡Hasta pronto, amigos!

Sancho: *(Buscando con trabajo la palabra correcta en inglés.)* We . . . have to leave you now. But . . . we . . . shall be with you . . . always. Siempre. Siempre.

(Los niños y las vagabundas empiezan a cantar "El mejor adiós", todavía rodeando a Efraín. Los cinco amigos saludan con las manos, incluyendo a Sancho, y se van.)

Cantantes:

> Cuando tú vienes a verme,
> cuando tú vienes aquí,
> dejo lo que estoy haciendo
> para correr hacia ti.
> Amiguito, no te vayas.
> Amiguito, quédate.
> Que si no, no habrá nadie
> que me acompañe feliz a mí.
> Que si no, no habrá nadie
> que me acompañe a mí.
> Hay miles de juegos
> que me gusta jugar.
> Hay nubes en el cielo
> que me encanta mirar.
> Pero sé que un gran amigo
> no es fácil de encontrar.
> Amiguito, cuando llegas,

una linda bienvenida te doy yo
y cuando te vayas te daré el mejor adiós,
que vuelvas otro día.
El mejor de los adioses para ti
guardo en mi corazón.

ESCENA 4

(Un poco después, en el apartamento de los González. Dana, Alicia y Jared están frente a la computadora, los ojos pegados a la pantalla, que todavía muestra las estatuas. Todos están tristes.)

Dana: I can't believe they're gone!

Jared: It was kind of neat to meet them in person. I wonder how . . . But never mind.

Alicia: Jared, me gustaría hablar en español, siempre.

Jared: ¿Para hablar con ellos?

Alicia: ¡Claro! *(Alicia y Jared ríen.)* Por lo menos, me he enterado que nos podemos identificar con algo del pasado de nuestros . . . padres.

Dana: I don't understand everything that you are saying. Will you teach me Spanish?

(Madre entra en la casa. Se quita la chaqueta, cansada.)

Mother: Hi, kids. Did you have supper?

Dana: Mama, will you teach me Spanish? We—Alicia and Jared and-

Mother: And who?

Dana: And those two guys who are in the CD that you gave Alicia for Christmas . . .

(Alicia and Jared look at each other, smile a bit, waiting to see what Dana will say and what they will have to explain. Mother looks at the computer, smiles, nods, and goes to the kitchen followed by Dana.)

Dana: They also speak Spanish, and I would like to know what they say.

Mother: Of course, honey. I'll ask Father to speak more Spanish at home. He speaks better than I do. Will you help me with the laundry, Dana?

Dana: Yes, Mama. And while we are doing the laundry, will you tell me all you know about those guys and whether you can get me a puzzle-

(Mother and Dana go inside the house. Alicia and Jared look after them and breathe with relief.)

Alicia: Wow! I thought she was going to tell the whole thing.

Jared: She will. The question is whether we will have to explain. And, why not? Father at least will love it.

Alicia: But how do we explain such a thing?

Jared: They were here! They were. I know it. We know it.

Alicia: *(Smiles, nods.)* Father will understand.

(They keep looking at the computer screen with Don Quijote and Sancho on it.)

FIN
_____

VOCABULARY–VOCABULARIO

Nouns–Nombres

belly: *panza*
donkey: *burro, rucio*
hawk: *halcón, gavilán*
heritage: *herencia, patrimonio*
damsel: *damisela, doncella*
saxophone: *saxofón*
surgeon: *cirujano*

Adjectives–Adjetivos

bored: *aburrido*
evil: *malo, perverso*
frozen: *helado*
hellish: *infernal, horrible*
loony: *loco*

Verbs–Verbos

to be disappointed: *estar desilusionado*
to be smashed: *ser destruído*
to carve: *trinchar, tallar, labrar*
to crave: *ansiar, anhelar*
to mock: *ridiculizar, burlarse de*

Index

Notes on the Author and Contributors

About the Author

Resurrección Espinosa was born in 1956 in a small village in Andalucía, in southern Spain. She is a graduate of the University of Granada. Resurrección has taught English as a second language at New London High School and Spanish at Connecticut College and the University of Rhode Island (URI). She founded Teatro Latino Estudiantil at URI and has directed the group for four years. She is the founder and director of Teatro Latino de New London; a Master Teaching Artist in Theater for the Connecticut Commission on the Arts, for which she does residencies around the state; and a public speaker for the Rhode Island Committee for the Humanities. She has pub-

lished *Waking Dream*, a collection of poems in English, and a book of plays, *El Gaucho Vegetariano and Other Plays for Students of Spanish*. Currently, she is working on another collection of plays for high school Spanish students, *Los padres incorregibles*. Since 1995, Resurrección has been publishing a weekly comic strip in Spanish, *Amanda y Rocinante*, illustrated by Dorothy L. Hall. It is featured in *Tiempo*, the Spanish-language supplement to the *Record Journal* (Meriden, Connecticut) and in *The Day* (New London, Connecticut).

About the Contributors

Dorothy Louise Hall is assistant managing editor, graphics/design, for the *Record Journal* in Meriden, Connecticut. She has illustrated several children's books, the latest of which, *Forever Friends*, was published by Tallfellows Press in 2002. She has acted with the William Billings Institute of American Music Theater Group, and in 1987 she received a Eugene O'Neill award for acting. Dorothy is the illustrator of the comic strip *Amanda y Rocinante* and has served on many community boards. In 1997, she received a YMCA Woman in Leadership Award.

Charles Frink's music has been performed by such groups as the Eastern Connecticut Symphony, the William Billings Institute of American Music, and the Hartford Ballet. He is one of the early O'Neill Memorial Theater playwrights and received one of the first composers' grants awarded by the National Endowment for the Arts, to write a composition about Joe Hill, the martyred songwriter and labor organizer for the Industrial Workers of the World. Dr. Frink holds three degrees from Yale University, and his music manuscripts are being collected at the Frink Archives at the Yale Music Library. He arranges traditional Spanish songs and writes original compositions for Resurrección's plays.